Presented to

_____

_____

_____

From _____

Date _____

More RECIPES WORTH SHARING

More
RECIPES WORTH
SHARING

A Second Helping of Recipes and Stories from
America's Most-Loved Community Cookbooks

Copyright © 2010 by

Favorite Recipes® Press

An imprint of

FRP.INC

A wholly owned subsidiary of Southwestern/Great American, Inc.
P.O. Box 305142
Nashville, Tennessee 37230
1-800-358-0560

Photography © by Abe Ogden
Illustrations © by Mary Stetson
Cover Design: Rikki Campbell Ogden/pixiedesign, LLC
Essayist: Carol Boker

Library of Congress Control Number: 2010932200
ISBN: 978-0-87197-549-2

Executive Editor: Sheila Thomas
Project Editor: Tanis Westbrook
Art Director: Steve Newman
Book Design: Travis Rader

Manufactured in the United States of America
First Printing: 2010

This cookbook is a collection of favorite recipes from community cookbooks generously shared as personal
favorites by cookbook committee members, FRP family, friends, and fans of *Recipes Worth Sharing*. We would
have loved to include every recipe submitted; however, due to limited space, duplications, and similarities, it
was impossible to include them all. The FRP team worked diligently to verify the proper names and spellings of
the many organizations and individual contributors. Should there be an error, please accept our sincere
apologies, and let us know so that we can correct it for subsequent printings.

ACKNOWLEDGMENTS

Welcome back for *More Recipes Worth Sharing*…serving up a second helping of favorite family recipes from America's most-loved community cookbooks. The second in the Favorite Recipes Press series celebrating community cookbooks, *More Recipes Worth Sharing* offers *More* recipes from *More* cookbooks and represents *More* states, capturing the unique spirit of community cookbooks with over 500 recipes from 198 community cookbooks representing 40 states and Bermuda. These regional specialties, classic selections, and new twists on old favorites will soon have you turning to *More Recipes Worth Sharing* again and again!

I have immense gratitude to so many for helping *Recipes Worth Sharing* become the success it is and *More Recipes Worth Sharing* a reality. As with the first book, I once again received a plethora of responses from organizations that have published community cookbooks. They submitted their "recipes worth sharing," and I'd like to thank those cookbook committees. I was delighted to find after the publication of *Recipes Worth Sharing* that many people approached me, wanting to share their own favorite recipes from their favorite community cookbooks. This led me to extend the request for recipes to the FRP family and others, and I got a tremendous response. I thank all who submitted recipes as well as stories to go with them. Thanks to Rikki Campbell Odgen for yet again capturing the vision of *More Recipes Worth Sharing* through her photography and cover design. Thanks to Carol Boker, who was a tremendous asset to the publication through her delightful accounts of conversations with many cookbook committee members. I am so glad that this collaboration brought us together again. Thanks to the very talented Mary Stetson, who contributed the beautiful line art recipe boxes that are sprinkled throughout the book. I look forward to following your career as you continue to grow as an artist. Mindy Henderson, thank you for always believing in me; I would not be where I am without you. To the many special people in my life, your support and encouragement means so much—Lisa, Renee, Holly, Martha, MMA and Karen (my personal publicists), and of course Jimmy and Layne for putting up with my crazy schedule and for being such good sports in the kitchen. To the entire team at FRP, thank you for caring about community cookbooks as much as I do.

And thank you to all of the community cookbook collectors out there. Your continued support of this book form helps not only to preserve a slice of history—and what a rich history it is—but to foster a vibrant, living snapshot of America's dinner table.

Sheila Thomas
FAVORITE RECIPES PRESS,
A DIVISION OF FRP, INC.

INTRODUCTION

"If a community cookbook could talk…[it] would deny that it was just a cookbook. It would say, 'Here, in my pages, it is true that you will find the best recipes of your neighbors, but my purpose is not solely to indulge the appetite. I also inform the mind…I serve both historical notes of value to the reader as well as recipes that afford a peep into the good eating of present and the days that are gone forever…But best of all, I know that I have an intrinsic value, for it is through my success, assured by the excellent recipes contributed by interested people, that I help the [organizations and volunteers] to carry on their services to the community."

Adapted from Old North State Cook Book, *JUNIOR LEAGUE OF CHARLOTTE, NC (1942)*

Since 1961 Favorite Recipes Press has been privileged to partner with literally hundreds of nonprofit organizations in the development, manufacturing, marketing, and distribution of their community cookbooks. Many things have changed in the publishing world over the past half century: the invasion of the internet into our daily lives, the increasing number of on-line book stores, the availability of on-line recipes, and fewer locally owned independent book and gift stores, stores that often partnered with organizations to support and do their part to contribute back to the community, have been replaced with chain and on-line stores. The one constant in this rapidly changing world of ours is, always has been, and hopefully always will be the dedication, loyalty, and shared passion shown by the countless volunteers who create, sell, or market these culinary and cultural bibles. The volunteers share an energy and passion for their organization's aspirations, and their work on the committees is a special time and a shared meaningful experience. The work on the committee is life-changing in and of itself, but this shared collaboration also produces life-changing funds for a multitude of noble causes. These volunteers make a difference; they make life better for those less fortunate. And in the meantime, perhaps unbeknownst to them, they have left a legacy, a documentation of their culinary traditions for home cooks and their families to enjoy for generations to come. This book is dedicated to those volunteers. So much has been made possible by their selfless, generous, and tireless work, including the publication of *Recipes Worth Sharing* and *More Recipes Worth Sharing*. I hope you enjoy reading and learning about the different regional cuisines and cultures that we have across our great country!

CONTENTS

APPETIZERS & BEVERAGES

GETTING STARTED

Billie Rose had been involved with Junior Leagues in Evanston, Indiana, and San Antonio, Texas, so when she and her husband moved to Chattanooga, Tennessee, she joined the league there immediately, knowing that it was the perfect way to get involved in the community as well as to make new friends. Her small but enjoyable involvement in cookbook development in the Evanston league led her to volunteer to chair the cookbook committee in Chattanooga. The group had not published a cookbook since 1982 when they created *Dinner on the Diner*, a successful cookbook still in print today.

"We put out the call for recipes for the new book, and although it began slowly, we ended up with about 800 submissions," Billie said. "One of the unique things we came up with was a cookbook mascot. We took a picture of Rosie the Riveter [the cultural icon from World War II] and renamed her Rosie the Triveter. She is holding a whisk and has a Junior League button on her lapel. We put her on all our fliers and our Facebook page and everything else we sent out. Rosie put out the call that 'the cookbook committee needs your help.'"

When testing the recipes, the committee got the whole membership involved by encouraging them to make and test food on their families,

SEASONED TO TASTE
JUNIOR LEAGUE OF CHATTANOOGA

The Perfect Way to Get Involved in the Community

book clubs, or whatever groups the members might be hosting in the community.

"Our sustainers have a group called the Garden Club, and they meet monthly," said Billie. "Our active members began catering their luncheons as part of the tastings. They appreciated the opportunity to be involved by helping with testing, tasting, and rating the recipes."

Proceeds from the sale of the cookbook help fund many of the league's community projects, including Healthy Starts, a children's health initiative.

"This was a wonderful bonding experience," Billie said. "I discovered so many delicious recipes, and the cookbook group is so enthusiastic and so much fun. My husband was extremely supportive. He understood how much involvement these projects take. He jokingly said we should call our new bulldog puppy 'Cookbook' just to get in the spirit of things, but I vetoed that."

Savory Rosemary Almonds

4 tablespoons butter
2 tablespoons finely minced fresh rosemary
1 teaspoon kosher salt
¼ teaspoon cayenne pepper
½ teaspoon garlic powder
2 cups almonds

Melt butter in a skillet over low heat. Stir rosemary, kosher salt, cayenne pepper, and garlic powder into melted buttter. Remove butter mixture from heat and let sit for 30 minutes. Preheat oven to 300 degrees. Stir and coat almonds with butter spice mixture. Line a baking sheet with heavy-duty aluminum foil. Place almonds coated with butter mixture in a single layer on aluminum foil. Bake in preheated 300-degree oven for 30 minutes, stirring nuts every 10 minutes. Let cool. Store in airtight container.

Toast to Tidewater
Junior League of Norfolk-Virginia Beach, Virginia

Rosemary Roasted Cashews

SERVES 8

1½ pounds cashew nuts (about 4½ cups)
3 tablespoons finely minced rosemary leaves
½ teaspoon red pepper
3 teaspoons dark brown sugar
½ teaspoon ground coriander
2 teaspoons kosher salt
2 tablespoons melted butter

Preheat oven to 375 degrees. Place the nuts on a baking sheet and toast for about 10 minutes until they are warmed through. Meanwhile, combine the rosemary with the remaining ingredients in a large bowl. Toss the warm nuts with the rosemary mixture until the nuts are completely coated.

You're Invited Back: A Second Helping of Raleigh's Favorite Recipes
Junior League of Raleigh, North Carolina

8   MORE RECIPES WORTH SHARING

CHEESE BENNES

MAKES 10 TO 12 DOZEN

½ pound sharp Cheddar cheese, grated
¼ pound margarine or butter, softened
½ teaspoon salt
Pinch cayenne
1¼ cups sifted flour
½ cup benne seeds (sesame seeds), roasted

Cream first four ingredients together. Add flour and knead. Add seeds and knead. Form into four or five long thin rolls. Chill in waxed paper several hours or freeze. Slice rolls into "thin dimes." Bake at 350 degrees for 10 to 15 minutes. If desired, sprinkle with salt while hot. Keep in tightly covered tin.

An old Charleston favorite!

Charleston Receipts Repeats
Junior League of Charleston, South Carolina

NANCY VARELLA'S CHEESIES

MAKES 3 DOZEN

1 medium egg white
1 teaspoon water
¼ cup fresh Parmesan cheese, grated
1½ cups Swiss cheese, grated
½ cup butter, softened
¾ cup flour
¾ teaspoon salt
⅛ teaspoon ground nutmeg

Preheat oven to 425 degrees. Mix egg white and water, beat lightly and set aside. Combine Parmesan cheese, Swiss cheese and butter. Add flour, salt and nutmeg. Stir with a fork until stiff dough is formed. Cover and chill at least 15 minutes. Shape dough into ¾-inch balls and place on greased cookie sheet. Flatten with a fork and brush with egg white mixture. Bake at 425 degrees for 10 minutes.

Georgia on My Menu
Junior League of Cobb-Marietta, Georgia

APPETIZERS 9

Ice Box Cheese Wafers

½ pound grated sharp cheese

¼ pound butter, creamed

½ teaspoon salt

Heavy pinch cayenne pepper

1½ cups sifted flour

Cream together cheese, butter, salt and pepper. Add flour. Make into roll. Wrap in waxed paper and put in ice box. Will keep for a month. When needed, slice into thin wafers and bake in moderate oven (350 degrees) for 8 to 10 minutes or until wafers are golden. For a decorative touch, place a pecan half on each wafer before baking.

Note: *Charleston Receipts*, first published in 1950, is the oldest Junior League cookbook still in print. Through its numerous printings over $1 million has been raised for the Junior League of Charleston's community projects.

Charleston Receipts, America's Oldest Junior League Cookbook in Print
Junior League of Charleston, South Carolina

Lemon-Rosemary Wafers

½ cup butter

½ cup sugar

1 egg white, beaten

½ teaspoon vanilla

2 tablespoons minced fresh rosemary

2 tablespoons shredded lemon zest

1 cup flour

Cream butter and sugar until light. Add egg and vanilla; beat well. Beat in rosemary and lemon zest. Mix in flour. Shape dough into a slender roll about 1½ inches in diameter. Cover with plastic wrap and refrigerate for at least 2 hours or overnight. Remove plastic wrap and slice roll into ¼-inch-thick rounds. Transfer to ungreased baking sheets. Bake at 350 degrees until set and just beginning to turn golden on the edges. Transfer wafers to rack and cool.

Variation and Improvisations
Friends of KEDM Radio, Monroe, Louisiana

GARLIC-ROASTED TOMATO BRUSCHETTA

SERVES 20 TO 24

6 Roma tomatoes
3 tablespoons olive oil
2 to 3 teaspoons balsamic vinegar
3 to 4 cloves garlic

1 to 2 teaspoons pepper
1 loaf French bread or Italian bread
Olive oil for brushing
Grated Parmesan cheese

Preheat the oven to 350 degrees. Slice the tomatoes ½ inch thick. Combine with 3 tablespoons olive oil, the vinegar, garlic and pepper in a bowl and mix gently to coat evenly. Arrange the tomatoes in a single layer in a baking pan. Bake for 15 to 20 minutes or just until tender.

Increase the oven temperature to 375 degrees. Slice the bread into 1-inch rounds. Brush lightly with olive oil and arrange on a baking sheet. Toast for 3 to 5 minutes. Place a tomato slice on each round and sprinkle with cheese. Broil until bubbly. Note: You can also cool the roasted tomatoes to room temperature and store in an airtight container in the refrigerator to serve on sandwiches, over your favorite pasta, or as a salad dressing.

Treasures from the Bend, Rich in History and Flavor
Fort Bend Junior Service League, Sugar Land, Texas

WESTSIDE BRUSCHETTA

SERVES 4 TO 6

1 baguette with sesame seeds
4 to 6 tablespoons extra-virgin olive oil
1 tablespoon minced garlic
1 tablespoon Romano cheese
¼ teaspoon ground pepper
1 red bell pepper, cut into ¼-inch pieces
1 yellow bell pepper, cut into ¼-inch pieces
2 plum tomatoes, cut into ¼-inch slices

3 green onions, cut into ¼-inch slices
½ cup shredded mozzarella, asiago or
    Gorgonzola cheese
4 ounces mushrooms, cut into ⅛-inch slices
4 ounces prosciutto or smoked ham,
    cut into ½-inch strips
Freshly grated pecorino Romano cheese

Slice the baguette lengthwise into halves. Place cut side up on a baking sheet. Combine the olive oil, garlic, 1 tablespoon Romano cheese and pepper in a bowl and mix well. Spread over the cut sides of the bread halves. Arrange the bell peppers, tomatoes and green onions on each bread half. Sprinkle with the mozzarella cheese. Top with the mushrooms and prosciutto.

Bake at 350 degrees for 5 to 10 minutes or until the cheese melts.

Broil for 2 to 3 minutes or just until the cheese begins to brown. Cut into 2-inch slices. Sprinkle with freshly grated pecorino Romano cheese.

Great Lake Effects
Junior League of Buffalo, New York

CROSTINI WITH BLUE CHEESE, HONEY AND WALNUTS

MAKES 24

24 diagonal slices baguette
2 tablespoons olive oil
6 ounces creamy blue cheese or Cambazola

2/3 cup toasted coarsely chopped walnuts
2/3 cup ripe figs, thinly sliced
3 tablespoons honey, warmed

Preheat the oven to 375 degrees. Arrange the baguette slices on a baking sheet and brush with olive oil. Toast until golden brown.

Combine the blue cheese and walnuts in a bowl and mix well. Spread evenly to the edges of the baguette slices. Bake just until the cheese melts. Arrange on a serving platter and top each with a slice of fig. Drizzle with honey and serve warm.

Note: You can substitute dried figs for the fresh figs, adding them to the crostini before baking.

Orange County Fare, A Culinary Journey through the California Riviera
Junior League of Orange County, California

NOT YOUR MOTHER'S HAM BISCUITS

MAKES 20 TO 24 BISCUITS

1 (20- to 24-roll) package dinner rolls in
  a foil pan
1/2 cup margarine, softened
1 1/2 tablespoons poppy seeds
1 1/2 tablespoons Dijon mustard

1 1/2 tablespoons grated onion
1 teaspoon Worcestershire sauce
8 ounces thinly sliced smoked ham
8 ounces thinly sliced Swiss cheese

Split the entire pan of rolls into halves horizontally with a serrated knife, leaving both halves intact. Combine the margarine, poppy seeds, Dijon mustard, onion and Worcestershire sauce in a bowl and mix well. Spread over the cut sides of the rolls. Layer the ham and cheese alternately on the bottom roll section and replace the top section.

Wrap the pan in foil and bake at 400 degrees for 20 minutes or until the cheese melts. Cut into rolls with a sharp knife to serve.

Note: You may use the rolls while they are still frozen and/or freeze the filled rolls before baking.

Notably Nashville, a medley of tastes and traditions
Junior League of Nashville, Tennessee

BUFFALO CHICKEN WINGS

MAKES 20 TO 25 WINGS

20 to 25 chicken wings
Vegetable oil for deep frying
¼ cup melted butter or margarine

Hot sauce
Bleu Cheese Dressing
Celery sticks

Disjoint the chicken wings and discard the tips. Rinse and pat dry. The wings must be completely dry to fry properly since there is no batter or breading.

Preheat the oil in a deep fryer or a large deep pan to 365 degrees. Add the chicken wings a few at a time to the hot oil. Do not allow the oil to cool as the chicken is added. Deep-fry for 6 to 10 minutes or until crisp and golden brown. Drain well by shaking in the fryer basket or a strainer.

Blend the butter with ½ bottle of hot sauce for medium-hot wings. Add additional hot sauce for hotter wings or additional butter for milder wings.

Combine the wings and the hot sauce in a large container. Let stand, covered.

Serve the chicken wings with Bleu Cheese Dressing and celery sticks.

BLEU CHEESE DRESSING

MAKES 3½ CUPS

2 cups mayonnaise
3 tablespoons cider vinegar
½ teaspoon dry mustard
½ teaspoon white pepper

¼ teaspoon salt
8 ounces bleu cheese, crumbled
¼ to ½ cup cold water

Combine the mayonnaise, vinegar, dry mustard, pepper and salt in a large bowl and beat until well blended. Mix in the bleu cheese. Add enough cold water gradually to make the dressing of the desired consistency, whisking constantly. Store in an airtight container in the refrigerator.

Great Lake Effects
Junior League of
Buffalo, New York

The origin of the culinary delight known as "chicken wings" began one Friday night in 1964 at Buffalo's Anchor Bar, owned by Frank and Teressa Bellissimo. Friends of the Bellissimo family had stopped at the bar for a late-night snack. While fixing the snack, Teressa was about to put chicken wings into a stockpot for soup when she thought, "It's a shame to put such beautiful wings into a stockpot." The rest is history!

APPETIZERS   13

CRANBERRY MEATBALLS

2 pounds ground beef

1 cup cornflakes

2 tablespoons grated onion

2 tablespoons Worcestershire sauce

½ teaspoon garlic powder

¼ teaspoon pepper

2 large eggs

½ cup ketchup

1 (12-ounce) can chili sauce

1 (16-ounce) can cranberry sauce

2 tablespoons sugar

2 tablespoons lemon juice

Mix the ground beef, cornflakes, onion, Worcestershire sauce, garlic powder, pepper, eggs and ketchup in a bowl until well combined. Shape gently into balls and arrange in a 9×13-inch baking dish. Mix the chili sauce, cranberry sauce, sugar and lemon juice in a bowl. Pour over the meatballs. Bake at 400 degrees for 35 to 40 minutes or until cooked through.

Dining with Pioneers, Volume 3
AT&T Pioneers, Tennessee Chapter 21

MEATBALLS EXTRAORDINAIRE

4 pounds ground beef

1 egg, slightly beaten

¼ large onion, grated

Salt to taste

1 (12-ounce) bottle chili sauce

1 (12-ounce) jar grape jelly

Juice of 1 lemon

Blend together meat, egg, onion and salt; form into 100 small meat balls. Combine chili sauce, jelly and lemon juice; pour over meatballs and simmer in electric skillet for 1 hour. Serve in heated chafing dish.

Dining with Pioneers, Volume 1
AT&T Pioneers, Tennessee Chapter 21

Hats-Off Stuffed Mushrooms

2 tablespoons butter
2 tablespoons all-purpose flour
Dash of pepper
1 cup half-and-half
1 (6-ounce) package frozen crab meat, thawed
½ cup dry bread crumbs

30 mushroom caps
⅓ cup butter, softened
3 tablespoons grated Parmesan cheese
3 tablespoons fresh lemon juice
1 teaspoon minced dill weed

Melt 2 tablespoons butter in a skillet over low heat. Add the flour and pepper and stir until blended. Add the half-and-half gradually, stirring constantly until thickened. Add the crab meat and half the bread crumbs and mix well. Spoon the mixture into the mushroom caps. Arrange the mushrooms on a baking sheet. Combine the remaining bread crumbs, 2 tablespons of the softened butter and the cheese in a bowl and mix well. Sprinkle over the filled mushrooms. Combine the remaining butter, the lemon juice and dill weed in a bowl and mix well. Drizzle over the mushrooms. Bake in a preheated 400-degree oven for 10 to 12 minutes or until heated through.

Rendezvous on the Ridge
Junior League of Jonesboro, Arkansas

Stuffed Mushrooms

2 pounds large mushrooms
2 tablespoons butter
2 cloves garlic, minced
8 ounces cream cheese, at room temperature
½ teaspoon dried dill weed

3 tablespoons grated Parmesan cheese
2 tablespoons bread crumbs
Salt and pepper to taste
2 tablespoons grated Parmesan cheese
2 tablespoons bread crumbs

Preheat oven to 400 degrees. Clean the mushrooms with a damp paper towel. Remove the stems from the mushrooms and dice. In a medium skillet, over medium-high heat, melt the butter. Sauté the chopped mushroom stems and the minced garlic for 3 to 5 minutes. Remove from the heat to cool. Add the cream cheese and mix thoroughly. Add the dill weed, Parmesan cheese and bread crumbs and mix well. Season to taste with salt and pepper. Spoon into a pastry bag fitted with a star tip and pipe into the mushroom caps. Sprinkle with the remaining 2 tablespoons of Parmesan cheese and 2 tablespoons of breadcrumbs. Bake for 10 minutes or until nicely browned.

Note: You may prepare the mushrooms a day ahead. Store in the refrigerator until ready to bake.

Tastes & Treasures, A Storytelling Cookbook of Historic Arizona
Historical League, Tempe, Arizona

$\mathcal{P}$IGS IN CASHMERE BLANKETS

SERVES 30

1¼ pounds sweet or hot Italian sausage links
½ cup peach preserves
¼ cup hot mustard

1 tablespoon honey
1 sheet puff pastry, thawed

Grill the sausage over hot coals or sauté in a skillet until cooked through; drain. Let stand until cool. Mix the preserves, mustard and honey in a bowl until of a sauce consistency.

Roll the puff pastry into a 10×10-inch square on a lightly floured surface; make sure the fold seams are smooth. Cut into thirty 1½×4-inch strips. Slice each sausage link lengthwise into halves and then into 2-inch chunks.

Spread some of the mustard sauce on each pastry strip. Place one chunk of sausage on each strip and enclose the sausage with the pastry, sealing the edges on the bottom. Arrange seam side down on a baking sheet lined with baking parchment. Chill for 30 to 60 minutes.

Bake in a preheated 400-degree oven for 15 to 20 minutes or until the pastry is puffed and golden brown. Serve warm with the remaining mustard sauce.

Excellent Courses, A Culinary Legacy of Ravenscroft
Ravenscroft School, Raleigh, North Carolina

$\mathcal{A}$NNAPOLIS OYSTER MELTS

SERVES 8 TO 12

24 fresh oysters
1½ cups barbeque sauce
1½ cups (6 ounces) shredded Cheddar cheese
6 slices bacon, cut into 2-inch pieces

Shuck and drain the oysters, leaving the oyster in one-half of its shell. Place oyster side up on a rack in a broiler pan. Top each with 1 tablespoon of the barbeque sauce, 1 tablespoon of the cheese and 1 piece of the bacon. Broil on the highest oven rack for 3 to 4 minutes or until the bacon is brown and the cheese is melted. Serve immediately.

A Thyme to Entertain—Menus & Traditions of Annapolis
Junior League of Annapolis, Maryland

GRILLED BACON-WRAPPED CHIPOTLE SHRIMP

VARIABLE SERVINGS

1 slice of bacon per shrimp used
1 pound shrimp, peeled and deveined
½ pound pepper Jack cheese, cut into
⅛×1-inch strips

3 jalapeño peppers, cut into ⅛×1-inch strips
1½ bottles roasted raspberry chipotle sauce

Preheat the oven to 350 degrees. Preheat the grill. Arrange bacon in a single layer on a baking sheet with sides. Bake for 7 minutes or until partially cooked. Let stand until cool. Butterfly the shrimp to form a small pocket in each. Insert one cheese strip and one jalapeño pepper strip in each shrimp. Wrap tightly with one slice of the bacon and thread on a skewer. Brush both sides of the shrimp with the sauce. Let stand for 10 minutes. Grill over indirect heat until the shrimp turn pink. Serve as an appetizer or as a main entrée over hot cooked rice.

Texas Tables
Junior League of North Harris and South Montgomery Counties, Texas

MINIATURE SHRIMP BURGERS

MAKES 20 TO 24 MINIATURE BURGERS

2 pounds uncooked medium shrimp
¾ cup mayonnaise, divided
1 Vidalia onion, minced
1 teaspoon Worcestershire sauce
Pinch cayenne pepper
Kosher salt to taste

Black pepper to taste
1 cup panko
Olive oil
¼ cup chili sauce
Tabasco sauce to taste
Bibb lettuce leaves

Peel and devein shrimp. Finely chop shrimp in a food processor. Put mixture into a bowl and add ¼ cup mayonnaise, onion and Worcestershire sauce and blend well. Stir in the cayenne pepper, kosher salt and black pepper. Shape into miniature patties. Dredge in the bread crumbs and place on a baking sheet. Chill, covered with plastic wrap, for 4 to 5 hours. Sauté the patties in olive oil in a skillet over medium heat for 3 minutes on each side or until crisp and golden brown. Drain and set aside. Combine the remaining ½ cup mayonnaise, chili sauce and Tabasco sauce in a bowl and mix well. To serve, place each shrimp patty on a Bibb lettuce leaf and top with a dollop of the chili mayonnaise.

A Savory Place, Culinary Favorites of Amelia Island
Micah's Place, Amelia Island, Florida

Shrimp and Asparagus Dijonnaise in Puff Pastry

Dijonnaise Dressing

⅓ cup mayonnaise

2 tablespoons Dijon mustard

½ teaspoon lemon zest

½ teaspoon lemon juice

To prepare the dressing, combine the mayonnaise, Dijon mustard, lemon zest and lemon juice in a small bowl and mix well.

Appetizers

18 asparagus spears, trimmed

1 (17-ounce) package frozen puff pastry sheets or 18 cocktail phyllo shells

18 shrimp, cooked and peeled

2 teaspoons chopped fresh citrus mint leaves, such as lemon or orange

To prepare the appetizers, place the asparagus in a large skillet and cover with cold water. Bring to a boil and remove from the heat. Let stand, covered, for 3 minutes. Drain and rinse with cold water. Drain and pat dry. Cut off the tips and reserve for garnish. Cut the remaining spears into ¼-inch pieces and place in a bowl. Add the dressing and toss to coat. Chill, covered, until ready to use.

Thaw the pastry for 30 minutes. Roll one pastry sheet into a 7½×15-inch rectangle on a lightly floured sheet of baking parchment. Cut out nine 2½-inch circles. Repeat with the remaining pastry sheet. (The pastry rounds may be frozen on a baking sheet at this point and stored in a sealable plastic freezer bag until ready to use. Thaw and continue with the recipe.)

Preheat the oven to 400 degrees. Press the pastry rounds into ungreased miniature muffin cups. Bake for 10 minutes or until golden brown, watching carefully to prevent overbrowning. Remove from the oven and tap down the centers while hot to form a shell. Let stand until cool. Spoon 1 teaspoon of the asparagus mixture into each shell. Place a reserved asparagus tip straight up in each and wrap with a shrimp. Sprinkle with the mint. Serve immediately or chill until serving time.

Note: These delectable and elegant little appetizers can be prepared the day before and assembled at the last minute. Our method for blanching asparagus is perfect every time.

Herbal Cookery
The St. Louis Herb Society, Missouri

CHRIST CHURCH SPANAKOPITA

1 (10-ounce) package frozen spinach, thawed
and well drained

1/3 cup minced onion

4 ounces freshly grated Parmesan cheese

3 tablespoons feta cheese

2 tablespoons soft bread crumbs

1/4 teaspoon salt

1/4 teaspoon ground nutmeg

1/2 (16-ounce) package frozen phyllo pastry

3 tablespoons butter or margarine, melted

Combine first 7 ingredients; chill mixture at least 1 hour.

Cut a 2-inch-wide strip through all layers of pastry. Cover remaining pastry with a damp cloth to keep from cracking.

Separate dough into stacks of 2 strips. Brush each stack of strips with melted butter; spoon 1 rounded teaspoon spinach mixture onto the top of each strip. Fold dough over filling like folding a flag. Place on a buttered baking sheet and brush with melted butter.

Repeat procedure with remaining spinach mixture, pastry, and melted butter.

Bake at 375 degrees for 20 minutes. Serve warm.

Back to the Table
Episcopal Church Women, Christ Church, Raleigh, North Carolina

TOMATO-FETA APPETIZERS

MAKES 2 DOZEN

1 frozen puff pastry sheet, thawed

1 cup mozzarella cheese, shredded

1 (4-ounce) package crumbled feta cheese

1/4 cup Vidalia or other sweet onion, minced

1 clove garlic, minced

2 tablespoons fresh basil, finely chopped

1 tablespoon fresh thyme or oregano,
finely chopped

1 tablespoon fresh chives, finely chopped

4 Roma tomatoes, thinly sliced

1 tablespoon virgin olive oil

Roll puff pastry into a square on a lightly floured surface. Transfer to an ungreased baking sheet. Bake at 400 degrees for 10 minutes or until golden brown. Carefully transfer to a wire rack to cool. When cool, return sheet to baking sheet. Sprinkle with cheeses, onions and garlic. Top with basil, thyme, and chives. Arrange tomato slices in a single layer on top and drizzle with oil. Bake at 400 degrees for 15 minutes or until cheese melts. Cut into squares with 1 tomato slice in each square.

Key Ingredients
Le Bonheur Club, Memphis, Tennessee

OMATO SANDWICHES

40 slices white bread, frozen
Unsalted butter to taste
Mayonnaise to taste
20 slices small peeled tomatoes, sliced
Salt and pepper to taste
Chopped fresh basil to taste

To assure ease in preparing, freeze bread. Cut rounds (2- to 3-inch size) from frozen bread and spread with butter, then mayonnaise. Using half the bread rounds, place a tomato slice on each. Sprinkle tomato slice with salt and pepper and a little basil. Top each sandwich with one of the remaining bread rounds. Serve at room temperature.

Party Potpourri
Junior League of Memphis, Tennessee

OLD-FASHIONED DEVILED EGGS

MAKES 12 DEVILED EGGS

6 large eggs, hard-boiled, cooled and peeled
3 to 4 tablespoons mayonnaise
3 to 4 tablespoons hot dog relish (a mixture
  of yellow mustard and sweet pickle relish)

Salt to taste
Parsley leaves, paprika, or thinly sliced olives
  for garnish

Slice eggs in half and carefully remove yolks. Put yolks in bowl and mash with fork until no lumps remain. Add mayonnaise and relish a little at a time until achieving a good consistency for stuffing. Add salt to taste and stuff eggs. Garnish, cover, and refrigerate or serve immediately. This recipe can be doubled or tripled, but for best results prepare in small batches.

Entertaining with Blue Grass Winners
Garden Club of Lexington, Kentucky

BERTHA'S CHEESE TART

MAKES 1 (7-INCH) TART

CRUST

1 cup finely chopped onion

1 cup finely chopped pecans

1 cup shredded Cheddar cheese

Blend all crust ingredients together and divide into two portions. Spray a 7-inch springform pan with nonstick cooking spray. Press half of crust mixture on the bottom.

FILLING

1 cup cooked chopped spinach, well drained

8 ounces cream cheese, softened

1 (9-ounce) jar mango chutney

½ teaspoon ground nutmeg

½ teaspoon ground white pepper

½ teaspoon garlic powder

½ teaspoon celery salt

Press spinach between paper towels to squeeze out excess moisture. In a food processor, blend filling ingredients. Spread over crust. Cover filling with remaining crust mixture. Apply light pressure with a spoon to the top crust to form tart. Refrigerate overnight. Carefully remove the pan's collar. Cover top with a serving plate and invert. Remove the bottom of the pan. Chill until ready to serve. Serve with your choice of party crackers.

Note: Doubling this recipe creates a "Big Bertha." For a "Big Bertha" use a 9-inch springform pan

Lamar School
Meridian, Mississippi

ONION TARTS

SERVES 36

6 to 8 ounces chopped onions

1 tablespoon butter

12 ounces cream cheese, softened

1 cup grated Parmesan cheese

¼ cup mayonnaise

36 frozen phyllo cups

Green onions and/or paprika to taste

Sauté the onions in the butter in a large skillet until translucent. Combine with the cream cheese, Parmesan cheese and mayonnaise in a bowl and mix well. Spoon into the phyllo cups and arrange on a baking sheet. Bake at 425 degrees for 6 to 8 minutes or until set. Garnish with green onions and/or paprika. You may also add salmon to the filling if desired.

Lone Star to Five Star
Junior League of Plano, Texas

Hot Mango Brie Cheese

SERVES 8 TO 10

1 (8-inch) round of Brie cheese
1 cup mango chutney or spicy mango chutney
8 slices bacon, crisp-cooked and crumbled

Place the cheese in a 10-inch quiche pan. Spread the chutney evenly over the top of the cheese and spread almost to the edge. Sprinkle the bacon on the top. Bake at 350 degrees for 30 to 45 minutes or until the chutney begins to bubble. Serve with bread or crackers.
   Note: For a vegetarian variation, substitute ½ cup toasted slivered almonds for the bacon.

A Thyme to Entertain—Menus & Traditions of Annapolis
Junior League of Annapolis, Maryland

Sun-Dried Tomato Mousse

SERVES 16

1 cup (2 sticks) unsalted butter, softened
16 ounces cream cheese, softened
½ cup oil-packed sun-dried tomatoes, drained, chopped
1 clove garlic, crushed
1 (6-ounce) can tomato paste
1 tablespoon dried basil
2 teaspoons salt
½ teaspoon pepper

Beat the butter in a mixing bowl until very smooth but not fluffy. Add the cream cheese and mix just until blended. Stir in the sun-dried tomatoes, garlic, tomato paste, basil, salt and pepper; do not overmix. Spoon the mixture into a 6-inch springform pan. Chill for 8 hours or until very firm. Place the pan in hot water for 15 seconds. Release the spring and invert the mousse onto a serving plate. Smooth the top with a warm spatula. Garnish by pressing chopped fresh parsley or chopped toasted pine nuts onto the side. Serve with breadsticks or crackers.

Savor the Moment, Entertaining Without Reservations
Junior League of Boca Raton, Florida

Party Cheese Pâté

3 (8-ounce) packages cream cheese, softened and divided
2 tablespoons milk
1 cup chopped pecans, toasted
1 (4.5-ounce) package Camembert cheese, softened
1 (4-ounce) package bleu cheese
1 cup (4 ounces) shredded Swiss cheese
Red and green grapes, cut in half, for garnish
Chive stems, for garnish
Assorted apples, gingersnaps or crackers

Line a lightly greased 8-inch round baking pan or 9-inch springform pan with plastic wrap. Set aside. Cream 1 package cream cheese and milk, in a medium bowl with an electric mixer, until smooth. Spread cream cheese mixture into prepared pan. Sprinkle evenly with chopped toasted pecans. Cover and chill. Combine remaining 2 packages of cream cheese, Camembert cheese, bleu cheese and Swiss cheese in a large mixing bowl. Beat until blended. Spoon mixture over pecan layer, spreading to edge of pan. Cover and chill at least 4 hours for flavors to blend. Can be stored up to one week in the refrigerator. Invert pâté carefully onto a serving plate, removing plastic wrap with care. Use grape halves and chive stems to decorate top along one edge to resemble a bunch of grapes. Serve with apple wedges, gingersnaps or assorted crackers.

Windows Across Missouri
Missouri State Medical Association Alliance, Jefferson City, Missouri

Black Olive Cheese Ball

8 ounces cream cheese, softened
1½ cups shredded Cheddar cheese
1 (5-ounce) jar of processed smoked cheese spread
1 teaspoon Worcestershire sauce
½ teaspoon dry mustard
1 (7-ounce) can chopped black olives
1 (6-ounce) can pitted black olives, drained and cut into halves
2 tablespoons chopped fresh parsley

Combine the cream cheese, Cheddar cheese, cheese spread, Worcestershire sauce and dry mustard in a bowl and mix well. Fold in the chopped olives. Shape into a ball. Decorate with the olive halves to form petals. Sprinkle all over with the parsley. Chill, covered, for 6 to 10 hours. Serve with crackers.

Oh Shenandoah!, A Cookbook From the Museum of the Shenandoah Valley
The Museum of the Shenandoah Valley, Virginia

Pineapple Cheese Ball

16 ounces cream cheese, softened

1 (8-ounce) can crushed pineapple, drained

¼ cup chopped green bell pepper

2 tablespoons minced onion

1 tablespoon minced jalapeño chile

Tabasco sauce to taste

1 tablespoon seasoned salt

2 cups chopped pecans

Combine the cream cheese, crushed pineapple, bell pepper, onion, jalapeño chile, Tabasco sauce, seasoned salt and 1 cup of the chopped pecans in a bowl and mix well. Chill in the refrigerator.

Shape into a ball and roll in the remaining 1 cup pecans, coating well. Place on a platter and serve with bite-sized crackers.

Beach Appétit
Junior League of the Emerald Coast, Fort Walton Beach, Florida

Garlic and Dill Feta Cheese Spread

8 ounces cream cheese, softened

4 ounces crumbled feta cheese

¼ cup mayonnaise

1 clove garlic, minced

1 tablespoon fresh dill, chopped

½ teaspoon seasoned pepper

¼ teaspoon salt

Process all ingredients in a food processor until smooth. Cover and chill 8 hours. Serve on cucumber slices drizzled with olive oil, or use as a spread for bagels, sandwiches or crackers.

This spread can be frozen for up to a month, tightly wrapped. Thaw in the fridge for 24 hours and stir before serving.

Seasoned to Taste
Junior League of Chattanooga, Tennessee

Spicy Olive Nut Spread

5 ounces green olives

8 ounces cream cheese, softened

1/2 teaspoon black pepper

1/2 teaspoon cayenne pepper

1/2 cup mayonnaise

1/2 cup chopped pecans

1 to 2 loaves white, French or sourdough
   baguettes

Drain the olives and chop, reserving 1 tablespoon brine. Beat the cream cheese and 1 tablespoon olive brine in a mixing bowl. Beat in the black pepper and cayenne pepper. Beat in the mayonnaise. Beat in the pecans and olives. Adjust the seasonings to taste. Chill, covered, for up to 1 week. Let stand at room temperature for a few minutes before serving. Slice the baguette and spread with the olive mixture.

Marshes to Mansions
Junior League of Lake Charles, Louisiana

Swiss and Chive Spread

3 cups (12 ounces) finely shredded
   Swiss cheese

3/4 cup mayonnaise

1/4 cup chopped chives

1/2 teaspoon salt

1/4 teaspoon ground white pepper

Combine Swiss cheese and mayonnaise in a bowl; add chives, salt, and pepper and stir well. Cover and chill until ready to serve. Serve with crackers. I prefer Wheat Thins.

Creating a Stir
Fayette County
Medical Auxiliary,
Lexington, Kentucky

FRP Family Favorites

"Almost one year after serving this simple spread at an open house, I received a phone call requesting the recipe. The caller claimed she had been thinking about the recipe since tasting it and would like to serve it at an upcoming dinner party she was hosting."

Sheila Thomas
FRP Publishing Consultant

Fabulous Pesto-Feta Spread

8 ounces cream cheese, softened
2 ounces grated Parmesan cheese
½ cup basil pesto sauce

5 medium Roma tomatoes, diced
½ cup chopped red onion
½ cup crumbled feta cheese

Preheat oven to 350 degrees. Spray shallow 2-cup oval baking dish with cooking spray. Mix cream cheese and Parmesan cheese; stir in pesto; mix well. Stir in Roma tomatoes and red onion; mix well. Place mixture in prepared baking dish. Sprinkle top of tomato mixture with feta cheese. Bake in preheated 350-degree oven for 20 minutes or until bubbly. Serve with crackers or baguette.

Toast to Tidewater: Celebrating Virginia's Finest Food & Beverages
Junior League of Norfolk-Virginia Beach, Virginia

Avocado Dip

SERVES 18

3 small avocados, chopped
1 cup chopped green onions
1 (10-ounce) can diced tomatoes with
   green chiles

½ cup vegetable oil
2½ tablespoons apple cider vinegar
1 teaspoon garlic salt
1 teaspoon pepper

Combine the avocados, green onions and undrained tomatoes with green chiles in a bowl. Add the oil and vinegar and toss to coat well. Season with the garlic salt and pepper. Chill in the refrigerator. Serve with tortilla chips.

Note: Fort Bend Seniors Meals on Wheels is committed to helping seniors remain independent by enhancing their quality of life through services and resources. Fort Bend Seniors provides services to over 1,000 seniors daily.

Treasures from the Bend, Rich in History and Flavor
Fort Bend Junior Service League, Sugar Land, Texas

> "I have advice for any group publishing a cookbook. You may agree on a pathway for your cookbook, but don't let it get in the way of a few fanciful and whimsical detours. Listen to that little voice in your head. It's the fanciful in life that brings you the most joy, so be sure it's part of your cookbook."
>
> STEPHANIE PRADE
> *HERBAL COOKERY*, THE ST. LOUIS HERB SOCIETY

Avocado Feta Dip

SERVES 6

2 tomatoes, chopped
1 avocado, chopped
6 ounces feta cheese, crumbled
1/4 cup chopped red onion
1 garlic clove, minced
1 tablespoon chopped parsley

1 tablespoon olive oil
1 tablespoon white wine vinegar
Chopped jalapeño chiles to taste
Red pepper flakes to taste
Oregano, salt and pepper to taste

Combine the tomatoes, avocado, feta cheese, onion, garlic and parsley in a bowl. Add the olive oil and wine vinegar and mix gently. Stir in jalapeño chiles and red pepper. Season with oregano, salt and pepper. Place the avocado pit in the bowl until ready to serve to keep the avocado from turning brown.

Orange County Fare, A Culinary Journey through the California Riviera
Junior League of Orange County, California

BLT Dip

SERVES 8 TO 10

2 pounds bacon
1 cup mayonnaise
1 cup sour cream
3 or 4 lettuce leaves

4 or 5 medium tomatoes, seeded and
finely diced
Bagel chips or choice of crackers

Cook bacon until very crisp. Drain and blot on paper towels; crumble. Combine bacon, mayonnaise and sour cream and refrigerate serveral hours or overnight. Line a serving dish with lettuce leaves. Spoon bacon mixture on top of lettuce; cover mixture with tomatoes. Serve with bagel chips or crackers.

Note: This recipe is easily doubled to feed a crowd. Use 3 pounds of bacon and double all other ingredients.

First Come, First Served...in Savannah!
St. Andrew's School, Savannah, Georgia

APPETIZERS

27

Green Chile and Bacon Dip

16 ounces cream cheese, softened
½ cup mayonnaise
1 tablespoon lemon juice
1 (4-ounce) can chopped green chiles
½ large onion, minced

½ large green bell pepper, minced
10 slices bacon, crisp-fried and crumbled
1 clove garlic, crushed
1 large green or red bell pepper

Combine the cream cheese, mayonnaise and lemon juice in a food processor. Process until smooth. Combine the cream cheese mixture, chiles, onion, minced green pepper, bacon and garlic in a bowl and mix well. Chill, covered, for 3 to 4 hours. Cut a slice from the top of the green or red pepper and discard. Remove the seeds and membranes. Spoon the cream cheese mixture into the pepper. Serve with corn chips.

Southern On Occasion
Junior League of Cobb-Marietta, Georgia

"Catch a Man" Dip

2 cups freshly shredded sharp Cheddar cheese
2 cups freshly shredded mild Cheddar cheese
1 bunch chopped green onions
1½ bottles real bacon bits
1 teaspoon cayenne pepper
1½ cups mayonnaise (may need more to moisten)

Combine all ingredients and mix well. Chill for at least 4 hours. Serve with tortilla chips or corn chips.

Seasoned to Taste
Junior League of Chattanooga, Tennessee

Delaware Crab Delight

1 (8-ounce) package cream cheese, softened
  with 1 tablespoon milk
10 ounces crab meat, shelled and
  picked through
2 tablespoons minced Vidalia onion
1 tablespoon horseradish

1/4 teaspoon salt
1/8 teaspoon pepper
1/3 cup sliced almonds
1/4 cup mayonnaise
1 1/2 to 3 tablespoons cream sherry

Preheat the oven to 325 degrees. Combine all the ingredients in a medium casserole dish. (If planning to serve cold, use 1 1/2 tablespoons of cream sherry; if planning to serve warm, use 3 tablespoons.) Bake for 25 minutes, or until heated through. Serve hot in a chafing dish or refrigerate to chill. Serve with butter or wheat crackers.

Dancing on the Table
Junior League of Wilmington, Delaware

Chunky Gorgonzola Dip

1 cup mascarpone cheese
1/3 cup sour cream
1/3 cup chopped fresh chives
1/2 teaspoon salt
1/4 teaspoon ground white pepper

1 cup (4 ounces) crumbled
  Gorgonzola cheese
Chopped fresh chives for garnish
Pear and apple slices
Crackers or toasted crostini

Combine mascarpone cheese and sour cream. Mix until smooth. Add chives, salt and white pepper. Mix. Fold in Gorgonzola, leaving crumbles of cheese in dip. Garnish with chopped chives. Serve with sliced pears, apples, crackers or on toasted crostini.

Note: Dip pear and apple slices in lemon water to prevent browning.

Windows Across Missouri
Missouri State Medical Association Alliance, Jefferson City, Missouri

EMON BASIL DIP

¾ cup mayonnaise	1 tablespoon fresh lemon juice
¾ cup low-fat plain yogurt	⅛ teaspoon cayenne pepper
⅓ cup chopped fresh basil	1¼ pounds fresh peeled shrimp
½ teaspoon grated lemon zest	1 pound sugar snap peas

Combine the mayonnaise, yogurt, basil, lemon zest, lemon juice and cayenne pepper in a bowl and mix well. Chill, covered, for up to 24 hours. Cook the shrimp in a saucepan of boiling seasoned water until the shrimp turn pink. Drain and place in a bowl. Chill, covered, until cold. Cook the sugar snap peas in a saucepan of boiling salted water for 45 seconds. Drain and plunge into ice water until cold. Drain and pat dry. Spoon the dip into a serving bowl and place on a platter. Surround with the shrimp and add sugar snap peas. For a thicker dip, drain the yogurt in a sieve before adding. This dip is also good on poached, baked or grilled salmon.

Recipes of Note
Greensboro Symphony Guild, North Carolina

ℱETA BLACK BEAN DIP

½ cup sugar	4 (11-ounce) cans Shoe Peg corn, drained
¾ cup apple cider vinegar	and rinsed
¾ cup vegetable oil	1 bunch scallions, chopped
3 (15-ounce) cans black beans, drained	1 bunch cilantro, chopped
and rinsed	1 (8-ounce) block feta cheese, crumbled

Whisk the sugar, vinegar and oil in a large bowl. Add the black beans, corn, scallions, cilantro and cheese and mix well. Chill until serving time. Serve with tortilla chips or corn chips.

A Thyme to Celebrate
Junior League of Tallahassee, Florida

Avocado Feta Salsa

1 cup chopped seeded plum tomatoes
4 ounces feta cheese, crumbled into
    large pieces
3 tablespoons red wine vinegar
2 tablespoons olive oil
2 tablespoons finely chopped red onion

2 cloves garlic, minced
1 tablespoon chopped parsley
1/2 teaspoon dried oregano
1/2 teaspoon salt
2 avocados, chopped

Combine the tomatoes, cheese, vinegar, olive oil, onion, garlic, parsley, oregano and salt in a bowl. Mix gently to prevent breaking up the cheese. Fold in the avocados. Serve immediately with tortilla chips, or store, covered, in the refrigerator. If preparing in advance and storing in the refrigerator, fold the avocados into the salsa just before serving to prevent discoloration.

Texas Tables
Junior League of North Harris and South Montgomery Counties, Texas

Bulldog Salsa

1/4 cup extra-virgin olive oil
1/2 cup fresh lime juice
1/2 cup fresh cilantro, chopped
1/2 cup fresh parsley, chopped
3 cloves garlic, crushed and minced
1 1/2 teaspoons cumin
1 teaspoon crushed red pepper

1 teaspoon freshly ground black pepper
1/2 teaspoon salt
2 cans seasoned black beans, drained
    and rinsed
1 large can white Shoe Peg corn, drained
1 red bell pepper, diced
1 Vidalia onion, diced

In a small mixing bowl, combine oil, lime juice, cilantro, parsley, garlic, cumin, red pepper, black pepper and salt, whisking well. In large serving bowl, combine beans, corn, bell pepper and onion. Pour marinade over bean mixture, tossing gently to coat. Chill overnight. Serve with tortilla chips.

Beyond the Hedges
Junior League of Athens, Georgia

Spicy Melon Salsa

SERVES 16

2½ cups diced cantaloupe

1 cup diced fresh or canned pineapple

1 red bell pepper, diced

2 scallions, thinly sliced

2 tablespoons chopped fresh cilantro

1 jalapeño chile, seeded and finely chopped

2 tablespoons lime juice

2 tablespoons mild olive oil

Combine the cantaloupe, pineapple, bell pepper, scallions, cilantro, jalapeño, lime juice and olive oil in a large bowl and toss gently. Chill, covered, until ready to serve.

Savor the Seasons, Vol. 3-The Culinary Collection
Junior League of Tampa, Florida

Tomato and Maui Onion Salsa

MAKES 12 (¼-CUP) SERVINGS

4 small tomatoes, chopped

1 small Maui onion, finely chopped

1 cup chopped fresh cilantro leaves

½ teaspoon cumin

½ fresh jalapeño pepper, minced

Juice of ½ lime or ¼ lemon, to taste

1 clove garlic, minced

1 small avocado, diced

Freshly ground pepper and salt to taste

Combine all ingredients. Refrigerate 1 hour to allow flavors to blend. Serve with your favorite chips.

Flavors of Hawaii, Recipes that Celebrate Hawaii's Diversity
Child and Family Service Guild, Honolulu, Hawaii

Tomatillo Verde Sauce with Avocado

2 to 4 medium serrano chiles
10 ounces tomatillos, husks removed
1 clove garlic
1 tablespoon chopped pickled jalapeño chile
1 tablespoon pickled jalapeño chile vinegar

½ cup cilantro
1 teaspoon salt
1 large avocado
⅓ cup finely chopped onion

Bring a saucepan of water to a boil and add the serrano chiles. Boil for 5 minutes and add the tomatillos. Boil for five minutes longer and remove from heat; drain.

Combine the serrano chiles, tomatillos, garlic, jalapeño chile and vinegar in a blender and process until puréed. Add the cilantro and salt and process until blended. Combine the purée, avocado, and onion in a bowl and mix well. Taste and adjust the seasonings and serve with tortilla chips.

Pomegranates and Prickly Pears
Junior League of Phoenix, Arizona

Bloody Mary

2 (32-ounce) bottles Clamato juice
9 ounces vodka
4 tablespoons lime juice
½ cup Worcestershire sauce
Celery salt to taste

In a 3½- to 4-quart container, combine Clamato juice, vodka, lime juice and Worcestershire. Sprinkle with a generous amount of celery salt. Stir. Serve in tall glasses with celery sticks as a garnish.

Note: Best when made ahead and refrigerated overnight.

The Heart of Pittsburgh
Sacred Heart Elementary School, Pittsburgh, Pennsylvania

Hot Spiked Cider

2 quarts apple cider
1 cup dried apricot halves
1 cup golden raisins
1 cup dried apple slices
3/4 cup peach- or ginger-flavored brandy
2 cloves, wrapped in cheesecloth for
    easy removal

1/2 teaspoon ground ginger
1/4 teaspoon ground cinnamon
1 cup bourbon
2 sticks cinnamon

Mix apple cider, apricot halves, golden raisins, apple slices, brandy, whole cloves, ground ginger and ground cinnamon in a large stainless saucepan. Let stand at room temperature for at least one hour. Heat cider mixture over medium heat until hot. Remove from heat; discard cloves. Stir in bourbon. Serve hot. Garnish with cinnamon sticks.

Toast to Tidewater, Celebrating Virginia's Finest Food & Beverages
Junior League of Norfolk-Virginia Beach, Virginia

Lemon Verbena Champagne Cocktail

1 cup sugar
2 cups water
20 to 25 organically grown fresh lemon verbena leaves
1 (750-milliliter) bottle Champagne, chilled

Bring the sugar and water to a boil in a small saucepan, stirring until the sugar dissolves. Remove from the heat. Add the lemon verbena leaves. Let stand, covered, until cool. Strain through a sieve into a pitcher, discarding the leaves. Store in the refrigerator. To serve, fill chilled Champagne glasses one-half full with the cold syrup and top with the Champagne.

Note: The essence of fresh lemon verbena will hit your nose just before your first sip of this cooling summer cocktail. You may want it all for yourself!

Herbal Cookery, From the Kitchens and Gardens of the St. Louis Herb Society
The St. Louis Herb Society, Missouri

Iced Lemonade with Vodka and Mint

1 1/3 cups sugar

1 cup packed fresh mint, stemmed

2 lemons, sliced

2 cups freshly squeezed lemon juice
   (about 10 lemons)

2 cups good-quality vodka

1/2 cup water

Ice cubes

1 liter club soda

8 lemon slices

8 mint sprigs

Combine the sugar, mint and lemons in a pitcher and mash lightly with the back of a wooden spoon. Let stand for 30 minutes. Add the lemon juice, vodka and water and stir until the sugar is dissolved. Chill for 30 minutes to 2 hours. Strain the lemonade and discard the mint. To serve, fill a tall glass or goblet with ice. Pour the lemonade to fill 1/3 of the glass and top with the club soda. Stir to blend. Garnish with a lemon slice and a mint sprig.

EveryDay Feasts, Volume 2: The Culinary Collection
Junior League of Tampa, Florida

Pretty-in-Pink Lemonade

2 (12-ounce) cans frozen pink
   lemonade concentrate

1 (750-milliliter) bottle sparkling wine

1 (2-liter) bottle Sprite

2 pints fresh strawberries, sliced, or
   1 (16-ounce) package frozen strawberries

Fill a punch bowl halfway with ice. Add the lemonade concentrate, wine, soda and strawberries to the punch bowl and mix well. Serve immediately in punch cups.

Worth Tasting, A Culinary Tour Through the Architecture of the Palm Beaches
Junior League of the Palm Beaches, Florida

WATERMELON LEMONADE

1 cup sugar, or to taste
1 cup water
2 cups chopped seeded watermelon
1 cup fresh lemon juice
3 cups carbonated water

Bring the sugar and water to a boil in a saucepan. Boil for 2 minutes or until the sugar dissolves, stirring occasionally. Pour into a container with a cover. Chill in the refrigerator. Press the watermelon with the back of a spoon through a fine mesh strainer into a bowl, discarding the pulp. Combine the watermelon juice, simple syrup and lemon juice in a container with a cover and mix well. Chill in the refrigerator. Pour into a 2-quart pitcher. Stir in the carbonated water just before serving. Pour over ice in glasses.

Splendor in the Bluegrass
Junior League of Louisville, Kentucky

VODKA BUCKETS

26 ounces vodka
2 (6-ounce) cans frozen lemonade concentrate, thawed
2 (6-ounce) cans frozen limeade concentrate, thawed
2 (32-ounce) bottles lemon-lime soda, chilled

Combine the vodka, lemonade concentrate and limeade concentrate in a large container; mix well. Chill until serving time. Add the lemon-lime soda at serving time and mix gently. Serve in glasses with sugared rims. Garnish with mint sprigs.

Oh My Stars!, Recipes that shine!
Junior League of the Roanoke Valley, Virginia

BLUE BAYOU BERRY MARGARITAS

SERVES 4

2½ cups crushed ice
⅓ cup tequila
¼ cup Grand Marnier

¼ cup confectioners' sugar
1 cup fresh or frozen blueberries
1 (6-ounce) can frozen limeade concentrate

Combine the ice, tequila, Grand Marnier, confectioners' sugar, blueberries and limeade concentrate in a blender container. Process until smooth. Pour into glasses, straining if desired.

Marshes to Mansions
Junior League of Lake Charles, Louisiana

PRICKLY PEAR MARGARITAS

SERVES 4

12 ounces tequila
8 ounces Triple Sec
8 ounces lime juice

4 ounces prickly pear cactus syrup
2 ounces orange juice

To serve on the rocks, combine the tequila, Triple Sec, lime juice, cactus syrup and orange juice in a cocktail shaker and shake to mix. Pour over ice in margarita glasses.

To serve blended, combine 4 cups ice, tequila, Triple Sec, lime juice, cactus syrup and orange juice in a blender and process until the desired consistency. Pour into margarita glasses. Rim the glasses with sugar or salt if desired.

Note: Prickly pear cactus syrup may be purchased at specialty supermarkets.

Pomegranates & Prickly Pears, Flavorful Entertaining from the Junior League of Phoenix
Junior League of Phoenix, Arizona

# Mojito

16 mint leaves

3 tablespoons sugar

2 tablespoons fresh lime juice

6 tablespoons white rum

Crushed ice

1 cup club soda

Crush the mint leaves, sugar and lime juice in a small glass with the back of a spoon. Add the rum and mix until the sugar dissolves. Fill 2 wine glasses with ice. Strain the rum mixture through a sieve into the wine glasses, pressing the mint leaves to extract all the juice. Top with club soda and garnish with mint leaves or lime wedges.

The Life of the Party, Volume 1: The Culinary Collection
Junior League of Tampa, Florida

# Café au Lait Punch

1 cup sugar

1 cup dark roast coffee or coffee extract,
   at room temperature

1 liter ginger ale, at room temperature

1 liter club soda, at room temperature

2 cups half-and-half

½ gallon vanilla ice cream

Combine the sugar, coffee, ginger ale, club soda and half-and-half in a large punch bowl and mix well. Fold in the ice cream and ladle into punch cups.

Editor's Note: Instead of coffee, you may use ¼ cup freeze-dried coffee dissolved in 1 cup of water.

Warm Welcomes: River Road Recipes IV
Junior League of Baton Rouge, Louisiana

Frozen Maraschino Punch

4 (16-ounce) jars maraschino cherries
1 (16-ounce) can crushed pineapple in
   heavy syrup
1 (48-ounce) can pineapple juice
1 (12-ounce) can frozen orange juice
   concentrate, thawed
1½ cups water
1½ to 1¾ cups vodka
2 (2-liter) bottles lemon-lime soda

Drain 2 jars of the maraschino cherries. Combine the drained and undrained jars of cherries with the crushed pineapple, pineapple juice, orange juice concentrate, water, vodka and 1 bottle of the lemon-lime soda in a 2½-gallon freezer container; mix well. Freeze for 24 to 36 hours, stirring every 3 to 5 hours for the first few hours.

Let stand at room temperature for 2 to 3 hours or until slushy. Combine with the remaining bottle of lemon-lime soda in a punch bowl and mix gently.

Treasures from the Bend, Rich in History and Flavor
Fort Bend Junior Service League, Sugar Land, Texas

Berry Sherbet Punch

16 ounces cranberry juice drink
1½ cups fresh lemon juice (no substitutions)
1 cup sugar

2 (28-ounce) bottles ginger ale
1 quart raspberry sherbet

Combine first 3 ingredients, stirring well. Chill until ready to serve. Stir in ginger ale and sherbet just before serving. Serve in a punch bowl with an ice ring.

Back to the Table
Episcopal Church Women, Christ Church, Raleigh, North Carolina

PIRATE PUNCH

2 (1.75-liter) bottles light rum
1 (1.75-liter) bottle Captain Morgan's
    Parrot Bay coconut-flavored rum
9 (46-ounce) cans pineapple juice
1 (46-ounce) can Hawaiian Punch

Combine the rums in a 5-gallon container. Add the pineapple juice and punch and mix well. Serve over ice. This recipe can be reduced to serve a smaller gathering.

Beach Appétit
Junior League of the Emerald Coast, Fort Walton Beach, Florida

SUSTAINER PUNCH

3 bottles sauterne
2 cups sugar
2 cups brandy, chilled
6 bottles Champagne
Ginger ale
Frozen grape clusters

Combine the sauterne and sugar in a punch bowl and stir gently to dissolve the sugar. Stir in the brandy and Champagne. Add enough ginger ale to dilute the punch to taste and mix gently. Ladle over frozen grape clusters in punch cups to serve.

Beach Appétit
Junior League of the Emerald Coast, Fort Walton Beach, Florida

SANGRIA

1 cup orange juice

½ cup sugar

1 (750-milliliter) bottle white zinfandel

¼ cup lime juice

¼ cup lemon juice

1 lemon, sliced

1 lime, sliced

1 orange, sliced

1 kiwifruit, sliced

20 grapes

Combine the orange juice and sugar in a saucepan. Heat over low heat until the sugar dissolves. Pour into a 2-quart pitcher. Stir in the zinfandel, lime juice and lemon juice. Add the lemon, lime, orange, kiwifruit and grapes. Cover the pitcher tightly with plastic wrap. Chill for 4 to 12 hours to allow the fruit to absorb the flavors. Serve some of the fruit in each glass.

Once Upon a Time, Recipes and Recollections from a River City
Junior League of Evansville, Indiana

BOURBON SLUSH

4 tea bags

2 cups boiling water

6 ounces frozen lemonade concentrate

12 ounces frozen orange juice concentrate

1 cup bourbon

7 cups water

2 cups sugar

Ginger ale or lemon-lime drink

Put tea bags into 2 cups boiling water. Steep for 5 minutes. Mix together the lemonade concentrate, orange juice concentrate, bourbon, water and sugar and add tea, removing bags. Pour into several containers and freeze at least 24 hours. Using an ice cream dipper, put 1 scoop of frozen mixture in a highball glass. Pour ginger ale or lemon-lime drink over top. Stir and serve.

Cordon Bluegrass
Junior League of Louisville, Kentucky

OUCHDOWN TODDY

8 cups apple cider

4 cinnamon sticks

1 whole nutmeg, cut in half

6 whole cloves

4 whole allspice

½ cup packed brown sugar

6 ounces frozen lemonade concentrate

6 ounces frozen pineapple-orange
  juice concentrate

1 liter Canadian whiskey

½ cup packed brown sugar

Combine apple cider, cinnamon sticks, nutmeg, cloves, allspice and ½ cup brown sugar in a saucepan and simmer for 10 minutes, stirring occasionally. Stir in the lemonade concentrate and pineapple-orange juice concentrate and simmer for a few minutes. Stir in the whiskey and ½ cup brown sugar. Cook until heated through, but do not let boil. Strain through a wire mesh strainer into a heatproof pitcher. Serve immediately or pour into thermos bottles to keep warm.

Note: For a nonalcoholic version, you may use ginger ale instead of whiskey.

Five Forks
Kerr-Vance Academy, Henderson, North Carolina

BERRY YOGURT SMOOTHIE

1 cup frozen unsweetened raspberries

1 cup frozen unsweetened blackberries

1 cup nonfat vanilla yogurt

1 cup 2% milk

3 tablespoons honey

1 teaspoon grated orange zest

1 teaspoon vanilla extract

Large pinch of cinnamon

Combine the ingredients in an electric blender. Place the top on the blender and blend until everything is well combined. Pour the smoothie carefully into tall glasses.

Junior Leagues In the Kitchen with Kids
Association of Junior Leagues International, FRP.INC

Hot Tia Maria and Coffee

1 teaspoon sugar

Hot coffee

1½ ounces Tia Maria

3 tablespoons heavy cream, lightly whipped

Chocolate shavings

In an Irish coffee glass or mug combine the sugar and enough hot coffee to dissolve the sugar. Add the Tia Maria and fill the glass to within 1 inch of the rim with hot coffee. Float 3 tablespoons lightly whipped cream on the coffee and sprinkle it with chocolate shavings to taste.

Simply Simpatico, The Home of Authentic Southwest Cooking
Junior League of Albuquerque, New Mexico

Citrus Tea

3 cups water

2 cloves

1 family-size tea bag

2/3 cup sugar

1½ cups pineapple juice

½ cup orange juice

2 to 4 tablespoons fresh lemon juice

Combine the water and cloves in a saucepan and bring to a boil. Boil for 10 minutes. Remove from the heat and add the tea bag. Let stand to steep for 10 minutes. Remove and discard the tea bag and cloves. Stir the sugar, pineapple juice, orange juice and lemon juice into the tea. Chill for 2 to 10 hours.

Simply Southern
Newnan Junior Service League, Georgia

Front Porch Tea

10 cups water, divided
1 cup sugar
2 cups boiling water
2 large family-size tea bags
1 (12-ounce) can frozen lemonade concentrate, thawed
1 tablespoon vanilla
1 tablespoon almond extract
Fresh peach slices

To make sugar syrup, in a 1-quart saucepan, combine 2 cups of the water and the sugar. Cook and stir until sugar dissolves. Set aside. In a 4-quart pitcher or bowl, pour the boiling water over the tea bags. Let stand 5 minutes. Remove tea bags. Add the remaining 8 cups water, the sugar syrup, lemonade concentrate, vanilla and almond extract. Serve over ice. Garnish with fresh peach slices, if desired.

Heart & Soul
Junior League of Memphis, Tennessee

Plantation Tea

Makes ½ gallon

1 quart boiling water
7 tea bags
12 stems mint
1 cup sugar
1 small can frozen lemonade
4 lemonade cans of water
1½ cups pineapple juice

In large punch bowl or pitcher, pour boiling water over tea bags, mint, and sugar. Stir. Let sit for 30 minutes, then discard tea bags and mint, squeezing them out into liquid. Add lemonade, water, and pineapple juice. Chill to serve.

Cordon Bluegrass
Junior League of Louisville, Kentucky

SPICED TEA MIX

2 cups Tang
1 cup powdered instant tea
1 cup apple cider mix
½ cup sugar
2 (6-ounce) packages lemon gelatin

2 (6-ounce) packages orange/pineapple
  gelatin
2 teaspoons apple pie spice
2 teaspoons cinnamon

Mix all ingredients together. Add 3 heaping teaspoons to a large cup. Pour hot water into cup. Stir until mixture is dissolved. Store mix in airtight container.

Wild Wild West, Cuisine from the Land of Cactus & Cowboys
Junior League of Odessa, Texas

CAJUN JUICE

2 cups water
6 regular tea bags
1 cup sugar

1 (6-ounce) can frozen limeade concentrate
1 can frozen pink lemonade concentrate
Mint leaves for garnish

Bring the water to a boil in a saucepan. Remove from the heat and add the tea bags. Let steep, covered, for 10 to 15 minutes. Remove the tea bags and add the sugar. Stir until the sugar is dissolved. Pour into a 4-quart pitcher. Add the limeade and lemonade concentrates and stir until melted. Add enough cold water to make 2 quarts. Add ice to fill the pitcher. Serve garnished with mint leaves.

Marshes to Mansions
Junior League of
Lake Charles, Louisiana

Faced with the coming heat, what goes down easier than cool, icy water? Water flavored with the irresistible tang of blackberries. We found that you can turn blackberries into luscious ice cubes that will flavor a glass of water as they thaw. Try it to create a refreshing drink that looks—and tastes—like the essence of summer.

VOLUNTEERISM ROCKS

What do you do as new cookbook chair for the Junior League of Baton Rouge, Louisiana, when your league already has a blockbuster cookbook, *River Road Recipes,* which is in its 50th year of printing and has sold 1.3 million copies?

For Holly Sides, the answer was simple. "There are still people out there who don't have the cookbook and still national avenues we have not explored," she said. "We are just fortunate that the ladies 50 years ago put out a product that makes it easy to build on."

River Road Recipes annually outsells all the other cookbooks combined that have been produced by the league. The other cookbooks are *River Road Recipes II, River Road Recipes III (A Healthy Collection),* and *River Road Recipes IV (Warm Welcomes).*

Cookbook sales alone have given $3 million back to the Baton Rouge community over the last 50 years to support children and education, physical health and well-being. Some of the money helped produce Baton Rouge facilities such as the Louisiana Arts and Science Museum and the Speech and Hearing Foundation.

RIVER ROAD RECIPES
JUNIOR LEAGUE OF BATON ROUGE

Celebrating 50 Years of Cajun Cooking

Besides marketing the league's four books, Holly's committee of 40 also had the challenge of looking at new projects within the cookbook realm—and they met the challenge head on. They have become the first Junior League to create an interactive on-line cooking/entertaining program, called River Road Recipes—A Louisiana Tradition.

Savvy cooks buying the on-line cookbook gets 125 top-rated recipes taken from all four of the original cookbooks. They can chose the recipes they want to make, organize a menu, print out a grocery list, and print out place cards for seating the guests. The recipes can even be altered through the system according to how many people the cook wants to feed.

As an attorney, Holly used to think that most people were cynical and selfish, but volunteering with the Junior League has changed her mind. "I am always touched about the simplicity of the help, excitement, and goodness that can come out of volunteering."

Breakfast Blintzes

1 cup sugar
4 teaspoons cinnamon
8 ounces cream cheese
½ cup sugar
2 egg yolks
2 large loaves white bread, sliced and crusts trimmed
1 cup margarine, melted

Mix 1 cup sugar and the cinnamon in a shallow dish. Combine the cream cheese, ½ cup sugar and the egg yolks in a mixing bowl. Beat until creamy, scraping the sides of the bowl as needed. Flatten each slice of the bread with a rolling pin. Spread one side of each slice of bread thinly with the cream cheese mixture. Roll each lengthwise to enclose the filling. Dip in the margarine and roll in the cinnamon-sugar. Arrange on a baking sheet and freeze until firm. Place in resealable plastic freezer bags. Freeze until baking time. Do not thaw before baking. Bake at 400 degrees for 15 minutes.

Silver Spoons, Blueberry Afternoons
National Association of Junior Auxiliaries, Greenville, Mississippi

Chiliquillas

10 or 11 tortillas, cut in bite-size pieces
1 large tomato, peeled and chopped
½ onion, chopped
1 or ½ fresh jalapeño pepper, minced
4 eggs
Sour cream
Mozzarella cheese, finely grated

Fry the tortillas until crisp in hot oil. Pour off most of the grease, leaving enough to cook the eggs in. Salt the pan of tortillas well. Mix together the tomato, onion, jalapeño, and eggs. Add to the skillet of crisp tortillas and scramble together until the eggs are done. Put the sour cream and grated cheese over each serving. Excellent with a fresh fruit salad and hot coffee or Mexican hot chocolate.

A Mexican brunch dish.

Junior League of Dallas Cookbook
Junior League of Dallas, Texas

Copper Mountain Quiche

1 pound fresh spinach
2 tablespoons all-purpose flour
1 cup (4 ounces) shredded Cheddar cheese
1 cup (4 ounces) shredded Swiss cheese
3 eggs, beaten
½ cup mayonnaise

½ cup cream
10 slices bacon, crisp-cooked and crumbled
8 ounces fresh mushrooms, sliced
1 bunch green onions, sliced
1 unbaked (9-inch) pie shell

Rinse and trim the spinach. Cook the spinach in a small amount of water in a saucepan just until tender. Drain well and chop. Combine the spinach and flour in a large bowl. Add the Cheddar cheese, Swiss cheese, eggs, mayonnaise, cream, bacon, mushrooms and green onions and mix well. Pour into the pie shell. Bake at 350 degrees for 1 hour or until set.

A Savory Place, Culinary Favorites of Amelia Island
Micah's Place, Amelia Island, Florida

"There's a great feeling of satisfaction when you work with a large group of people and you end up with this beautiful cookbook, *A Savory Place*. I learned a lot about people during the process. Sometimes you just don't know what they can bring to a project, talents you never knew they had."

IRIS JACOBSEN
MICAH'S PLACE, AMELIA ISLAND, FLORIDA

COWBOY QUICHE

1 pound ground sirloin
1 cup finely chopped green onions
½ cup finely chopped red bell pepper
½ cup canned diced green chiles
2 garlic cloves, minced
1 tablespoon salt-free seasoned salt
   (Mrs. Dash preferred)
1 teaspoon salt

1 teaspoon pepper
12 eggs, or 4 cups pasteurized egg substitute
1½ cups milk or soy milk
2 cups (8 ounces) shredded sharp
   Cheddar cheese
Sour cream
Additional chopped green onions and
   shredded Cheddar cheese

Preheat the oven to 350 degrees. Sauté the ground sirloin, green onions, bell pepper, green chiles, garlic, seasoned salt, salt and pepper in a large nonstick skillet, stirring until the beef is brown and crumbly. Whisk the eggs in a large bowl until frothy. Whisk in the milk. Add the beef mixture and 2 cups cheese and mix well. Pour into a greased 9×13-inch baking dish. Bake for 1 hour or until a wooden pick inserted comes out clean. Let stand for 5 minutes before cutting into squares. Garnish with sour cream, green onions, and cheese. Serve with your favorite salsa.

Black Tie & Boots, Timeless Traditions from the New West
The University of Wyoming, Laramie, Wyoming

FIVE-LAYER QUICHE

16 ounces whole green chiles, drained
1 pound bacon, cooked crisp and crumbled
1 small onion, chopped
1 pound Monterey Jack cheese, shredded
1 pound Cheddar cheese, shredded
12 eggs

Preheat oven to 350 degrees. Slit the green chiles lengthwise to but not through the other side and lay flat over the bottom of a 9×13 inch baking pan. Sprinkle with the bacon, onion, Monterey Jack cheese and Cheddar cheese in the order listed. Whisk eggs in a bowl until blended and pour over the prepared layers. Bake for 45 minutes or until a wooden pick inserted in the center comes out clean. For variety, add some of your favorite ingredients prior to the cheese layers.

Pomegranates & Prickly Pears—flavorful entertaining from the Junior League of Phoenix
Junior League of Phoenix, Arizona

SOUTHWESTERN CRUSTLESS QUICHE

½ cup butter (1 stick)

½ cup flour

6 extra-large eggs

1 pound Monterey Jack cheese,
   cubed or shredded

2 cups cottage cheese

1 cup milk

3 ounces cream cheese, softened

1 teaspoon baking powder

1 teaspoon salt

¼ teaspoon white pepper

2 (14-ounce) cans artichoke hearts,
   drained, chopped

Melt the butter in a saucepan until melted. Stir in the flour. Cook over medium-low heat until smooth, stirring constantly. Whisk the eggs in a bowl until blended. Stir in the flour mixture, Monterey Jack cheese, cottage cheese, milk, cream cheese, baking powder, salt and white pepper. Arrange the chopped artichokes over the bottom of a greased 9×13 inch baking pan. Spoon the cheese mixture over the top. Bake at 350 degrees for 40 minutes.

A Taste of Enchantment
Junior League of Albuquerque, New Mexico

MILANO OMELETTE

¼ cup grated carrot

2 tablespoons minced onion

1 clove garlic, minced

1½ teaspoons olive oil

1½ teaspoons butter

1 teaspoon brown sugar

¼ cup cream cheese, softened

3 eggs

Salt to taste

Pepper to taste

1 cup marinara sauce, heated

Sauté the carrot, onion and garlic in a mixture of the olive oil and butter in a skillet. Stir in the brown sugar. Cook until caramelized. Add the vegetable mixture to the cream cheese in a bowl and mix well. Whisk the eggs, salt and pepper in a bowl until blended. Pour the eggs into a large nonstick sauté pan. Cook as for an omelet, lifting the edge of the omelet as the eggs set to allow the uncooked egg to flow underneath; do not stir.

Microwave the cream cheese mixture in a microwave-safe dish just until heated through. Spread over the omelet. Top with half the marinara sauce. Fold the omelet over to enclose the filling. Transfer the omelet to a heated plate. Drizzle with the remaining marinara sauce.

Splendor in the Bluegrass
Junior League of Louisville, Kentucky

Make-Ahead Sausage Breakfast Casserole

SERVES 8 TO 10

9 medium eggs
3 cups milk
1½ teaspoons salt
1½ teaspoons prepared mustard
3 slices bread, cubed
1 pound sausage, cooked, drained and cooled
1½ cups shredded cheese

Combine the eggs, milk, salt and prepared mustard in a bowl and mix well. Stir in the bread, sausage and cheese. Chill, covered, for 8 to 12 hours.

Preheat the oven to 350 degrees. Spoon the sausage mixture into a 9×13-inch baking dish and bake for 45 minutes or until a knife inserted in the center comes out clean.

Creating Comfort
Genesis Women's Shelter, Dallas, Texas

Yankee-Pleaser Casserole

SERVES 8 SOUTHERNERS OR 6 YANKEES

1 pound bulk sausage with sage
4 ounces (1 cup) shredded sharp
 Cheddar cheese
1 (8-ounce) package corn muffin mix
1 cup hot cooked grits

½ cup (1 stick) butter, melted
4 eggs
1¾ cups milk, heated
2 ounces (½ cup) shredded sharp
 Cheddar cheese

Brown the sausage in a skillet, stirring until crumbly; drain. Sprinkle into a greased 2-quart baking dish and top with 1 cup shredded cheese. Combine the corn muffin mix, grits, butter, eggs and milk in a bowl and mix well. Pour into the prepared dish. Top with ½ cup cheese. Bake at 325 degrees for 45 minutes.

You may prepare the dish in advance and store in the refrigerator or freezer until needed. Allow a frozen casserole to thaw before baking and increase the baking time to 55 minutes for a refrigerated casserole.

Notably Nashville
Junior League of Nashville, Tennessee

Green Chile Strata

1 loaf French bread
1½ cups shredded Monterey Jack cheese
1½ cups shredded Cheddar cheese
8 ounces cream cheese, chopped
8 slices bacon, crisp-fried and crumbled
3 to 5 roasted fresh green chiles, peeled,
   seeded and chopped

10 large eggs
2 cups milk
½ teaspoon dry mustard
Cayenne pepper to taste

Cut the crust from the French bread and tear the bread into pieces. Spread in a greased 9×13-inch baking dish. Layer the Monterey Jack cheese, Cheddar cheese, and cream cheese over the bread. Top with the bacon and green chiles. Beat the eggs in a bowl and stir in the milk, dry mustard, and cayenne pepper. Pour over the layers. Bake at 350 degrees for 55 to 60 minutes or until set and golden brown. Let stand for 10 minutes before serving.

Lone Star to Five Star
Junior League of Plano, Texas

Texas Breakfast Strata

1 pound mild or hot bulk pork sausage
1 small onion, finely chopped
½ medium red or green bell pepper, chopped
2 (10-ounce) cans diced tomatoes with
   green chiles
10 (10-inch) small flour tortillas, torn into
   bite-size pieces

3 cups (12 ounces) shredded
   Mexican-blend cheese
6 eggs
2 cups buttermilk
Salt and pepper to taste

Preheat the oven to 350 degrees. Brown the sausage in a large skillet over medium-high heat, stirring until crumbly; drain. Add the onion and bell pepper to the sausage in the skillet and sauté until the vegetables are tender. Stir in the tomatoes with green chiles. Reduce the heat and simmer for 10 minutes.

Layer the tortillas, sausage mixture and cheese one-half at a time in a lightly greased 9×13-inch baking pan. Whisk the eggs, buttermilk, salt and pepper in a bowl until smooth. Pour evenly over layers. Bake, covered lightly with foil, for 30 minutes or until golden brown and bubbly.

Treasures from the Bend, Rich in History and Flavor
Fort Bend Junior Service League, Sugar Land, Texas

Tidewater Tortillas

4 (8-inch) spinach tortillas

5.2 ounces Boursin cheese

4 ounces country cured Smithfield ham

4 eggs, scrambled and kept warm

4 ounces Brie cheese, rind removed, sliced

3 tablespoons balsamic vinegar

3 to 4 cups baby greens

Place tortillas on a flat surface. Spread Boursin cheese thinly over one side of tortilla. Divide ham evenly between tortillas to cover Boursin cheese. Sprinkle cooked eggs over ham. Place a layer of Brie cheese over eggs. Toss balsamic vinegar and greens in a small bowl. Place one cup of tossed greens with dressing on each tortilla. Roll up tortilla and enjoy.

Toast to Tidewater
Junior League of Norfolk-Virginia Beach, Virginia

Green Grits

1 cup quick-cooking grits

Salt to taste

4 scallions

1 tablespoon butter

1 (10-ounce) package frozen whole leaf spinach, thawed, squeezed dry and coarsely chopped

½ cup heavy cream

1½ cups freshly grated Parmigiano-Reggiano cheese

Freshly ground pepper to taste

2 large eggs, beaten

Cook the grits using the package directions and season with salt. Cover to keep warm. Trim the scallions, leaving the bulb and 2 inches of the green tops. Thinly slice the scallions. Melt the butter in a large heavy skillet over medium heat. Add the scallions. Sauté for 3 to 4 minutes or until wilted. Add the spinach. Sauté for 2 minutes. Remove from the heat.

Stir the cream into the warm grits until smooth. Add the spinach mixture, 1 cup of the cheese, salt and pepper and mix until combined. Add the eggs and beat with a wooden spoon until combined and smooth. Pour into a greased 10-inch baking dish. Sprinkle with the remaining ½ cup cheese. Bake at 350 degrees for 30 to 40 minutes or until set and the top is brown. Serve hot.

Note: This casserole is excellent to serve in place of potatoes. It can also be made a day ahead and then just baked the day you serve it.

Oh, Shenandoah! A Cookbook from the Museum of the Shenandoah Valley
The Museum of the Shenandoah Valley, Virginia

Pasta with Purple Sage and Browned Butter

1 pound tagliatelle or similar pasta
Salt to taste
¼ cup (½ stick) unsalted butter
35 fresh purple sage leaves, coarsely chopped
1 teaspoon coarse salt
¼ teaspoon (scant) freshly ground pepper
1 cup (4 ounces) freshly grated
    Parmesan cheese
Pepper to taste

Cook the pasta in boiling salted water in a large stockpot until al dente. Melt the butter in a large skillet over medium to medium-high heat. Add the sage, 1 teaspoon coarse salt and ¼ teaspoon pepper. Sauté for 10 minutes or until the butter is brown and the edges of the sage are crisp. Remove from the heat.

Place 2 or 3 tablespoons of the pasta cooking water in a warm serving bowl. Drain the pasta in a colander and place in the bowl. Add the butter mixture and ½ cup or more of the Parmesan cheese and toss to combine. Season with salt and pepper to taste. Serve with the remaining Parmesan cheese.

Note: Butter lovers will appreciate this pasta dish that highlights the mild flavor of the purple variety of this easily grown perennial herb. You will love the crisp edge on the sage if you do not chop it too finely.

Herbal Cookery
The St. Louis Herb Society, Missouri

Spinach Mushroom Florentine

1 pound cremini, sliced
2 (10-ounce) packages frozen chopped
  spinach, thawed and drained
¼ cup chopped onion

¼ cup butter, melted
1 cup shredded Cheddar cheese
1 teaspoon salt
Garlic powder to taste

Preheat the oven to 350 degrees. Sauté the mushrooms in a nonstick skillet until tender. Cool slightly. Press the excess moisture from the spinach. Combine the spinach, onion, butter, ½ cup of the cheese and salt in a bowl and mix well. Spoon half the spinach mixture into a buttered 9×13 inch baking dish and top with half the mushrooms. Sprinkle with garlic powder. Top with the remaining spinach mixture, remaining mushrooms and garlic powder. Sprinkle with the remaining ½ cup cheese and bake for 20 minutes or until bubbly.

Tastes & Treasures
Historical League, Tempe, Arizona

Double Decker French Toast

4 slices whole wheat bread
2 ounces softened cream cheese
2 eggs
1 tablespoon milk
1 teaspoon vanilla extract
¼ teaspoon ground cinnamon
3 tablespoons butter or margarine

Spread 2 slices of the bread with the softened cream cheese. Top each slice with another slice of bread. Beat the eggs until frothy in a flat soup plate or pie plate. Beat in the milk, vanilla and cinnamon. Melt the butter on a griddle or in a large frying pan. While the butter is melting, soak each of the sandwiches on both sides in the egg mixture until well saturated. Place the soaked sandwiches on the griddle and cook, turning once until golden brown on both sides. Serve at once sprinkled with additional cinnamon or drizzled with maple syrup.

Of Tide and Thyme
Junior League of Annapolis, Maryland

OVERNIGHT FRENCH TOAST

1 loaf French bread, cut into ¾-inch slices
8 ounces cream cheese, softened
1½ cups milk
⅓ cup maple syrup
12 eggs
Maple syrup
Whipped cream
Fresh fruit

Arrange a layer of bread in a 9×13-inch baking pan sprayed with nonstick cooking spray. Spread half the cream cheese over the bread. Arrange the remaining bread on the cream cheese layer. Spread the remaining cream cheese on the bread. Whisk together the milk and syrup in a bowl. Add the eggs one at a time, whisking constantly until blended. Pour over the prepared layers. Cover the dish with plastic wrap. Weight the plastic wrap with two boxes confectioners' sugar or cake mix so that the plastic is touching the layers. Chill overnight in the refrigerator.

Preheat the oven to 350 degrees. Bake, uncovered, for 30 to 40 minutes or until the eggs are set. Let stand for 10 minutes loosely covered with aluminum foil. Serve with warm maple syrup, whipped cream and fresh fruit. You may spread your favorite flavor preserves over each layer of cream cheese for extra flavor, if desired.

Savor the Seasons, Vol. 3:
The Culinary Collection
Junior League of
Tampa, Florida

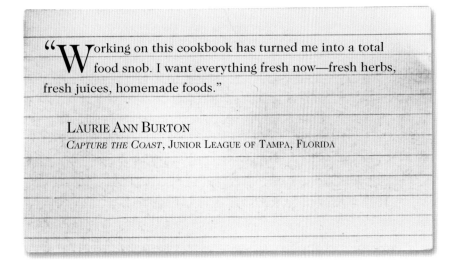

"Working on this cookbook has turned me into a total food snob. I want everything fresh now—fresh herbs, fresh juices, homemade foods."

LAURIE ANN BURTON
CAPTURE THE COAST, JUNIOR LEAGUE OF TAMPA, FLORIDA

CORNMEAL PANCAKES WITH CORN SALSA

1 (10-ounce) package frozen corn

1 cup salsa

1/2 cup yellow cornmeal

1 tablespoon all-purpose flour

1 teaspoon sugar

1/2 teaspoon baking soda

1/2 teaspoon salt

1 cup buttermilk

2 egg yolks

2 egg whites

1/2 cup (2 ounces) shredded Cheddar cheese

1/2 cup sour cream

Microwave the corn in a microwave-safe dish for 2 minutes; drain. Or cook the corn with 1/2 cup boiling water in a saucepan for 1 minute or just until tender; drain. Mix 1/2 cup of the corn with the salsa in a bowl.

Sift the cornmeal, flour, sugar, baking soda and salt into a bowl and mix well. Whisk the buttermilk and egg yolks in a bowl until blended and stir into the cornmeal mixture. Beat the egg whites in a mixing bowl until stiff but not dry peaks form. Fold the egg whites into the cornmeal batter.

Preheat a skillet and spray the hot skillet with nonstick cooking spray. Pour 2 tablespoons of the batter into the hot skillet for each pancake and sprinkle with the remaining corn. Cook until the underside is golden brown and turn. Sprinkle with the cheese and cook until brown on the remaining side. Roll each pancake and top with 1 tablespoon of the corn salsa and a dollop of sour cream.

Dallas Dish
Junior League of Dallas, Texas

Willamette Valley Waffles

½ cup margarine

1 tablespoon granulated sugar

2 egg yolks

1 cup plus 1 tablespoon flour

Dash of salt

4 teaspoons baking powder

1 cup buttermilk

⅛ teaspoon almond flavoring

2 egg whites

⅔ cup chopped hazelnuts

Cream together the margarine and sugar. Add the egg yolks and blend. In a separate container, mix the flour, salt and baking powder. Using low speed on mixer, alternately add the buttermilk and flour to the egg yolk mixture. Add the almond flavoring. Beat the egg whites until stiff and fold into the batter. Spoon batter onto a preheated waffle iron; spread out the batter and sprinkle with approximately 2 tablespoons of nuts. Cook waffles according to directions on waffle iron. Repeat.

Taste of Oregon
Junior League of Eugene, Oregon

Anne's Banana Breakfast Bars

¾ cup unsweetened applesauce

¾ cup packed brown sugar

1 egg, beaten

1 teaspoon cinnamon

¼ teaspoon baking soda

1½ cups ripe bananas, mashed

4 cups rolled oats

½ cup dried cranberries

½ cup walnuts or pecans, chopped

Preheat the oven to 350 degrees. Combine the applesauce, brown sugar, egg, cinnamon, baking soda, bananas, oats, cranberries and walnuts in a large bowl and mix well. The batter will be very stiff. Spread the batter evenly in a 9×13-inch baking pan lightly coated with nonstick cooking spray. Bake for 30 to 35 minutes or until golden brown and a wooden pick inserted into the center comes out clean. Remove from the oven to cool completely. Cut into bars. Store in an airtight container or freeze in freezer bags.

Living Well, More Than a Cookbook
National Extension Association of Family and Consumer Sciences, Dallas, Texas

Deep-Fried Bread (Sopaipillas)

4 cups flour
1½ teaspoons salt
1 teaspoon baking powder
1 tablespoon lard or butter
1 envelope dry yeast

¼ cup warm water (105 to 115 degrees)
1¼ cups scalded milk, cooled to
    room temperature
Oil for deep-frying

Combine the flour, salt and baking powder in a bowl and mix well. Cut in the lard until crumbly. Dissolve the yeast in the warm water. Stir into the cooled scalded milk. Add 1¼ cups of the liquid to the dry ingredients, stirring to form a dough. Add enough of the remaining ¼ cup liquid gradually to make a dough that is firm and holds its shape. Knead the dough on a floured surface for 5 minutes or until smooth and elastic. Invert the bowl over the dough. Let rest for 10 minutes or until dough will yield a hole when poked. Separate dough into 4 equal portions. Roll 1 portion ¼ inch thick or slightly thinner, keeping the remaining portions covered with plastic wrap. Cut the rolled dough into triangles or squares; do not reroll any of the dough. Fry the sopaipillas, in batches, in the hot oil until puffed and hollow; holding under the surface of the oil if needed. Repeat with the remaining portions of dough.

Note: You may omit the yeast and water and increase the milk to 1½ cups.

A Taste of Enchantment
Junior League of Albuquerque, New Mexico

New Orleans Doughnuts

1 package active dry yeast
1½ cups warm water
½ cup sugar
1 teaspoon salt
2 eggs

1 cup undiluted evaporated milk
7 cups all-purpose flour
¼ cup soft shortening
Oil for frying
Confectioners' sugar

In large bowl, sprinkle yeast over water; stir to dissolve. Add sugar, salt, eggs and milk. Blend with rotary beater. Add 4 cups of the flour; beat smooth. Add shortening; beat in remaining flour. Cover and chill overnight. Roll out on floured board to ⅛-inch thickness. Cut into 2½-inch squares. Deep fry at 360 degrees 2 to 3 minutes or until lightly browned on each side. Drain on paper towels. Sprinkle heavily with confectioners' sugar. Dough keeps well in refrigerator for several days. Cover bowl with plastic wrap and punch down occasionally.

Talk About Good!
Junior League of Lafayette, Louisiana

BANANA BREAD

SERVES 10 TO 12

½ cup shortening, or 1 stick of margarine

1 cup sugar

2 eggs

1½ cups mashed bananas (3 to 5 bananas)

2 cups sifted flour

1 teaspoon salt

½ teaspoon baking soda

1 teaspoon vanilla

⅔ cup chopped nuts

Cream shortening; add sugar slowly and cream well. Add eggs and beat. Add bananas; then add flour, salt, and soda which have been sifted together. Add vanilla and nuts. Bake for approximately 1 hour and 15 minutes at 325 degrees in a greased 2-quart loaf pan. Test center for doneness. Cool thoroughly, wrap in foil, and keep in refrigerator. Best for slicing after at least one day.

The Gasparilla Cookbook
Junior League of Tampa, Florida

Through Children's Literacy, The Junior League of Tampa promotes literacy by sending trained volunteers into kindergarten classrooms at Hillsborough County Title I schools to conduct storytelling sessions and give each child 16 books per year to take home. For some of the children, these are the first of their very own. The project has also provided classrooms with multilingual literacy backpacks, teaching materials for centers, butterfly gardens, and additional books.

CARROT BREAD

1½ cups flour
1 cup sugar
1 teaspoon baking powder
1 teaspoon baking soda
1 teaspoon cinnamon
¼ teaspoon salt

½ cup vegetable oil
2 large eggs
1 teaspoon vanilla extract
1 cup grated carrots
½ cup chopped pecans (optional)

Mix first 6 ingredients in bowl. Add the oil, eggs and vanilla and mix well. Stir in grated carrots and pecans. Spoon into a greased loaf pan. Bake at 325 degrees for 1 hour. Remove to a wire rack to cool.

Tropical Settings
Junior League of Fort Myers, Florida

HAWAIIAN NUT BREAD

SERVES 20 TO 24

3 cups flour
2 cups sugar
1 teaspoon baking soda
1 teaspoon salt
1 teaspoon cinnamon
1 cup chopped pecans or walnuts

3 eggs, beaten
1 (8-ounce) can crushed pineapple, drained
1½ cups vegetable oil
2 cups mashed bananas
2 teaspoons vanilla extract

Combine the flour, sugar, baking soda, salt and cinnamon in a medium bowl and mix well. Stir in the pecans. Combine the eggs, pineapple, vegetable oil, bananas and vanilla in a large bowl and mix well. Add the dry ingredients to the egg mixture and stir just until moistened.

Spoon the batter into 2 greased and floured loaf pans. Bake at 350 degrees for 1 hour and 5 minutes or until a wooden pick inserted near the center comes out clean. Remove to a wire rack to cool.

Las Vegas: Glitter to Gourmet
Junior League of Las Vegas, Nevada

HOOD RIVER APPLESAUCE BREAD

MAKES 2 LOAVES

4 cups flour

2 tablespoons cornstarch

2 cups sugar

4 teaspoons baking soda

1 teaspoon cinnamon

½ teaspoon ground cloves

½ teaspoon allspice

½ teaspoon nutmeg

¼ teaspoon salt

1 cup vegetable oil

3 cups applesauce

1 cup raisins

½ cup chopped walnuts

Mix the flour, cornstarch, sugar, baking soda, cinnamon, cloves, allspice, nutmeg and salt in a large bowl. Mix the oil, applesauce, raisins and walnuts in a medium bowl. Add to the dry ingredients and stir to mix well. Divide the batter between 2 greased 5×9-inch loaf pans.

Bake at 350 degrees for 1 hour or until a wooden pick inserted in the center comes out clean. Cool in the pans for 10 minutes. Invert the bread onto wire racks and let cool completely.

Cooking from the Coast to the Cascades
Junior League of Eugene, Oregon

LUSCIOUS LEMON LOAF

MAKES 1 LOAF

1½ cups all-purpose flour

1 teaspoon baking powder

¼ teaspoon salt

1 cup sugar

½ cup (1 stick) butter

2 large eggs

½ cup milk

¼ cup grated lemon zest

¼ cup fresh lemon juice

1 cup walnuts, chopped

1 teaspoon lemon extract

Preheat the oven to 350 degrees. Grease or line a 5×8-inch loaf pan with baking parchment paper. Sift the flour, baking powder and salt together. Combine the sugar, butter and eggs in a mixing bowl. Beat using a mixer fitted with a paddle attachment until light and fluffy, scraping the bowl occasionally. Add the flour mixture alternately with the milk, mixing well after each addition. Stir in the lemon zest, lemon juice, walnuts and flavoring.

Spoon the batter into the prepared pan and bake for 55 to 60 minutes or until the loaf tests done. Cool in the pan for 5 minutes. Remove to a wire rack to cool completely.

Note: You may drizzle with a mixture of ¼ cup confectioners' sugar, 1 teaspoon half-and-half and 1 teaspoon lemon juice.

Tastes & Treasures, A Storytelling Cookbook of Historic Arizona
Historical League, Tempe, Arizona

Strawberry Bread

MAKES 1 LOAF

1 cup all-purpose flour	2 eggs, beaten
½ cup sugar	¾ cup cooking oil
1½ teaspoons cinnamon	1 (10-ounce) package frozen strawberries, thawed
½ teaspoon salt	
½ teaspoon baking soda	¾ cup chopped nuts

Mix dry ingredients. Add liquid ingredients. Add strawberries and nuts. Mix well and pour into greased 9×5×3-inch loaf pan. Bake at 350 degrees for 1 hour.

The Stenciled Strawberry Cookbook
Junior League of Albany, New York

Sailor's Skillet Bread

MAKES 1 LOAF

½ cup sugar	½ teaspoon baking soda
1 tablespoon butter or margarine	4 cups flour
2 cups buttermilk	1 tablespoon baking powder
½ cup raisins	1½ teaspoons salt
2 tablespoons caraway seeds	

Preheat oven to 350 degrees.

Beat sugar and butter together in a large mixing bowl. In another bowl, combine buttermilk, raisins, caraway seeds and baking soda. Stir into sugar mixture. Sift together flour, baking powder and salt. Gradually stir into buttermilk mixture. Turn into a greased heavy 9-inch skillet with an ovenproof handle. (Wrap a plastic-handled skillet in a double thickness of aluminum foil.)

Bake in preheated oven for 60 minutes. Turn out of pan onto a clean towel and let stand for 30 minutes. Cut into wedges and serve warm.

Simply Classic
Junior League of Seattle, Washington

Texas Panhandle Bread

1 cup milk
½ cup (1 stick) butter
1 envelope dry or fast-rising yeast
½ cup warm water (100 to 110 degrees)
2 eggs

½ cup sugar
⅓ teaspoon salt
3 cups all-purpose flour
6 tablespoons butter

Scald the milk with ½ cup butter in a saucepan; cool. Dissolve the yeast in the water. Beat the eggs in a mixing bowl until light and fluffy. Add the sugar and salt and beat well. Stir in the milk mixture. Beat in 1½ cups of the flour until smooth. Stir in the yeast mixture. Let rise, uncovered, for 1 hour. Add the remaining 1½ cups flour and mix well. Cover with a damp cloth and chill for 8 to 10 hours. Let stand at room temperature for 2 hours. Melt 6 tablespoons butter in a bundt pan, turning to coat the sides. Place the dough in the prepared pan and let rise for 30 minutes. Bake at 350 degrees for 30 minutes or until a wooden pick inserted in the center comes out clean. Cool in the pan for 10 minutes. Invert onto a wire rack to cool completely.

Settings Sunrise to Sunset
Assistance League of the Bay Area, Houston, Texas

Spoon Bread Berea Style

SERVES 4 TO 6

3 cups milk
1 cup cornmeal
3 eggs, well beaten
1 teaspoon salt
3 tablespoons baking powder
3 tablespoons butter, melted
1 tablespoon butter (additional)

Combine 2 cups milk with cornmeal in a saucepan. Bring to a boil, stirring constantly. Remove from heat. Add remainder of milk, well-beaten eggs, salt, baking powder, and melted butter. Pour into a greased deep-dish casserole and bake at 350 degrees for 30 minutes, or until brown. Top with additional tablespoon of butter and allow to melt before serving.

Cordon Bluegrass
Junior League of Louisville, Kentucky

CRAWFISH CORN BREAD

1 yellow onion, chopped
1/2 cup chopped bell pepper
1/4 cup chopped green onions
1/4 cup (1/2 stick) butter
2 jalapeño chiles, chopped
2 cups yellow cornmeal
1 tablespoon baking powder
1 teaspoon salt

1/2 teaspoon baking soda
1 1/2 cups (6 ounces) shredded
   Cheddar cheese
1 (15-ounce) can cream-style corn
1 cup milk
1/2 cup vegetable oil
3 eggs, lightly beaten
1 pound frozen crawfish tails, thawed

Sauté the yellow onion, bell pepper and green onions in the butter in a skillet until tender. Stir in the jalapeño chiles. Combine the cornmeal, baking powder, salt and baking soda in a bowl and mix well. Stir the cheese, corn, milk, oil and eggs into the cornmeal mixture. Add the onion mixture and mix well. Stir in the crawfish tails.

Spoon the batter into a greased 9-inch cast-iron skillet. Bake at 400 degrees for 35 to 45 minutes or until light brown. Serve with a bowl of soup and/or a mixed green salad. You may bake the corn bread in a greased 9×13-inch baking pan.

Warm Welcomes: River Road Recipes IV
Junior League of Baton Rouge, Louisiana

THE BEST LITTLE JALAPEÑO CORN BREAD IN TEXAS

1 package corn bread mix
1 egg
1/2 cup chopped green onions
1 (8-ounce) can cream-style corn

1/4 cup chopped jalapeño chiles
3/4 cup shredded Cheddar cheese
1 tablespoon sugar
2 tablespoons vegetable oil

Preheat the oven to 425 degrees. Combine the corn bread mix, egg, green onions, corn, jalapeño chiles, cheese, sugar and oil in a bowl and mix well. Pour into a greased cast-iron skillet or 9-inch pie plate. Bake for 25 minutes or until golden brown.

Note: Omit the sugar if using Jiffy brand corn bread mix.

Tuxedos to Tailgates
Dallas Junior Forum, Texas

Angel Biscuits

1 envelope dry yeast
2 tablespoons lukewarm water
5 cups self-rising flour
¼ cup sugar

1 cup shortening
2 cups buttermilk
6 tablespoons butter, melted

Dissolve the yeast in the lukewarm water in a small bowl. Let stand for 5 minutes or until bubbly. Mix the flour and sugar in a large bowl. Cut in the shortening with a pastry blender until crumbly. Add the yeast mixture and buttermilk and stir just until moistened. Cover and chill for 8 to 10 hours. Knead the dough on a floured work surface 10 to 12 times. Roll the dough ½ inch thick. Cut with a biscuit cutter. Dip the biscuits in the melted butter and fold in half. Place on a greased baking sheet. Let rise for 2 hours. Bake at 400 degrees for 12 to 15 minutes or until golden brown.

Dining with Pioneers, Volume 3
AT&T Pioneers, Tennessee Chapter 21

Banana Chip Praline Muffins

SERVES 12

3 small ripe bananas
1 egg
1½ cups pancake mix
½ cup granulated sugar
2 teaspoons vegetable oil

1 cup semi-sweet chocolate chips
⅓ cup pecans, toasted and chopped
3 tablespoons brown sugar
2 tablespoons butter, melted

Mash the bananas in a bowl. Add the egg, pancake mix, granulated sugar and oil and stir just until combined. Fold in the chocolate chips. Place paper liners in muffin cups and coat with nonstick cooking spray. Fill the prepared muffin cups three-fourths full. Combine the pecans, brown sugar and butter in a bowl and mix well. Spoon equal amounts of the pecan mixture onto the center of the muffins. Bake at 400 degrees for 18 to 20 minutes or until golden brown. Remove the muffins from the pan to a wire rack to cool.

Note: If you want to use mini chocolate chips, reduce the amount to ½ cup.

Five Forks
Kerr-Vance Academy, Henderson, North Carolina

3 cups all-purpose flour
1 tablespoon baking powder
1/2 teaspoon baking soda
1/2 teaspoon salt
10 tablespoons unsalted butter, softened
1 cup minus 1 tablespoon sugar
2 eggs
1 1/2 cups plain low-fat yogurt

Preheat oven to 375 degrees. Spray muffin pan with nonstick cooking spray. Combine flour, baking powder, baking soda and salt and set aside. Beat butter and sugar on medium-high speed with electric mixer until light and fluffy. Add eggs one at a time, beating well after each addition. Beat in half of flour mixture and half of yogurt, mixing well. Repeat. Pour evenly into muffin pans. Bake for 25 minutes or until golden. Cool 5 minutes on wire rack and serve warm.

Note: To make Cinnamon-Coated Muffins, combine 1/2 cup sugar and 2 teaspoons cinnamon. Dip warm muffins in melted butter, then in sugar mixture.

To make Poppy Seed Muffins, add 3 tablespoons poppy seeds to flour mixture and 1 tablespoon lemon zest to butter and sugar mixture. Heat 1/4 cup sugar and 1/2 cup lemon juice until sugar dissolves and a light syrup forms. Brush over warm muffins.

Full Moon—High Tide
Beaufort Academy, South Carolina

"What I miss most about the end of the cookbook tasting process is meeting with the committee for coffee and recipe tasting at a local coffee shop. Even the owner would love it because he would add opinions as well."

KATHRYN TORTORICI
TABLES OF CONTENT, JUNIOR LEAGUE OF BIRMINGHAM, ALABAMA

Pumpkin Muffins

2/3 cup vegetable oil

1 cup sugar

2 eggs

1 (16-ounce) can pumpkin

1½ cups flour

1 teaspoon baking powder

1 teaspoon baking soda

½ teaspoon salt

1½ teaspoons pumpkin pie or apple pie spice

½ teaspoon grated orange zest

½ teaspoon grated lemon zest

Beat the oil and sugar in a large bowl until well mixed. Add the eggs and pumpkin and beat well. Sift the flour, baking powder, baking soda, salt and pumpkin pie spice into a bowl and mix well. Add the orange zest and lemon zest and toss to mix. Stir into the pumpkin mixture. Pour the batter into greased muffin cups. Bake at 350 degrees for 20 to 25 minutes or until the muffins test done.

The Swan's Palette
Forward Arts Foundation, Atlanta, Georgia

Tennessee Spice Muffins

MAKES 7 DOZEN MINI MUFFINS

1 cup (2 sticks) butter or margarine, softened

2 cups sugar

2 eggs

2 cups applesauce (preferably unsweetened)

1 tablespoon cinnamon

2 teaspoons allspice

1 teaspoon ground cloves

4 cups flour

2 teaspoons baking soda

1 teaspoon salt

1 cup nuts, chopped

Confectioners' sugar

Cream the butter and sugar in a mixing bowl until light and fluffy. Add the eggs 1 at a time, mixing well after each addition. Add the applesauce, cinnamon, allspice and cloves; mix well. Sift the flour, baking soda and salt together. Add to the applesauce mixture and beat well. Stir in the nuts. Spoon the batter into lightly greased miniature muffin cups. Bake at 350 degrees for 8 to 10 minutes or until the muffins test done. Remove to a wire rack to cool. Sprinkle with confectioners' sugar.

Note: May refrigerate the batter in an airtight container for up to 2 weeks. Baked muffins freeze well. Reheat before serving.

Open House
Junior League of Murfreesboro, Tennessee

BREADS   69

BASIL POPOVERS WITH GARLIC CHIVE BUTTER

GARLIC CHIVE BUTTER

½ cup (1 stick) unsalted butter, softened

2 tablespoons finely chopped garlic chives

Pinch of salt

To prepare the garlic chive butter, combine the butter, garlic chives and salt in a small bowl and mix well. Chill, covered, until serving time. Make ahead so the flavors can meld. Note: Instead of garlic chives, try 1 tablespoon finely chopped basil leaves with a few drops of garlic juice, or ⅛ teaspoon porcini mushroom powder with garlic chives and garlic juice.

POPOVERS

1¼ cups all-purpose flour

½ teaspoon salt

3 eggs

1¼ cups milk

1 tablespoon unsalted butter, melted

¼ cup chopped fresh basil leaves

¼ cup chopped fresh garlic chives (stems only)

2 tablespoons unsalted butter

To prepare the popovers, mix the flour and salt in a medium mixing bowl. Beat the eggs with the milk in a mixing bowl with an electric hand mixer until light and frothy. Add 1 tablespoon melted butter and beat at low speed until well mixed. Add to the flour mixture and beat at medium speed for 1 to 2 minutes or until the batter is the consistency of heavy cream. Add the basil and garlic chives and mix gently by hand. (The batter may be made in advance up to this point and chilled in the refrigerator. Bring to room temperature before baking.)

Place an oven rack in the middle of the oven. Preheat the oven to 400 degrees. Spray the popover cups with butter-flavor nonstick cooking spray. Heat the popover pan in the oven for 2 minutes. Cut 2 tablespoons butter into six equal pieces. Place one butter piece in each preheated popover cup. Return the pan to the oven and heat for 1 minute or until the butter is bubbly. Fill each cup one-half full with the batter. Bake for 20 minutes. Do not open the oven door. Reduce the oven temperature to 300 degrees. Bake for 20 minutes longer. Serve immediately with the garlic chive butter.

Herbal Cookery
The St. Louis Herb Society,
Missouri

There are three rules to making good popovers: ingredients should be at room temperature; fill cups no more than one-half full; and do not open the oven door. When garlic chives are in season, their blossoms make a lovely garnish. The popovers are best served immediately, but can be held in the oven for up to 30 minutes. Turn off the oven. Pierce the side of each popover to allow the steam to escape and set back in the pan. Let the oven cool for 5 minutes and return the pan to the oven.

Popovers with Strawberry Butter

SERVES 12

Strawberry Butter

½ cup (1 stick) salted butter, softened
½ cup strawberry preserves

To prepare the strawberry butter, blend the butter and preserves in a bowl until smooth.

Popovers

2 large eggs
1 cup milk
1 cup all-purpose flour
½ teaspoon salt
Butter for coating

To prepare the popovers, beat the eggs and milk in a mixing bowl until frothy. Add the flour and salt and beat for 1 minute or until large bubbles form. Let stand at room temperature for 30 to 45 minutes. Beat again for 1 minute or until large bubbles form. Liberally coat twelve muffin cups with butter. Fill each cup two-thirds full with the batter. Bake at 400 degrees for 35 to 40 minutes or until the popovers swell up and are golden brown. Do not open the oven door while baking. Remove from the oven and immediately pierce the tops with a knife to relieve the steam. Serve warm with the strawberry butter.

A Thyme to Entertain—Menus & Traditions of Annapolis
Junior League of Annapolis, Maryland

JUNIOR LEAGUE CINNAMON ROLLS

CINNAMON MIXTURE

1 cup sugar (or to taste)

4 teaspoons cinnamon

Combine sugar and cinnamon in a small bowl. Set aside.

ROLLS

1 teaspoon active dry yeast
  (about 1½ packages)

¼ cup warm water (105 to 115 degrees)

5 tablespoons butter

1 cup milk

½ cup sugar

1 teaspoon salt

1 egg

4 cups flour

½ cup (1 stick) melted butter

Sprinkle yeast into the water in a glass measuring cup; set aside to foam. In a small saucepan, melt the 5 tablespoons of butter in milk; add sugar and salt. Pour the warmed milk mixture from the pan into a large mixing bowl. Mix in the egg and flour. Use an electric mixer with a pastry hook or paddle, or mix by hand with a wooden spoon. Add yeast mixture to the dough. Dough will be sticky. (You may need to add up to ½ cup more flour for ease in handling.) Cover the bowl with a damp cloth. Let dough rise in a warm place about 1½ to 2 hours.

Meanwhile, prepare 9×13-inch pan by brushing a small portion of the melted butter or by spreading the butter with a paper towel. Punch dough down. Roll out dough onto a lightly floured surface, ¼ inch thick. Spread on about half of the remaining melted butter, and half of the cinnamon mixture. Cut strips of dough 3 inches wide and 3 inches long. Roll into cigar-shaped rolls 1 inch wide and 3 inches long. Dip rolls into melted butter and then roll them in the cinnamon mixture. Arrange rolls, seam sides down, into pan. Rolls should touch each other without being crowded. Bake at 350 degrees for 25 to 30 minutes.

Note: To make lighter rolls, let the uncooked rolls rise a second time before baking. For gooey rolls, drizzle additional butter and sprinkle more cinnamon mixture before baking.

Saint Louis Days/
Saint Louis Nights
Junior League of Saint Louis, Missouri

These rolls have been made since the 1940s. Our members still make them weekly, deliver them to several local markets and raise more than $20,000 a year.

ORANGE ROLLS

¼ cup sugar, divided

1 tablespoon fresh orange juice

2 teaspoons (heaping) orange zest, divided

1 (8-count) can refrigerator crescent rolls

⅛ teaspoon cinnamon (optional)

4 teaspoons butter, melted

Combine 2 tablespoons of the sugar, the orange juice and 1 heaping teaspoon of the orange zest in a bowl and mix well. Set the topping aside. Unroll the crescent roll dough. Separate the dough into two rectangles, pressing the perforations to seal.

Combine the remaining 2 tablespoons sugar, remaining 1 heaping teaspoon orange zest and the cinnamon in a small bowl. Brush each rectangle with the butter. Sprinkle with the cinnamon mixture. Roll up each rectangle to enclose the filling, beginning with the short end. Freeze the roll-ups for 10 to 15 minutes.

Remove from the freezer and cut into eight rolls. Place cut side down in a generously buttered 8-inch round baking pan. Top each roll with 2 teaspoons of the topping. Bake at 375 degrees for 18 to 22 minutes or until golden brown. Invert onto a serving plate and immediately invert each roll so that the topping is on top. Delicious served warm.

A Savory Place, Culinary Favorites of Amelia Island
Micah's Place, Amelia Island, Florida

MOTHER'S REFRIGERATOR ROLLS

1 cup scalded milk

½ cup cooking oil

½ cup sugar

1 teaspoon salt

1 package yeast

¼ cup warm water

2 eggs, slightly beaten

4 cups all-purpose flour

Mix the first 4 ingredients and cool to lukewarm. Dissolve yeast in water. Add to the milk mixture. Add eggs and flour. Knead and let rise in a warm place until doubled in bulk. Pat down and put in refrigerator overnight. Pinch off and roll out on a floured surface as needed. Cut out circles and fold in half. Place on a greased cookie sheet and let rise 30 to 40 minutes. Bake in a preheated oven at 400 degrees for 12 minutes.

Note: For cinnamon rolls, ice with a mixture of melted butter or margarine, cinnamon, and powdered sugar.

A Southern Collection—Then and Now
Junior League of Columbus, Georgia

CHERRY ALMOND SCONES

3¼ cups all-purpose flour
¾ cup sugar
2 tablespoons baking powder
1 tablespoon salt
1½ sticks butter, chilled and sliced
¾ cup heavy whipping cream
¾ cup milk
1 tablespoon almond extract
¼ cup dried cherries
¾ cup almonds, blanched and sliced
1 egg, beaten
Sliced almonds

This recipe requires 1 hour of refrigeration. Preheat the oven to 375 degrees. Mix the flour, sugar, baking powder and salt in a bowl. Cut the butter into the flour mixture using a pastry blender until the consistency of coarse meal. Add the cream, milk, flavoring and cherries and mix until a dough forms. Gently mix in ¾ cup almonds.

Divide the dough into two equal portions. Roll or pat each portion into a 1-inch-thick round on a lightly floured surface. Cut each round into six to eight wedges.

Arrange the wedges on a baking sheet lined with baking parchment. Brush the tops with the egg using a pastry brush. Sprinkle with sliced almonds to taste and gently press to adhere. Or, you can sprinkle with coarse sugar. Chill, covered, for at least 1 hour or overnight. You may freeze at this point for future use. Bake for 20 to 30 minutes or until golden brown. Cool on the baking sheet for 2 minutes. Remove to a wire rack. Store in an airtight container.

Texas Tables
Junior League of North Harris and South Montgomery Counties, Texas

John Flynn's Irish Scones

1 cup raisins (optional)
1¼ cups each bread flour and cake flour
2 tablespoons (heaping) baking powder
½ cup shortening

¼ cup sugar
1¼ teaspoons salt
1 egg
½ cup milk

Combine the raisins in enough hot water to cover in a bowl. Let stand for 20 minutes; drain. Combine the bread flour, cake flour and baking powder in a bowl and mix well. Combine the shortening, sugar and salt in a bowl and mix until blended. Stir in the egg. Add the flour mixture gradually and stir until a dough forms. Add the milk gradually and mix well. Stir in the raisins. Shape the dough into 12 rounds and arrange on a baking sheet. Bake at 400 degrees for 20 minutes. Remove to a wire rack to cool.

Explore the Tastes of Maryland, From Mountains to Sea
Maryland Dietetic Association, Brooklandville, Maryland

Gooey Cheese Bread

2 loaves French bread
¾ cup unsalted butter, softened
1 teaspoon (or more) hot red pepper sauce
   (such as Texas Pete)

1 teaspoon dried thyme
1 red onion to taste
4 cups (16 ounces) shredded Cheddar cheese

Slice the bread in half horizontally. Mix the butter, hot sauce and thyme in a bowl. Spread the butter mixture over the cut sides of the bread. Arrange onion slices over the bottom half of the loaves and sprinkle with the cheese. Replace the tops of the loaves and wrap each loaf in foil. Bake at 400 degrees for 25 minutes or until cheese is melted and bread is crusty.

Note: Preshredded cheese is fine to use in this recipe. You may increase the heat by adding more hot sauce, if desired. Make sure you slice the onions very thin. This bread is fabulous with barbeque chicken or ribs.

Five Forks
Kerr-Vance Academy, Henderson, North Carolina

CHALLENGES OF COOKBOOK PUBLISHING

The Junior League of Tampa published *The Gasparilla Cookbook* in 1961. The cookbook remains the standard bearer of the league's cookbook successes, with 22 printings, a 50-year anniversary in the works, and Southern Living Hall of Fame award recognition. Although that cookbook was a hard act to follow, the league has since published *Tampa Treasures* and a four-book series called The Culinary Collection. The proceeds from all these cookbooks go back into the league to help with its commitment to build a healthier, more educated, and safer community for Tampa Bay's children and their families.

As development chairperson for *Capture the Coast,* the fourth book in the Culinary Collection, Laurie Ann Burton discovered a major challenge—the advent of the Internet.

"The explosion of recipes on line made us compare the recipes not only against our other cookbooks but also against high-profile food Web sites, including Southern Living, Food Network, and Epicurious.com," said Laurie Ann. "Part of the process was to vet recipes using Google. We didn't just vet them by title, because titles can change, but by a string of directions in the recipes to find out if they overlapped a recipe on line. It was a tedious process but well worth it."

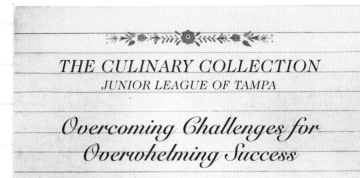

THE CULINARY COLLECTION
JUNIOR LEAGUE OF TAMPA

Overcoming Challenges for Overwhelming Success

Occasionally if an excellent recipe was found on line but they wanted to use it, the committee was able to vary it slightly and add the local Tampa flair.

Betsy Graham, marketing chair for *Everyday Feasts,* the second book in the Culinary Collection, discovered some different challenges.

"We found that our younger league members didn't cook much, plus most of them were working fulltime," Betsy said. "This made it difficult to gather new recipes from them or to get the time commitment for the cookbook committee. However, we realized a cookbook committee of 10 worked just fine in making decisions and keeping on top of things."

Kristie Salzer worked on *Tampa Treasures* and then became food stylist for the culinary series of books.

"My biggest challenge was keeping the books stylistically consistent and current while still reflecting the personality of the committee that was organizing each one," she said.

²/₃ pound beef chuck	2 small potatoes, peeled and cut into
2 tablespoons prepared mustard	⅓-inch cubes
1 tablespoon butter	2 mushrooms, thinly sliced
1 tablespoon vegetable oil	½ green bell pepper, seeded and chopped
1 teaspoon paprika	½ red bell pepper, seeded and chopped
½ teaspoon salt	1 tablespoon ketchup
2 teaspoons all-purpose flour	2 tablespoons red wine
2 onions	Salt to taste
3 cups hot beef stock	Fresh ground pepper to taste
½ cup dry sherry	Tabasco sauce to taste
1 bay leaf	

Cut the beef into ½-inch cubes, removing all fat and skin. Mix the beef with the mustard in a bowl until all the pieces are coated. Sear the beef in the hot butter and oil in a heavy medium saucepan for 5 minutes or until brown. Season with 1 teaspoon paprika and ½ teaspoon salt. Add the flour and cook for 5 minutes or until the mixture is thick and dark brown, stirring constantly. Add the onions, beef stock, wine and bay leaf. Cover and return to a boil. Reduce the heat and simmer for 45 minutes, stirring occasionally. Add the potatoes, mushrooms and bell peppers. Simmer for 30 minutes, stirring occasionally. Stir in the ketchup and wine. Add additional beef stock if needed for the desired consistency. Season with salt, pepper and Tabasco sauce. Discard the bay leaf before serving.

Now Serving
Junior League of
Wichita Falls, Texas

The Junior League of Wichita Falls, is very proud of their relationship with Sheppard Air Force Base, in particular, the Euro-NATO Joint Jet Pilot Training program. This relationship is fostered in large part by the League's International Friendship Committee. The ENJJPT program is made up of instructors and student pilots from Canada.

GRANDMA IDA'S SWEDISH STEW

3 ribs celery, cut into ½-inch pieces

2 tablespoons vegetable oil

2 pounds veal, cut into medium cubes

6 medium potatoes, peeled and cut into
  medium cubes

4 cups water

1 chicken bouillon cube

10 black peppercorns

1 teaspoon salt

4 large carrots, cut into ½-inch pieces

3 cups water

2 tablespoons flour

½ cup milk

Few drops of Kitchen Bouquet (optional)

Salt and pepper to taste

Sauté the celery in 1 tablespoon of the vegetable oil in a 4-quart Dutch oven until wilted. Remove to a bowl. Add the remaining 1 tablespoon vegetable oil to the Dutch oven. Add the veal. Sauté over high heat until the veal is brown and the juices are sealed in. Reduce the heat. Simmer for 10 minutes. Drain, leaving 1 tablespoon of the pan drippings in the Dutch oven. Return the celery to the Dutch oven. Add the potatoes and enough of the 4 cups of water to cover. Stir in the bouillon cube until dissolved. Tie the peppercorns in cheesecloth or place in a tea ball. Add to the Dutch oven and season with 1 teaspoon salt. Cook over medium heat for 20 minutes or until the potatoes are tender.

Cook the carrots in 3 cups water in a 2-quart saucepan over medium heat for 15 minutes; drain. Add to the Dutch oven.

Remove ½ cup liquid from the Dutch oven and place in a bowl. Add the flour and stir until smooth. Add the milk and mix well. Add gradually to the Dutch oven, stirring constantly. Simmer over low heat until thickened; stirring constantly and adding additional milk as needed for the desired consistency. Add Kitchen Bouquet to darken the color of the stew.

Before serving remove 6 to 8 potato pieces from the stew and mash with a fork; return to the stew and stir to mix well. Remove and discard the peppercorns. Season with salt and pepper to taste. Ladle into soup bowls. Serve with Swedish hardtack and butter.

More Enchanted Eating
Friends of the West Shore Symphony, Muskegon, Michigan

KENTUCKY BURGOO

FIRST DAY: STOCK

1 hen, 4 to 5 pounds

1 pound beef stew meat

1 pound veal stew meat

1½ to 2 pounds beef or knuckle bones

1 stalk celery

1 carrot, peeled

1 small onion, peeled

5 to 6 sprigs parsley

1 (10½-ounce) can tomato purée

4 quarts water

1 red pepper pod

¼ cup salt

1 tablespoon lemon juice

1 tablespoon Worcestershire sauce

1 tablespoon sugar

1½ teaspoons black pepper

½ teaspoon cayenne pepper

Combine the 17 stock ingredients in large pot; bring to a boil. Cover and simmer 4 hours. Cool. Strain meat mixture. Reserve meat and stock. Discard vegetables. Remove skin, bone, and gristle from meat, then chop meat. Return meat to stock and refrigerate overnight.

SECOND DAY: BURGOO

6 onions, finely chopped

8 to 10 tomatoes, peeled and chopped

1 turnip, peeled and finely chopped

2 green peppers, chopped

2 cups fresh butter beans

2 cups thinly sliced celery

2 cups finely chopped cabbage

2 cups sliced fresh okra

2 cups fresh corn

½ unpeeled lemon, seeded

The next day, remove and discard fat layer from stock. Add onions, tomatoes, turnip, peppers, beans, celery, cabbage, okra, corn and lemon to the meat and stock. Cover and simmer 1 hour. Uncover and simmer 2 hours longer, stirring frequently to prevent sticking. Burgoo is ready when it reaches the consistency of thick stew.

To Market, To Market
Junior League of Owensboro, Kentucky

Kentucky Burgoo is a thick, often spicy stew that's a famous regional food of Kentucky. Burgoo experts disagree about what meats actually go into burgoo. Each area of Kentucky, and even individual burgoo cooks, use different types of meat in their burgoo. About the only point on which burgoo experts agree is the consistency of the soup. A good burgoo should be thick, but still soupy. This is the reason for the long, slow cooking time. It gives the burgoo time to thicken naturally. In Owensboro, cooks prefer to use mutton, beef, and chicken. Mutton gives burgoo a wild game like flavor that holds its own against the pepper and vegetables in the burgoo.

"Who, excepting Kentuckians and their favored Southern Friends and kinsmen has ever really known the bliss of genuine burgoo?"
—*Washington Post* 16 June, 1906

OYSTER STEW

½ cup water

1 small white onion, chopped

½ cup celery, chopped

1 pint stewing size oysters

½ teaspoon salt

¼ teaspoon pepper

2 tablespoons butter

1 pint half-and-half

Pour water into medium-size saucepan. Add onion and celery and boil until slightly tender. Add oysters and cook until oysters curl. Add salt and pepper. Reduce heat and add butter. Pour in 1 pint of half-and-half.

Savannah Style
Junior League of Savannah, Georgia

CHILI QUEEN'S CHILI

2 pounds lean chili meat

½ pound lean ground chuck

1 onion, chopped

¼ cup green pepper, chopped

2 cloves garlic, minced

1 tablespoon chili powder

1 tablespoon cumin

¾ teaspoon oregano

½ teaspoon sage

2 tablespoons cornmeal

1 (1-ounce) package Williams chili seasoning

1 teaspoon salt

¼ teaspoon black pepper

1 tablespoon Worcestershire sauce

¼ to ½ cup chili sauce

1 (6-ounce) can tomato paste

1 (1-pound) can whole tomatoes

Sauté ground meats, onion, green pepper and garlic in six-quart roasting pan. Add remaining ingredients, blending well. Bring to a boiling point. Reduce heat and simmer, covered, two hours. Beans may be added, if desired.

Stir-Ups
Junior Welfare League of Enid, Oklahoma

Vegetarian Chili

SERVES 8

1 large onion, chopped
5 cloves garlic, minced
2 teaspoons canola oil
1½ cups diced carrots
1 cup diced celery
1½ cups diced zucchini
1 (28-ounce) can crushed tomatoes
1 (48-ounce) can tomato juice
3 tablespoons molasses
5 tablespoons chili powder

5 tablespoons ground cumin
1 tablespoon crumbled dried oregano leaves
½ teaspoon coriander
¼ teaspoon ground cloves
¼ teaspoon ground allspice
3 cups cooked kidney beans
3 cups cooked garbanzo beans
1 cup diced green pepper
2 cups frozen corn kernels
Finely chopped jalapeño peppers, for passing

In a large stockpot, sauté the onion and garlic in the oil until softened. Add the carrots, celery, and zucchini. Partially cook.

Add the crushed tomatoes, tomato juice, molasses, chili powder, cumin, oregano, coriander, cloves and allspice. Bring to a boil, then add both beans, green pepper and corn. Simmer for 10 minutes.

Serve with the jalapeño peppers passed at the table for individual tastes.

Note: It is advisable to wear gloves when handling jalapeño peppers.

Cooking with Music
Boston Symphony Orchestra, Massachusetts

Woodlawn Chicken Mull

VARIABLE SERVINGS

1 small hen (about 4 pounds)
4 large onions, chopped
1 quart milk
1 stick butter or margarine

Catsup
Worcestershire sauce
Red pepper
Saltine crackers, crumbled

Cook hen in a small amount of water. Debone and cut into small pieces. Cook down in stock (add water if necessary) with onions. Add milk, butter, catsup, Worcestershire sauce, and red pepper. Add saltine crackers gradually until mull reaches desired consistency. It is easier if you season hen and stock a little and then add crackers and finish seasoning.

Note: The dish known in northeast Georgia as chicken mull is a stew of chicken meat, broth, milk, butter, vegetables, and seasonings. In South Georgia it is called chicken jallop.

Beyond the Hedges
Junior League of Athens, Georgia

8 slices unsmoked bacon, cut into ½-inch pieces
2 large onions, chopped
8 stalks celery, chopped
12 unpeeled small red potatoes
3 quarts clam juice
1 tablespoon marjoram
1 tablespoon dill
Salt and pepper to taste
1 quart shucked clams with juice

Cook the bacon in a skillet until the drippings are rendered. Drain, reserving 2 tablespoons of the drippings in the skillet. Add the onions and celery and sauté in the drippings over medium-high heat for 5 minutes. Combine with the potatoes, clam juice, marjoram, dill, salt and pepper in a large saucepan. Simmer, covered, until the potatoes are tender. Add the clams. Simmer over medium-high heat for 5 minutes; do not boil. Sprinkle servings with the bacon.

Windows
Junior League of Rhode Island, Rhode Island

In coastal towns, the Native Americans taught early settlers to prepare a feast called an Appanaug or clambake. An authentic Rhode Island clambake includes corn, onions, potatoes, sausages, steamers, fish, and lobsters, which are covered with seaweed and steamed in a rock-filled fire pit by a "bakemaster." Shore dinners may also include clam chowder, clam cakes, brown bread, and watermelon.

Sweet Potato and Corn Chowder with Chicken

6 slices bacon, finely chopped
½ medium onion, chopped
¼ cup (½ stick) butter
1 teaspoon fresh basil, chopped
1 teaspoon fresh thyme, chopped
½ cup flour
2 cups frozen corn kernels
1 large red bell pepper, chopped
1 pound sweet potatoes, diced and blanched
1 cup water
6 cups chicken broth
4 cups chopped cooked chicken
1½ cups milk
1 teaspoon salt
¼ teaspoon pepper
1 tablespoon chopped parsley

Place the bacon in a saucepan and cook over medium-high heat until crisp-cooked. Drain off most of the drippings. Add the onion, butter, basil and thyme to the remaining drippings. Cook until the onion is soft. Add the flour and mix well. Stir in the corn, bell pepper and sweet potatoes. Sauté for 5 minutes. Add the water, chicken broth and chicken. Bring to a boil. Add the milk, salt and pepper. Reduce heat and simmer until thickened, stirring constantly. Stir in the parsley.

Note: If you are in a hurry, it is helpful to simply purchase a rotisserie chicken from the market.

Between the Lakes, A Collection of Michigan Recipes
Junior League of Saginaw Valley, Michigan

CORN CHOWDER

1 onion, chopped

2 large garlic cloves, minced

¼ cup (½ stick) butter

1 cup minced bell pepper

1 stalk celery, minced

1½ cups corn kernels

1 (14-ounce) can cream-style corn

2 cups whipping cream

2 fresh cayenne chiles, minced

1 tablespoon honey

½ teaspoon white pepper

Salt and pepper to taste

1 pound shrimp, peeled and deveined

Sauté the onion and garlic in the butter in a skillet for 1 minute. Add the bell pepper and celery. Cook for 1 minute. Stir in the corn kernels, cream-style corn, whipping cream, cayenne chiles, honey and white pepper. Simmer for 15 minutes, stirring occasionally. Season with salt and pepper. Add shrimp and simmer for 5 minutes. If shrimp are frozen, simmer for 15 minutes.

Peeling the Wild Onion
Junior League of Chicago, Illinois

This was a hit at FRP's awards luncheon, which featured recipes from the 2008 Tabasco Community Cookbook Award winners.

FRP Family Favorites

RED POTATO, LEEK, AND CORN CHOWDER

MAKES 6 QUARTS

4 unpeeled diced red potatoes

2 sticks butter, divided

4 tablespoons flour

2½ quarts half-and-half

½ cup chopped parsley

1 to 2 teaspoons honey

1 bay leaf

¼ teaspoon black pepper

¼ teaspoon salt

¼ teaspoon nutmeg

1 large Spanish onion, minced

4 cloves garlic, minced

1 leek, (white part only) sliced

3 scallions, white and green parts, chopped

¾ teaspoon dry mustard

½ teaspoon cayenne pepper

6 stalks diced celery

4 (20-ounce) boxes frozen whole kernel corn

3 vegetable bouillon cubes

1½ teaspoons ground thyme

Parboil potatoes in water to cover for 7 to 8 minutes. Drain and reserve. To make sauce, in heavy saucepan, melt ½ stick butter. Add flour and a pinch of salt. Cook over low flame for 10 minutes. Add half-and-half, stirring constantly for 10 minutes. Add parsley, honey, bay leaf, pepper, salt, and nutmeg. To make chowder, sauté onion, garlic, leek, and scallions for 20 to 25 minutes in remaining butter. Season with mustard, cayenne, and salt to taste. Raise the heat and add celery. Cook 3 to 4 minutes. Add corn and bouillon cubes. Cook 3 to 4 minutes more. To combine, add the potatoes and corn mixture to the sauce and season with thyme. Remove the bay leaf. Taste and add salt if necessary. Serve piping hot!

Of Tide and Thyme
Junior League of Annapolis, Maryland

Salmon and Salmon Chowder

4 slices thick bacon, slivered

1 cup onion, chopped

2 medium cloves garlic, minced

5 cups chicken stock

2 cups potatoes, sliced

1¼ cups clam juice

2 tablespoons cognac or brandy

2 small bay leaves

1 cup heavy cream

½ cup fresh parsley, chopped

¾ pound salmon, skinned, cut into 1-inch dice

½ cup smoked salmon, flaked

¼ teaspoon white pepper

In a large stockpot over medium heat, cook bacon until fat is rendered, but bacon is not crisp. Remove bacon from pot with a slotted spoon. Set aside. Drain all but 2 tablespoons bacon drippings from pot. Add onion and cook until soft but not brown, about 7 minutes. Add garlic and cook 2 minutes more. Add stock, potatoes, clam juice, cognac or brandy and bay leaves. Bring to a low boil and simmer over medium heat until potatoes are tender, about 20 minutes. Add cream and parsley. Heat through. Add fresh and smoked salmon, white pepper and cooked bacon. Heat without boiling, about 5 minutes to cook fresh salmon. Remove the bay leaves. Serve hot.

Simply Classic
Junior League of Seattle, Washington

Chilled Alderwood-Smoked Salmon Bisque

3 tablespoons unsalted butter

⅓ cup finely chopped shallots

1 (8-ounce) piece of alderwood-smoked salmon

6 ounces cream cheese, softened

1½ cups heavy cream

3 cups milk

½ cup plus 2 tablespoons sour cream

Sprigs of dill weed

Melt the butter in a medium saucepan over low heat. Sauté the shallots in the butter until tender. Add the salmon and cook for 1 minute. Add the cream cheese. Cook until the cream cheese is melted, stirring constantly. Purée the mixture in a blender or food processor until smooth. Combine the cream, milk and sour cream in a bowl and mix well. Add to the salmon mixture and process until smooth. Chill, covered, in the refrigerator for several hours. Garnish with fresh dill weed and serve with dark wheat bread.

Still Gold'n
Junior League of Spokane, Washington

CAROLINA CRAB BISQUE

½ cup butter

2 cups sliced mushrooms

2 medium scallions, chopped

½ cup chopped onion

½ cup chopped green bell pepper

½ cup chopped parsley

¼ cup butter

¼ cup all-purpose flour

4 cups milk

2 chicken bouillon cubes

½ teaspoon nutmeg

Tabasco sauce to taste

2 teaspoons salt

½ teaspoon pepper

2 cups half-and-half

2 cups crab meat

6 to 8 tablespoons sherry

Melt ½ cup butter in a medium skillet. Add the mushrooms, scallions, onion, bell pepper and parsley. Sauté until tender but not brown. Melt ¼ cup butter in a stockpot and remove from the heat. Stir in the flour. Return to the heat. Add the milk gradually and cook until the mixture thickens, stirring constantly. Stir in the bouillon cubes, nutmeg, Tabasco sauce, salt and pepper. Add the sautéed vegetables and half-and-half. Bring to a boil. Reduce the heat and add the crab meat. Simmer for 5 minutes. Ladle into bowls and top each serving with 1 tablespoon sherry.

You're Invited Back: A Second Helping of Raleigh's Favorite Recipes
Junior League of Raleigh, North Carolina

CRAB GAZPACHO

1 (46-ounce) bottle or can vegetable
  juice cocktail

6 ripe tomatoes, chopped or puréed

2 red bell peppers, chopped or puréed

2 cucumbers, peeled and chopped or puréed

1 bunch scallion bulbs, chopped or puréed

3 garlic cloves, crushed

Chopped fresh basil to taste

Tabasco sauce to taste

Salt and pepper to taste

6 to 8 tablespoons fresh lump crab meat,
  drained and flaked

Pour the vegetable juice cocktail into a large bowl. Stir in the tomatoes with juice, bell peppers, cucumbers, scallions and garlic. Mix in the basil, Tabasco sauce, salt and pepper, tasting as needed for the desired flavor; the seasoning will intensify with time. Chill, covered, until serving time. Ladle into the soup bowls and top each serving with 1 tablespoon of crab meat.

Note: Prepare 1 day in advance to enhance the flavor.

Appetizers at Devon
Devon Horse Show and Country Fair, Pennsylvania

CORN AND CRAB SOUP

¼ cup finely chopped onion

Butter for sautéing

1½ cups thawed frozen corn kernels, or
   3 ears of corn

1 tablespoon olive oil

5 tablespoons butter

5 tablespoons all-purpose flour

2½ cups milk

2 cups chicken broth

¾ cup fresh crab meat, shells removed and meat flaked

Salt and pepper to taste

½ cup heavy cream

1 dash of cayenne pepper

4 slices applewood-smoked bacon, crisp-cooked and
   crumbled (optional)

Sauté the onion in butter in a skillet until tender. Remove the corn kernels from the cob using a sharp knife. This should measure about 1½ cups. Sauté the corn in the olive oil in a skillet over medium-high heat until tender.

Melt 5 tablespoons butter in a Dutch oven and stir in the flour until blended. Cook until bubbly, stirring constantly. Whisk in the milk and broth until blended. Cook for about 10 minutes or until thickened, whisking frequently. Stir in the onion, corn, crab meat, salt, black pepper, cream and cayenne pepper.

Bring to a boil and then reduce the heat. Simmer for 5 minutes and stir in the bacon. Ladle into soup bowls and serve immediately.

Excellent Courses, A Culinary Legacy of Ravenscroft
Ravenscroft School, Raleigh, North Carolina

Combo Gumbo Josephs

1 (3-pound) broiler-fryer
2 quarts water
½ cup bacon drippings
½ cup flour
4 stalks celery, chopped
2 medium onions, chopped
1 large green bell pepper, chopped
2 cloves garlic, minced
½ cup chopped fresh parsley
2 pounds shrimp
1 pound okra, sliced
2 tablespoons bacon dripping
4 medium tomatoes, peeled, seeded and
   coarsely chopped
2 tablespoons Worcestershire sauce

¼ tablespoon Tabasco sauce
1 bay leaf
2 teaspoons thyme
½ teaspoon rosemary
½ teaspoon pepper
1 teaspoon paprika
1 teaspoon salt
1 ham hock
1½ cups cubed cooked ham
4 crabs
2 teaspoons molasses
Juice of 1 large lemon
Hot cooked rice
Gumbo filé

Combine chicken and water in a Dutch oven. Bring to a boil; cover and simmer 1½ hours or until chicken is tender. Remove chicken from broth; cut into 1-inch cubes. Strain broth, reserving 6 cups.

Heat ½ cup bacon drippings in an 8-quart Dutch oven; stir in flour. Cook over medium heat, stirring occasionally, until roux is the color of a copper penny (20 to 30 minutes). Add celery, onions, green pepper, garlic and parsley; cook over low heat for 45 minutes. Mixture will be dry.

Peel shrimp, reserving shells. Refrigerate shrimp until needed. Combine shells and enough water to cover in a saucepan. Bring to a boil and boil 20 minutes. Strain shell stock, reserving 2 cups.

Cook okra in 2 tablespoon bacon drippings until tender, stirring occasionally. Add okra, chicken stock, shell stock, and next 9 ingredients to roux mixture. Bring to a boil; reduce heat and simmer 2½ hours, stirring occasionally. Add chicken, ham hock, cubed ham, crabs and molasses; simmer 30 minutes. Add shrimp and simmer 10 minutes longer. Stir in lemon juice. Serve over rice. Add a small amount of filé to each serving, if desired.

Editor's Note: You may use 1 pound fresh or frozen crab fingers, if desired.

Some Like It South
Junior League of Pensacola,
Florida

Gumbo is generally a southern U.S. regional term for a stew-like dish that can have any of many ingredients, including vegetables such as okra, tomatoes, and onions and one or several meats or shellfish such as chicken, sausage, ham, shrimp, crab, or oysters. *Gumbo z'herbes* ("with herbs") was once traditionally served on Good Friday and contains at least seven greens (for good luck) such as spinach, mustard greens, collard greens, and so on. The name gumbo is a derivation of the African word for "okra."

ZARZUELA DE MARISCO

6 slices bacon

1 tablespoons olive oil

3 yellow onions, chopped

2 green bell peppers, chopped

2 carrots, chopped

3 ribs celery, chopped

3 garlic cloves, minced

2 dashes of Tabasco sauce

1 (28-ounce) can Italian-style tomatoes

1 (28-ounce) can crushed tomatoes

1 cup sherry

3 tablespoons lemon juice

1 teaspoon thyme

1 teaspoon dried basil

1 teaspoon sugar

1 teaspoon salt

1 teaspoon freshly ground pepper

1 tablespoon Old Bay seasoning

1 bay leaf

1/4 cup parsley

1 pound crab meat, drained and flaked

12 ounces snapper, grouper or tilapia fillets

8 ounces medium shrimp, peeled
    and deveined

12 ounces scallops

Hot cooked white rice

Cook the bacon in a large heavy saucepan until crisp. Remove the bacon to paper towels to drain, reserving the drippings in the saucepan. Crumble the bacon and set aside. Add the olive oil, onions, bell peppers, carrots, celery and garlic to the reserved drippings in the saucepan and sauté for 5 minutes. Stir in the Tabasco sauce, tomatoes, sherry, lemon juice, thyme, basil, sugar, salt, pepper, Old Bay seasoning, bay leaf, parsley and bacon and simmer for 30 minutes. Add the crab meat and fish and cook for 10 minutes. Stir in the shrimp and scallops and cook for 5 minutes or until the shrimp turn pink. Discard the bay leaf. Serve over rice.

Sunny Days, Balmy Nights
The Young Patronesses
of the Opera,
Coral Gables, Florida

Community cookbooks are widely recognized for their documentation and preservation of regional specialties and comfort foods such as this delectable soup full of the flavors of South Florida.

CREAMY ASPARAGUS SOUP

SERVES 8

1½ pounds asparagus
¼ cup (½ stick) butter
1 cup chopped yellow onion
½ cup chopped celery
2 tablespoons minced garlic
¼ cup dry white wine
1 to 3 tablespoons all-purpose flour
4 cups chicken broth
1 to 2 teaspoons salt
½ teaspoon freshly cracked black pepper
¼ teaspoon cayenne pepper
2 cups heavy whipping cream

Snap off the thick woody ends of the asparagus spears and discard. Chop the asparagus. Reserve half of the asparagus tips for garnish. Blanch the reserved asparagus tips in boiling water in a saucepan; drain.

Melt the butter in a sauté pan and add the onion and celery. Sauté until the onion is almost translucent. Add the remaining asparagus and the garlic. Sauté until the asparagus is tender. Stir in the wine and cook until most of the wine has evaporated. Add enough of the flour to make a roux and mix well. Cook for about 5 minutes, stirring frequently. Gradually whisk in the broth, salt, black pepper and cayenne pepper. Bring to a boil; reduce the heat.

Simmer for about 20 minutes and stir in the cream. Return to a boil; immediately reduce the heat. Simmer for 10 minutes. Purée the soup in batches in a blender or food processor. Strain through a sieve into the saucepan, discarding the solids. Taste and adjust the seasonings. Ladle into cups or soup bowls and garnish with the reserved blanched asparagus tips.

Texas Tables
Junior League of North Harris and South Montgomery Counties, Texas

Colorado Microbrew and Cheddar Cheese Soup

4 ounces bacon, coarsely chopped

½ cup chopped white onion

3 tablespoons all-purpose flour

3 cups half-and-half

2 cups chicken stock

12 ounces white or sharp Cheddar
  cheese, shredded

3 dashes of Tabasco sauce

½ teaspoon Worcestershire sauce

½ cup Colorado microbrew ale,
  at room temperature

Salt and freshly ground pepper to taste

1 tablespoon thinly sliced green onions

Cook the bacon in a large heavy-bottomed nonreactive stockpot over medium heat until limp but not brown. Add the white onion and cook until the onion is translucent and the bacon is crisp. Stir in the flour gradually. Cook for 2 minutes, stirring constantly. Add the half-and-half and stock a small amount at a time, stirring constantly to ensure there are no lumps. Bring to a boil and reduce the heat. Simmer, covered, over low heat for 15 minutes. Remove from the heat. Whisk in the cheese, Tabasco sauce, Worcestershire sauce, ale, salt and pepper. Ladle into a bowl and sprinkle with the green onions.

A Peak at the Springs
Junior League of Colorado Springs, Colorado

Pasta Fagioli

3 garlic cloves, minced

4 teaspoons olive oil

1 (28-ounce) can crushed tomatoes

Salt

Pepper

1 teaspoon oregano

1 can cannellini beans, undrained

1 pound ditalini, cooked firm
  (drain, reserve 1 cup liquid)

Grated Parmesan cheese

Red pepper flakes

Sauté garlic in olive oil, add tomatoes, salt and pepper; simmer 15 minutes. Add oregano and cannellini beans, simmer 10 minutes longer. Add cooked ditalini and some reserved water, if needed. Stir around; let set 5 minutes. Serve with grated cheese and hot pepper.

Note: Ditalini is a small tube-shaped pasta often used in soups; any small soup pasta may be used.

Preserving Our Italian Heritage
Sons of Italy Florida Foundation, Tampa, Florida

Exotic Mushroom and Sage Soup

4 ounces shiitake mushrooms, coarsely chopped

4 ounces portobello mushrooms, coarsely chopped

1 yellow onion, chopped

1 carrot, chopped

2 ribs celery, chopped

8 cups chicken stock (preferably homemade)

8 fresh sage leaves

3 tablespoons unsalted butter

4 ounces cremini, stems removed and mushrooms chopped

5 tablespoons unsalted butter

1 cup all-purpose flour

3 cups milk

¼ teaspoon Tabasco sauce

Salt and white pepper to taste

Combine the shiitake mushrooms, portobello mushrooms, onion, carrot, celery and stock in a 4-quart stockpot. Bring to a boil. Reduce the heat and simmer, covered, for 15 minutes. Add the sage. Simmer for 15 minutes. Strain into a bowl, discarding the solids. Set the mushroom stock aside.

Melt 3 tablespoons butter in the stockpot over medium heat. Add the cremini mushrooms and sauté for 4 minutes. Remove the cremini mushrooms and set aside.

Melt 5 tablespoons butter in the stockpot over medium heat. Whisk in the flour to form a blonde roux. Cook for 3 to 5 minutes or until the mixture turns a caramel color. Whisk in the milk gradually. Cook until thickened and smooth, whisking constantly. Add the reserved mushroom stock gradually. Cook until thickened, stirring constantly. Add the reserved cremini mushrooms, Tabasco sauce, salt and white pepper. Cook until heated through. Ladle into serving bowls.

Note: Portobello mushrooms are a larger, more mature cremini. Do not clean mushrooms with water, and never soak them, or they will absorb water and become mushy. Instead, use a pastry brush and remove any dirt.

Herbal Cookery
The St. Louis Herb Society, Missouri

WATERCRESS AND POTATO SOUP

1 small onion, finely chopped
2 bunches watercress, rinsed, finely chopped
8 ounces potatoes, peeled, chopped
1 tablespoon butter

1 cup half-and-half or milk
1⅓ cups chicken stock
Salt and pepper to taste

Cook onion, watercress and potatoes in butter in saucepan, covered, over low heat for 5 minutes, stirring occasionally. Stir in half-and-half, chicken stock, salt and pepper. Simmer, partially covered, for 30 minutes, stirring occasionally. Let stand until cool. Purée in blender. Heat to serving temperature. Ladle into bowls. Garnish with additional watercress leaves.

Main Line Classics II
Junior Saturday Club of Wayne, Pennsylvania

CREAM OF POBLANO WITH CROSTINI

3 poblano chiles, cut into halves
½ cup chopped onion
¼ cup chopped carrots
2 tablespoons clarified butter
2 tablespoons all-purpose flour
4 cups chicken stock

¾ cup heavy cream
1 tablespoon chopped fresh cilantro
Salt to taste
8 tortilla chips
4 slices Monterey Jack cheese

Discard the seeds from the poblano chiles using plastic gloves. Sauté the poblano chiles, onion and carrots in the clarified butter in a small saucepan for 5 minutes. Stir in the flour and cook over low heat for 5 minutes, stirring constantly. Whisk in the stock and simmer for 30 minutes or to the desired consistency, stirring occasionally.

Process the poblano chile mixture in a blender until puréed. Return the purée to the saucepan and continue to simmer, stirring occasionally. Stir in the heavy cream and cilantro and season to taste with salt.

Ladle the soup into ovenproof bowl and top each serving with 2 tortilla chips and 1 slice of cheese. Arrange the bowls on a baking sheet and broil until the cheese melts. Serve immediately.

Dallas Dish
Junior League of Dallas, Texas

Purée of Banana Squash Soup

2 tablespoons unsalted butter
1 cup chopped yellow onions
½ cup grated carrots
½ cup chopped red bell pepper
½ teaspoon grated lemon rind
1 teaspoon chopped parsley
¼ teaspoon celery seeds
¼ teaspoon crushed dried basil
¼ teaspoon crushed dried marjoram
⅛ teaspoon crushed dried thyme

1 pinch each crushed dried rosemary and
    dry mustard
½ teaspoon ginger
1½ pounds banana squash, split and seeded
2½ cups chicken stock
1 tablespoon honey
5 tablespoons cream sherry
Salt and pepper
Heavy cream for garnish

Melt butter in stockpot or large saucepan. Add onions, carrots, red pepper, lemon rind, parsley and seasonings. Mix well. Cover tightly and braise gently over low heat for 20 minutes. Rub surface of squash with butter and place in a foil-lined pan. Bake at 375 degrees for 30 minutes or until tender. Add stock to onion mixture and heat. Scoop pulp from squash and purée in a food processor. Add stock mixture to squash purée and return soup to pot. Stir in honey and cream sherry. Add salt and pepper. Serve garnished with 1 tablespoon cream swirled to create a marbled effect.

Celebrate
Junior League of Sacramento, California

Calabacitas Soup (Little Squash Soup)

1 pound lean ground beef
1 large onion, diced
1 teaspoon oregano, crushed
1 (20-ounce) can garlic-roasted
    chicken broth
1 (28-ounce) can diced tomatoes

2 to 3 medium zucchini, halved and sliced
2 to 3 medium yellow squash, halved
    and sliced
1 (12-ounce) can Shoe Peg Corn, drained
4 ounces diced green chiles
1 (16-ounce) jar reduced-fat Cheez Whiz

Brown the ground beef and onion in a large pan, stirring until crumbly; drain. Add oregano, diced tomatoes and chicken broth and heat. Stir in the zucchini, yellow squash, corn and chiles. Cook until the vegetables are tender. Stir in the Cheez Whiz and allow to melt. Serve the soup with chopped cilantro, shredded cheese, sour cream, sliced black olives and diced avocado for garnishes.

Beyond the Rim: A Taste of Amarillo
Junior League of Amarillo, Texas

CHIPOTLE SWEET POTATO SOUP

1 tablespoon unsalted butter

1½ cups thinly sliced onions

2 tablespoons brown sugar

1 teaspoon salt

¼ teaspoon ground cinnamon

4 cloves garlic, minced

6 cups (1-inch chunks) sweet potatoes
   (3 pounds)

1 chipotle chile in adobo sauce

4 cups fat-free low-sodium vegetable broth

1 cup half-and-half

3 tablespoons fresh lime juice

Sour cream for garnish

Chopped fresh chives for garnish

Melt the butter in a stockpot over medium-high heat. Add the onions, brown sugar, salt and cinnamon and sauté for 4 minutes or until the onions are light brown. Add the garlic and sauté for 1 minute. Stir in the sweet potatoes and chipotle chile and sauté for 10 minutes. Stir in the broth and bring to a boil. Reduce the heat to low.

Simmer for 25 minutes or until the sweet potatoes are tender, stirring occasionally. Remove from the heat and cool for 5 minutes. Pour ½ of the sweet potato mixture into a blender and process until puréed. Pour the purée into a soup tureen and cover to keep warm. Repeat the process with the remaining sweet potato mixture.

Heat the half-and-half in a microwave-safe bowl on high for 30 seconds or until hot. Stir the half-and-half and lime juice into the soup and garnish with sour cream and chives.

Tables of Content
Junior League of Birmingham, Alabama

"My daughter worked at a mission's campus, and often had to prepare dishes for large groups. When she made this soup for the staff and students, it was voted to go into the camp's 'Official Recipe Box' they all loved it so much!"

Anne Pritchard
FRP/Cookbook Marketplace

FRP Family Favorites

1½ pounds turtle meat, trimmed

¼ cup (½ stick) unsalted butter

8 garlic cloves, finely chopped

2 onions, finely chopped

4 ribs celery, finely chopped

2 green bell peppers, finely chopped

1½ tablespoons kosher salt

1 teaspoon freshly ground pepper

2 Creole tomatoes, finely chopped

¾ cup all-purpose flour

12 cups beef stock

1 cup Worcestershire sauce

2 tablespoons Crystal pepper sauce, or mild
   pepper sauce

2 tablespoons finely chopped flat-leaf parsley

2 tablespoons finely chopped fresh thyme

5 eggs, hard-cooked and finely chopped

6 ounces fresh spinach, sliced

Zest of 3 lemons, finely chopped

⅓ cup fresh lemon juice

½ cup pale sherry

Kosher salt to taste

Cut the turtle meat into ¼-inch pieces. Melt the butter in a heavy 7-quart saucepan over medium-high heat. Add the turtle meat and garlic and cook for 5 minutes or until the turtle meat is no longer pink, stirring occasionally. Stir in the onions, celery, bell peppers, 1½ tablespoons salt and the pepper.

Cook for 10 minutes or just until the vegetables begin to become translucent. Stir in the tomatoes. Cook for 5 minutes, stirring frequently to prevent scorching. Reduce the heat to medium and sprinkle with the flour. Cook for 5 minutes, stirring constantly and scraping the bottom of the pan to prevent the flour from scorching. Add the stock gradually, stirring and scraping the bottom of the pan constantly to prevent lumps from forming. Stir in the Worcestershire sauce, pepper sauce, parsley and thyme. Simmer for 30 minutes.

Add the eggs, spinach, lemon zest, lemon juice and sherry and mix well. Simmer for 10 minutes. Season with salt to taste. Ladle into heated cups or soup bowls.

*Crescent City Moons
Dishes and Spoons*
Junior League of
New Orleans, Louisiana

> "**C**ommunity cookbooks, compilations of recipes authored not by one but by many, not by chefs but by cooks."
>
> JOHN T. EDGE
> *A GRACIOUS PLENTY*

Swan Coach House Cream of Wild Rice Soup

2 large onions, finely chopped
2 carrots, finely chopped
2 celery ribs, finely chopped
2 cups finely chopped ham
1 cup (2 sticks) butter

½ cup flour
16 cups (1 gallon) chicken broth
Salt and white pepper to taste
2 cups light cream or half-and-half
4 cups cooked wild rice

Sauté the onions, carrots, celery and ham in the butter in a 4- to 5-quart saucepan over medium heat for 3 minutes or until tender-crisp. Sift in the flour, a small amount at a time, stirring until well mixed. Add the chicken broth slowly, stirring until well blended. Season with salt and white pepper. Cook until the mixture thickens, stirring constantly. Add the half-and-half and wild rice. Cook until heated through. Serve immediately.

The Swan's Palette
Forward Arts Foundation, Atlanta, Georgia

Chilled Blueberry Soup

1 cup blueberries
1 slice lemon
1 cinnamon stick
2 cups water
2 tablespoons sugar

Pinch of salt
½ tablespoon cornstarch
Water
¼ cup heavy cream
Frozen orange juice concentrate to taste

In a saucepan, combine blueberries, lemon, cinnamon, and 2 cups water. Bring to a boil and simmer 10 minutes. Add sugar and salt. Combine cornstarch with a little water and add to mixture. Bring to a boil again and simmer 1 minute. Remove cinnamon; purée mixture in blender until smooth. Add cream. Taste: if strong flavor is desired, add frozen orange juice, 1 teaspoon at a time, until desired flavor is achieved. Cool and chill well.

Cordon Bluegrass
Junior League of Louisville, Kentucky

STRAWBERRY CHAMPAGNE "SOUP"

1 pint fresh ripe strawberries
1 bottle champagne, chilled
Mint sprigs, if available

Purée strawberries by pushing them through a sieve to remove the seeds and skin. Chill puréed strawberries.

To serve: Pour purée into 4 soup bowls or champagne glasses. Open chilled champagne at the table to avoid it becoming flat. Pour champagne into purée. Garnish with a sprig of mint. Serve immediately.

The Stenciled Strawberry Cookbook
Junior League of Albany, New York

CHILLED STRAWBERRY SOUP IN MELON BOWLS

2 pints fresh strawberries, rinsed, hulled
1 cup orange juice
1¼ teaspoons tapioca instant pudding mix
⅛ teaspoon allspice
⅛ teaspoon cinnamon

½ cup sugar
1 teaspoon grated lemon zest
1 tablespoon lemon juice
1 cup buttermilk
2 cantaloupes, chilled

Reserve 6 of the strawberries. Purée the remaining strawberries in a food processor or blender. Strain the puréed strawberries into a medium saucepan. Add the orange juice and mix well. Set aside. Combine the pudding mix and ¼ cup of the strawberry mixture in a small bowl and mix well. Add to the remaining strawberry mixture in the saucepan with the allspice and cinnamon; mix well. Bring to a boil over medium heat, stirring constantly. Cook for 1 minute or until thickened, stirring constantly.

Remove from heat and combine with the sugar, lemon zest, lemon juice and buttermilk in a large bowl and mix well. Slice the reserved strawberries and fold into the soup. Chill, covered, for 8 hours or longer. Cut each cantaloupe into halves and discard the seeds. Remove enough of the pulp to leave a shell. Spoon the soup into the cantaloupe shells and garnish with thin lemon slices.

Oil & Vinegar
Junior League of Tulsa, Oklahoma

Broccoli Salad

1 large head broccoli, trimmed and chopped
   into small pieces
1 small sweet red onion, finely chopped
1 cup sunflower seeds
½ cup raisins

1 cup mayonnaise
¼ cup sugar
2 tablespoons vinegar
10 slices bacon, crisp-cooked and crumbled

Combine the broccoli, onion, sunflower seeds and raisins in a bowl and mix well. Mix the mayonnaise, sugar and vinegar in a bowl. Add to the broccoli mixture and stir until coated. Chill, covered, for 2 to 3 hours. Stir in the bacon just before serving.

Rendezvous on the Ridge
Junior League of Jonesboro, Arkansas

Walnut Cranberry Slaw

2 cups chopped or shredded green cabbage
2 cups chopped or shredded red cabbage
1 cup walnuts
1 cup dried cranberries
½ cup sliced purple onion
½ cup chopped red bell pepper

½ cup vegetable oil
⅓ cup cider vinegar
⅓ cup sugar
1 teaspoon celery seeds
½ teaspoon salt

Toss the cabbage, walnuts, cranberries, onion and bell pepper together in a bowl. Whisk the oil, vinegar, sugar, celery seeds and salt in a bowl until the sugar dissolves. Drizzle over the cabbage mixture. Chill, covered, for 4 hours. Drain before serving.

Texas Tables
Junior League of North Harris and South Montgomery Counties, Texas

Ramen Crunch Slaw

SERVES 8 TO 10

2 packages pork or oriental ramen noodles
1 (16-ounce) package coleslaw mix
Chopped green onions to taste
1 (3-ounce) package salted sunflower seeds

2 ounces slivered almonds, toasted
¾ cup vegetable oil
⅓ cup sugar
⅓ cup white vinegar

Crumble the ramen noodles, reserving the seasoning packets. Combine the ramen noodles, coleslaw mix, green onions, sunflower seeds and almonds in a bowl and mix well. Combine the oil, sugar, vinegar and reserved seasoning in a bowl and mix well. Add the dressing to the coleslaw mixture and mix well. Serve immediately. You may make the dressing ahead of time and let stand at room temperature until serving time.

Dining with Pioneers, Volume 3
AT&T Pioneers, Tennessee Chapter 21

Margarita Coleslaw

SERVES 12

Margarita Dressing

¾ can frozen margarita mix, thawed
¼ cup vinegar
¼ cup vegetable oil

1 to 2 tablespoons honey
1 teaspoon celery seeds

For the dressing, combine the margarita mix, vinegar, oil, honey and celery seeds in a jar with a tight-fitting lid. Shake to mix.

Salad

9 cups shredded green cabbage
3 cups shredded red cabbage

2 Granny Smith apples, peeled, chopped
1 cup dried cranberries

For the salad, combine the green cabbage, red cabbage, apples and cranberries in a bowl and mix well. Add the desired amount of dressing and toss to coat. Serve immediately.

A Taste of Enchantment
Junior League of Albuquerque, New Mexico

102   MORE RECIPES WORTH SHARING

1 large cauliflower, broken into florets
½ medium red onion, thinly sliced
¼ cup Parmesan cheese, grated
1 pound bacon, fried crisp and crumbled
1 cup mayonnaise
3 to 4 tablespoons sugar

Toss cauliflower, onion, cheese and bacon to mix. Combine mayonnaise and sugar. Pour over salad. Toss to coat. Cover and refrigerate at least 30 minutes.

100 Years of Cooking
The Ladies Ministry of The Hendersonville Church of Christ, Tennessee

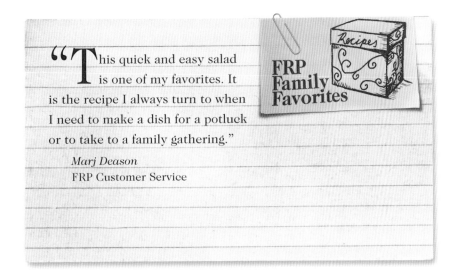

"This quick and easy salad is one of my favorites. It is the recipe I always turn to when I need to make a dish for a potluck or to take to a family gathering."

Marj Deason
FRP Customer Service

FRP Family Favorites

Corn Salad

2 cups Shoe Peg corn

¾ cup cucumber, chopped

1 medium tomato, chopped

¼ cup onion, chopped

½ teaspoon dry mustard

½ teaspoon celery seeds

4 tablespoons mayonnaise

2 tablespoons vinegar

2 teaspoons salt

½ cup sour cream

Combine corn, cucumber, tomato and onion; set aside. In small bowl, combine remaining ingredients and mix well. Pour over vegetables and toss. Cover and marinate in refrigerator for 12 hours.

Georgia on My Menu
Junior League of Cobb-Marietta, Georgia

Sultry Summer Shoe Peg Salad

½ cup cooking oil

¾ cup red wine vinegar

1 teaspoon salt

1 teaspoon pepper

1 (16-ounce) package frozen cut green
    beans, thawed

1 (16-ounce) package frozen green
    peas, thawed

1 medium can Shoe Peg corn, drained

1 bunch green onions, chopped

1 medium bell pepper, chopped

1 (7-ounce) jar diced pimientos, drained

1 cup chopped celery

1 small can water chestnuts, drained
    and chopped

Combine oil, vinegar, sugar, salt and pepper in a medium saucepan. Over medium heat, bring to a boil. Remove from heat and cool.

Combine all other ingredients in a large bowl; pour cooled dressing over vegetables and toss to coat. Chill before serving.

Note: Fresh vegetables can be used instead of frozen when available.

You're Invited Back—A Second Helping of Raleigh's Favorite Recipes
Junior League of Raleigh, North Carolina

Warm Balsamic Mushroom Salad

2 tablespoons olive oil
2 large shallots, thinly sliced
8 ounces white button mushrooms, sliced
4 ounces shiitake mushrooms, stems removed
    and sliced
4 ounces cremini mushrooms, sliced
2 tablespoons olive oil

Salt and pepper to taste
1 tablespoon balsamic vinegar
6 cups mixed baby greens
2 tablespoons olive oil
2 teaspoons balsamic vinegar
4 ounces Gorgonzola cheese or other blue
    cheese, crumbled

Heat 2 tablespoons olive oil in a large skillet over medium-high heat. Add the shallots and cook just until the shallots begin to brown and caramelize. Add the mushrooms, 2 tablespoons olive oil, salt and pepper and sauté for 5 minutes or until the mushrooms are tender. Stir in 1 tablespoon vinegar.

Toss the greens with 2 tablespoons olive oil and 2 teaspoons vinegar in a large salad bowl. Season with salt and pepper. Arrange the greens evenly on a rectangular or narrow oval platter. Spoon the warm mushroom mixture over the center of the greens and sprinkle the blue cheese over the top. Serve warm.

Excellent Courses, A Culinary Legacy of Ravenscroft
Ravenscroft School, Raleigh, North Carolina

Sandia Potato Salad

2 pounds new potatoes, cut into quarters
1 cup chopped peeled jicama
1/2 cup sliced black olives
1/4 cup sliced green olives
2 jalapeño chiles, finely chopped
2 tablespoons snipped fresh parsley
1 tablespoon snipped fresh cilantro

1/2 teaspoon salt
1/2 teaspoon pepper
1 (8-ounce) bottle ranch salad dressing
Leaf lettuce
18 cherry tomatoes, cut into halves
1 large avocado, sliced
Lime juice

Combine the new potatoes with enough water to cover in a saucepan. Bring to a boil. Boil for 10 minutes; drain. Combine the new potatoes, jicama, black olives, green olives, jalapeño chiles, parsley, cilantro, salt and pepper in a bowl and mix gently. Add the salad dressing and toss to coat. Chill, covered, for 6 to 24 hours. Line a salad bowl with leaf lettuce. Add the cherry tomato halves to the potato salad and mix gently. Spoon into the prepared bowl. Brush the avocado slices with lime juice and arrange over the top of the salad. Serve immediately.

A Taste of Enchantment
Junior League of Albuquerque, New Mexico

Shout Hallelujah Potato Salad

SERVES 20 TO 25

5 pounds petite gold potatoes
5 hard-boiled eggs, peeled and chopped
1 (4-ounce) jar diced pimientos
4 drops Louisiana Hot Sauce
2 teaspoons celery salt
¼ cup seasoned rice wine vinegar
1 cup sweet salad cube pickles or
   sweet pickle relish
1 tablespoon olive oil

1⅛ cups mayonnaise
¼ cup yellow mustard
1 to 2 jalapeño peppers, seeded and minced
½ cup chopped red onion
½ cup chopped green bell pepper
¼ cup chopped parsley
Salt and pepper to taste
Paprika for garnish

In a large pot of salted water over high heat, boil potatoes with skin on until tender; drain. Peel off skins with fingers while holding under cold, running water. Cool potatoes, chop into small pieces, and transfer to a large mixing bowl. Add eggs. In a small bowl mix drained pimientos with hot sauce. Add to potato mixture. Add all remaining ingredients except paprika. Do not stir. Mix by hand, mashing some potatoes and leaving others in chunks. Add salt and pepper, transfer to serving platter, and shape into mound. Dust with paprika. Cover and refrigerate 3 to 4 hours.

Note: This recipe was the winner of the Southern Foodways Symposium award in the potato salad competition.

Square Table
Yoknapatawpha Arts Council, Oxford, Mississippi

Lucky Seven Salad

SERVES 6 TO 8

1 head romaine, trimmed
1 cup chopped apple
½ cup crumbled blue cheese
½ cup dried cranberries
½ cup chopped seeded peeled cucumber
½ cup pecans
½ cup thinly sliced red onion

½ cup grapeseed oil, walnut oil or
   vegetable oil
¼ cup white wine vinegar
¼ cup balsamic vinegar
1 teaspoon garlic powder
¼ teaspoon freshly ground pepper
⅛ teaspoon sea salt

Tear the romaine into bite-size pieces. Toss with the apple, cheese, cranberries, cucumber, pecans and onion in a bowl. Whisk the grapeseed oil, vinegars, garlic powder, pepper and salt in a bowl until combined. Pour over the salad mixture and mix until coated.

California Mosaic, A Cookbook Celebrating Cultures and Cuisine
Junior League of Pasadena, California

Balsamic Apple and Spinach Salad

SERVES 6 TO 8

Balsamic Dressing

1 cup vegetable oil or olive oil
½ cup sugar
½ cup balsamic vinegar

1 teaspoon paprika
½ teaspoon ground dry mustard
½ teaspoon salt

Combine the oil, sugar, vinegar, paprika, dry mustard and salt in a bowl and mix until smooth.

Salad

2 medium Granny Smith apples, chopped
1 (10-ounce) package each fresh spinach and
    Italian salad greens

¼ cup chopped red onion
1 cup crumbled feta cheese
1 cup toasted pecans

Add the apples to the dressing and let stand for several minutes. Combine the spinach and salad greens with the onion, cheese and pecans in a salad bowl and mix well. Add the apples and dressing and toss to coat well.

Notably Nashville, A Medley of Tastes and Traditions
Junior League of Nashville, Tennessee

Smoky Autumn Salad

SERVES 6

¼ cup balsamic vinegar
¼ cup maple syrup
¼ cup olive oil
¼ teaspoon freshly ground pepper
12 ounces baby spinach leaves

2 large Granny Smith apples, cored and
    thinly sliced
1 cup (4 ounces) shredded smoked mozzarella
    cheese or smoked Gouda cheese
½ cup chopped pecans, toasted

Combine the vinegar, maple syrup, olive oil and pepper in a large salad bowl and whisk until combined. Add the spinach, apples, cheese and pecans and toss until coated. Serve immediately.

A Thyme to Entertain, Menus & Traditions of Annapolis
Junior League of Annapolis, Maryland

STRAWBERRY AND SPINACH SALAD

SERVES 8

SALAD

1 pound fresh spinach, washed, dried and broken into pieces

1 pint strawberries, washed, hulled and sliced

Prepare spinach and strawberries and return to refrigerator to chill.

SWEET FRENCH DRESSING

⅓ cup sugar
½ cup vegetable oil
¼ cup white vinegar

¼ teaspoon salt
¼ cup catsup
½ tablespoon Worcestershire sauce

Make dressing and chill.

Just prior to serving, toss spinach, strawberries, and dressing.

Of Tide and Thyme
Junior League of Annapolis, Maryland

SUCCOTASH SALAD

SERVES 6 TO 8

½ to 1 cup bow tie pasta
1 (8-ounce) package French-style green beans
1 (10-ounce) package frozen baby lima beans
1 (11-ounce) can nibblets corn, drained
1 cup (4 ounces) grated asiago cheese or Parmesan cheese

6 green onions, chopped
3 plum tomatoes, seeded and chopped
Newman's Own Caesar dressing to taste
Salt and pepper to taste
8 ounces bacon, crisp-cooked and crumbled

Cook the pasta, green beans and lima beans separately using the package directions; drain and cool. Combine the pasta, cooked vegetables, corn, cheese, green onions and tomatoes in a bowl. Add dressing and toss to coast. Sprinkle with salt and pepper. Stir in the bacon just before serving. Serve at room temperature.

Note: Julienned spinach or romaine may be substituted for the pasta. One pound of chopped blanched asparagus may be used for either of the green vegetables.

A Savory Place, Culinary Favorites of Amelia Island
Micah's Place, Amelia Island, Florida

6 large boneless skinless chicken breasts
2 green onions, sliced
1 cup almonds, toasted and crushed
1½ cups red seedless grapes, sliced into halves lengthwise
1 cup crumbled blue cheese, such as Gorgonzola
½ cup mayonnaise, or to taste
Salt and pepper to taste

Boil the chicken in water to cover for one hour; drain, discarding the liquid. Let stand to cool. Shred the chicken with a fork or process in a food processor. Place the chicken in a large bowl. Fold in the green onions, almonds, grapes, cheese and mayonnaise until well combined. Season with salt and pepper. Serve on a bed of lettuce or miniature croissants.

A Thyme to Entertain, Menus & Traditions of Annapolis
Junior League of Annapolis, Maryland

This was a hit at FRP's awards luncheon, which featured recipes from the 2008 Tabasco Community Cookbook Award winners.

FRP Family Favorites

River Street Salad

1 cup salad oil

½ cup each olive oil and red wine vinegar

2 tablespoons lemon juice

1 clove of garlic, minced

1 teaspoon Dijon mustard

1½ teaspoons Worcestershire sauce

1 teaspoon salt

½ teaspoon pepper

½ lemon

2 avocados, sliced

1 head Boston lettuce, torn

¾ to 1 cup watercress

¼ cup chopped green onions

2 cups chopped cooked chicken, chilled

1 tomato, chopped

¾ cup shredded Cheddar cheese

6 slices crisp-fried bacon, crumbled

2 hard-cooked eggs

Combine the salad oil, olive oil, vinegar, 2 tablespoons lemon juice, garlic, mustard, Worcestershire sauce, salt and pepper in a covered jar and shake to mix well. Chill until serving time. Squeeze the lemon over the avocado slices to prevent browning. Combine the remaining ingredients in a large salad bowl. Add the dressing and toss lightly.

Downtown Savannah Style
Junior League of Savannah, Georgia

Cilantro Lime Crab Salad

2 tomatoes, sliced and chopped

⅓ cup finely chopped red onion

2 tablespoons chopped fresh cilantro

½ teaspoon ground cumin

½ teaspoon grated lime zest

2 teaspoons fresh lime juice

3 tablespoons mayonnaise

8 ounces lump crab meat, drained and
    shells removed

Salt and pepper to taste

1 large ripe avocado, cut into halves

1 teaspoon fresh lime juice

1 small bunch chopped fresh cilantro

1 lime, peeled and cut into wedges

Combine the tomatoes, onion, 2 tablespoons cilantro, the cumin, lime zest and 2 teaspoons lime juice in a bowl and mix well. Stir in the mayonnaise. Fold in the crab meat and season with salt and pepper. Brush the cut sides of the avocado halves with 1 teaspoon lime juice to prevent discoloration. Mound equal portions of the crab meat salad in each avocado half and arrange each stuffed avocado half on a serving plate. Garnish with chopped cilantro. Arrange the lime wedges around the stuffed avocado halves. Serve immediately.

Texas Tables
Junior League of North Harris and South Montgomery Counties, Texas

Mexican Fiesta Salad with Cilantro Salad Dressing

Cilantro Salad Dressing

3 to 5 jalapeño chiles, seeded
¼ cup white wine vinegar
1 garlic clove

1 teaspoon salt
⅔ cup olive oil
½ cup packed fresh cilantro

For the cilantro salad dressing, place the jalapeño chiles, vinegar, garlic and salt in a blender or food processer and process until puréed. Add the olive oil in a fine stream, processing constantly until well mixed. Add the cilantro and process until finely chopped.

Salad

⅔ cup black beans, rinsed and drained
½ cup chopped red onion
1 cup corn kernels
½ cup chopped green bell pepper
1½ cups seeded chopped tomatoes
2 cups torn lettuce

1 cup (4 ounces) shredded Monterey
    Jack cheese
1 avocado, cut into 6 slices
4 slices lean bacon, crisp-cooked
    and crumbled

For the salad, combine the black beans and 2 tablespoons of Cilantro Salad Dressing in a bowl and mix well. Marinate, covered for 2 hours or longer. Add the onion and mix well. Combine the corn and bell pepper in a bowl and mix well. Reserve 2 tablespoons of the bean mixture, 1 tablespoon of the tomatoes and 1 tablespoon of the corn mixture. Layer the lettuce, remaining bean mixture, remaining tomatoes, remaining corn mixture and the cheese in a large glass bowl. Arrange the avocado slices on top to resemble the spokes of a wheel. Fill in the spaces between the spokes with the reserved bean mixture, tomatoes, corn mixture and the bacon. Garnish with a cilantro sprig. Serve with the remaining Cilantro Salad Dressing.

A Perfect Setting, A Collection of West Texas Recipes
Junior League of Lubbock, Texas

Yakima Tomato Pasta Salad

SERVES 8 TO 10

16 ounces bow tie pasta
1 (12-ounce) bottle zesty Italian salad
    dressing
4 large Yakima tomatoes, chopped

1 large green bell pepper, chopped
1 large Walla Walla onion, chopped
3 tablespoons Johnny's Salad Elegance
3 tablespoons grated Parmesan cheese

Cook the pasta using the package directions; drain. Add the salad dressing, tomatoes, bell pepper, onion, salad seasoning and cheese and toss to mix well. Spoon into a large bowl. Chill, uncovered, until ready to serve.

Fresh From the Valley. A Harvest of Recipes
Junior League of Yakima, Washington

Pear and Gorgonzola Salad Pizza

SERVES 8

1 (12-inch) commercial pizza crust
    (tested with Boboli crust)
1 teaspoon olive oil
2 Bosc pears, thinly sliced
1 cup (4 ounces) crumbled Gorgonzola cheese
1/2 cup walnut halves, toasted

1 1/2 to 2 cups (6 to 8 ounces) shredded
    mozzarella cheese
2 cups mixed spring salad greens
1/2 cup (2 ounces) crumbled
    Gorgonzola cheese
1/4 cup Champagne vinaigrette

Brush the pizza crust with the olive oil. Arrange the pear slices in a single layer over the crust. Sprinkle with 1 cup Gorgonzola cheese and the walnuts. Top with the mozzarella cheese. Bake at 350 degrees for 10 to 12 minutes or until the cheeses are melted. Combine the salad greens, 1/2 cup Gorgonzola cheese and the vinaigrette in a bowl and toss to mix well. Sprinkle over the pizza. Cut into wedges to serve.

Big Taste of Little Rock
Junior League of Little Rock, Arkansas

CURRIED RICE SALAD WITH CARROTS, COCONUT AND RAISINS

SERVES 12

4 (6-ounce) packages chicken-flavored
    Rice-A-Roni
6 tablespoons butter or margarine, melted
2¼ teaspoons curry powder
10 cups water
¾ cup olive oil
⅓ cup white wine vinegar
1 tablespoon lemon juice
⅓ cup chopped parsley

3 garlic cloves, pressed
6 tablespoons mango chutney
¾ cup dark raisins
¾ cup golden raisins
6 tablespoons sliced scallions
1½ cups grated coconut
2¼ cups shredded carrots
3 tablespoons mango chutney

Remove the seasoning packets from each package of the Rice-A-Roni and set aside. Brown the contents of each package of Rice-A-Roni separately with 1½ tablespoons of the butter and a little over ½ teaspoon of the curry powder in a large skillet. Place in a large saucepan. Add the water and the contents of the reserved seasoning packets. Bring to a boil and then reduce the heat to low. Simmer for 15 minutes. Drain the rice, stirring while the rice drains and cools. Cover and chill for 30 minutes. Combine the olive oil, vinegar, lemon juice, parsley and garlic in a large bowl and mix well. Stir in 6 tablespoons chutney and the raisins. Let stand for 15 minutes. Add the rice, scallions, coconut and carrots and toss to mix. Stir in 3 tablespoons chutney 1 tablespoon at a time, if desired.

Sunny Days, Balmy Nights
The Young Patronesses of the Opera, Coral Gables, Florida

SHRIMP RÉMOULADE

SERVES 6

2 pounds shrimp, boiled and picked
1 cup olive oil
½ cup tarragon vinegar
1¼ cups chopped celery
2½ teaspoons chopped green pepper
2 tablespoons chopped onion

5 tablespoons chopped parsley
¾ cup Creole mustard or mustard and
    horseradish
2½ teaspoons salt
½ teaspoon black pepper
¼ cup paprika

Mix all the ingredients and let marinate in the refrigerator for 24 hours, stirring often. Use as a salad, or on toast or crackers.

Charleston Receipts
Junior League of Charleston, South Carolina

TABOULI SALAD

½ cup cracked wheat (or bulgur)

4 tomatoes, chopped

3 bunches parsley, stemmed and chopped

1 bunch green onions, sliced

Small handful of fresh mint, stemmed and chopped

½ cup olive oil

½ cup lemon juice

Salt and freshly ground pepper to taste

Soak the cracked wheat in enough water to generously cover in a bowl for 30 minutes and drain. Press the excess moisture from the cracked wheat. Combine the cracked wheat, tomatoes, parsley, green onions and mint in a bowl and mix well. Stir in the olive oil and lemon juice and season to taste with salt and pepper. Delicious served cupped in a variety of lettuce or fresh grape leaves.

Tastes & Treasures
Historical League, Tempe, Arizona

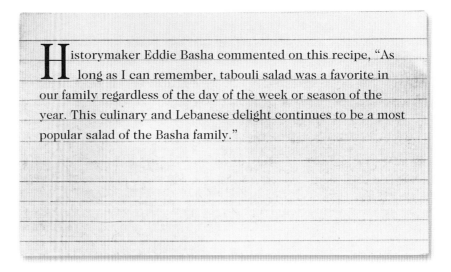

Historymaker Eddie Basha commented on this recipe, "As long as I can remember, tabouli salad was a favorite in our family regardless of the day of the week or season of the year. This culinary and Lebanese delight continues to be a most popular salad of the Basha family."

CREAMY APPLE SALAD

1 cup water

½ cup dried cranberries

¼ cup golden raisins

½ cup mayonnaise

3 tablespoons plain yogurt

2 tablespoons sugar

2 teaspoons lemon zest

1 tablespoon freshly squeezed lemon juice

1 Granny Smith apple, cored and chopped

3 Gala apples, cored and chopped

1 cup chopped celery

½ cup chopped pecans, toasted

In medium saucepan over medium-high heat, bring water to a boil. Remove from heat and stir in cranberries and raisins. Let stand 10 minutes and then drain. In large mixing bowl, combine mayonnaise, yogurt, sugar, zest and lemon juice. Stir in apples, celery, cranberries and raisins. Cover and chill. Sprinkle with pecans just before serving.

Beyond the Hedges
Junior League of Athens, Georgia

FROSTY HOLIDAY SALAD

8 ounces cream cheese, softened

1 (14-ounce) can sweetened condensed milk

½ cup mayonnaise

2 tablespoons fresh lemon juice

1 (15-ounce) can whole cranberry sauce

1 (10-ounce) package frozen dark sweet cherries

1 (20-ounce) can crushed pineapple, drained

¼ cup pecans, chopped and toasted

Beat the cream cheese, sweetened condensed milk, mayonnaise and lemon juice in a large mixing bowl until smooth. Add the cranberry sauce and beat at low speed until blended. Fold in the cherries and pineapple. Spread in a 9×13-inch baking pan and sprinkle with the pecans. Freeze until firm. Thaw slightly before cutting and serving.

Note: Since this is a frozen salad, it needs to be served when your family or guests sit down to eat. Allow about ten minutes to soften so that it cuts easily and serve immediately. This keeps extremely well. Can be made days in advance.

Five Forks
Kerr-Vance Academy, Henderson, North Carolina

GRAPE SALAD

SERVES 8 TO 12

8 cups seedless red grapes

8 ounces cream cheese, softened

½ cup sugar

1 teaspoon vanilla extract

1 cup sour cream

2 cups pecans, chopped

½ cup brown sugar

Arrange the grapes in a 9×13 glass dish lined with two layers of paper towels. Chill, covered with plastic wrap, for 8 to 10 hours. Remove the grapes and paper towels. Mix the cream cheese, sugar and vanilla in a bowl. Sir in the sour cream and grapes. Spoon into the 9×13 inch dish. Mix the pecans and brown sugar in a bowl. Spread over the grape mixture.

Silver Spoons, Blueberry Afternoons
National Association of Junior Auxiliaries, Greenville, Mississippi

MELON WITH FETA, RED ONION AND PINE NUTS

SERVES 8

2 medium red onions, sliced ¼ inch thick

1 tablespoon vegetable oil

2 medium cantaloupes

1 medium honeydew melon

¼ cup chopped fresh mint leaves

2 tablespoons fresh lime juice

Salt and pepper to taste

¼ cup pine nuts, toasted

½ cup crumbled feta cheese

Cook the onions in the oil in a large skillet over medium heat until softened, stirring occasionally. Remove from the heat and let stand until cool. Cut a slice from the top and bottom of each melon. Stand a melon on a cutting board with the cut side down. Remove the rind, cutting from the top to the bottom. Cut the melon into ¾-inch chunks, discarding the seeds. Place in a bowl. Repeat with the remaining melons. Add the mint, lime juice, salt and pepper to the melons and toss to combine. Spoon onto a platter. Top with the cooked onions. Sprinkle with the feta cheese and pine nuts. Toss just before serving.

Boston Uncommon
Junior League of Boston, Massachusetts

Mint Julep Melon Salad

½ cup sugar

½ cup water

1 tablespoon fresh mint leaves

2 cups fresh cantaloupe balls

2 cups fresh honeydew balls

2 cups fresh watermelon balls

Mix the sugar and water in a small saucepan. Cook over low heat until the sugar dissolves, stirring occasionally. Stir in the mint. Let stand for 30 minutes or longer; strain, discarding the mint. Let stand until cool. Toss the melon balls with the syrup in a salad bowl. Garnish with sprigs of fresh mint. You may store the mint syrup in an airtight container in the refrigerator for up to 2 weeks.

Warm Welcomes: River Road Recipes IV
Junior League of Baton Rouge, Louisiana

Mojito Salad with Honey Rum Dressing

Honey Rum Dressing

½ cup canola oil

½ cup fresh lime juice (about 3 limes)

⅓ cup honey

1 tablespoon dark rum

¾ teaspoon sea salt

To prepare the dressing, whisk the canola oil, lime juice, honey, rum and sea salt in a small bowl. Chill, covered, until serving time.

Salad

½ cup thinly sliced red onion halves

Juice of 1 lime

¼ jicama, peeled and julienned

½ cup blueberries

1 English cucumber, thinly sliced
  (about 3 cups)

½ (5-pound) seedless watermelon, cut into
  1-inch cubes

1 pound strawberries, cut into halves
  lengthwise

⅓ cup lightly packed fresh mint
  leaves, chopped

To prepare the salad, soak the onion in the lime juice in a small nonreactive bowl for 2 to 10 hours. Place the undrained onions in a large bowl. Add the remaining ingredients. Pour the dressing over the top and toss to mix. Serve cold or at room temperature.

Herbal Cookery
The St. Louis Herb Society, Missouri

Stardust Salad

First Layer

1 box lemon gelatin

1 box orange gelatin

2 cups hot water

1½ cups cold water

2 bananas, sliced

1 (No. 2) can crushed pineapple, drained

40 small marshmallows

Dissolve lemon gelatin and orange gelatin in hot water. Add cold water, bananas, pineapple and marshmallows or cover top with marshmallows and then let this congeal.

Second Layer

1 cup sugar

2 tablespoons flour

1 cup pineapple juice

1 large egg, beaten until foamy

Cook until thick and chill until cold.

Third Layer

½ pint (1 cup) heavy cream

1 small package cream cheese

Grated sharp Cheddar or American cheese

Whip heavy cream. Blend in cream cheese, then spread on second layer. Grate cheese on top.

Dining with Pioneers, Volume 1
AT&T Pioneers, Tennessee Chapter 21

"It wasn't difficult getting recipes to test for our book. Trading recipes these days is far more profitable than trading stock ... and much more everlasting."

STEPHANIE PRADE
Herbal Cookery, St. Louis Herb Society

Twenty-Four-Hour Fruit Salad

1 (20-ounce) can pineapple chunks

1 (8-ounce) can crushed pineapple

1 (10-ounce) package miniature
   marshmallows

1 pound red grapes, cut into halves

1/2 cup sugar

1 large egg, lightly beaten

1/8 teaspoon salt

1 cup chopped pecans

1 cup whipped cream

Drain the pineapple chunks and crushed pineapple, reserving 2 tablespoons of the juice. Combine the pineapple with the marshmallows and grapes in a bowl and mix gently.

Mix the reserved juice, sugar, egg and salt in a saucepan. Cook over low heat until thickened, stirring frequently. Let stand until cool. Add to the fruit mixture and mix gently. Stir in the pecans. Chill, covered, in the refrigerator for 1 hour. Fold in the whipped cream. Chill, covered, for 24 hours.

Southern On Occasion
Junior League of Cobb-Marietta, Georgia

BLT Wrap

3 ounces vegetable-flavor low-fat cream
   cheese, softened

4 medium flour tortillas

2 medium tomatoes, seeded and chopped

1 medium avocado, chopped

2 cups mixed salad greens

10 slices bacon, crisp-cooked and crumbled

1/3 cup reduced-calorie ranch salad dressing

Spread a thin layer of the cream cheese on each tortilla. Combine the tomatoes, avocado, salad greens, bacon and salad dressing in a large bowl and mix well. Place over the cream cheese layer and roll up. Serve immediately.

Living Well More Than a Cookbook
National Extension Association of Family and Consumer Sciences, Dallas, Texas

ini BLTs

12 slices party white bread
1 pound bacon
2 cups sour cream
2 tablespoons mayonnaise
½ teaspoon pepper

¼ teaspoon garlic salt
¼ teaspoon salt
1 pint cherry tomatoes, sliced and drained
1 head lettuce, shredded

Cut circles from each slice of bread with a 2-inch round cutter. Arrange the bread rounds on an ungreased baking sheet. Toast at 375 degrees until brown on both sides, turning once. Let stand until cool.

Fry the bacon in a skillet until crisp. Drain and crumble. Mix the bacon, sour cream, mayonnaise, pepper, garlic salt and salt in a bowl. Spread on the toasted rounds. Top each slice with 1 or 2 tomato slices 30 minutes before serving. Top each round with shredded lettuce.

Southern On Occasion
Junior League of Cobb-Marietta, Georgia

Bite-Size Sloppy Joes with Cheese

SERVES 6 TO 8

1 (10-ounce) can refrigerated buttermilk biscuits

1 pound ground chuck

1 (6-ounce) can tomato paste

1 cup water

1 package Sloppy Joe seasoning mix

2 cups (8 ounces) shredded Cheddar cheese

Flatten biscuits into greased muffin pan cups. Brown ground chuck in a skillet over medium heat, stirring until it crumbles and is no longer pink; drain and return to skillet. Add tomato paste, 1 cup water, and seasoning mix to meat, sitrring well. Spoon mixture evenly into muffin pan cups and sprinkle with cheese. Bake at 375 for 15 to 20 minutes or until golden. Let cool before removing from pan.

Easy to make, easy to eat...watch them disappear!

Creating a Stir
Fayette County Medical Auxiliary, Lexington, Kentucky

Kraut Runza

KRAUT

1 head cabbage, cored, chopped

1 medium-large onion, chopped

2 medium garlic cloves, crushed

3 tablespoons vegetable oil

1 pound lean ground beef

1 tablespoon (or more) salt

Pepper to taste

1 recipe Runza Bread

Sauté the cabbage, onion and garlic in the heated oil in a heavy large saucepan over medium-high heat until the cabbage is translucent. Add the ground beef and mix well. Stir in the salt and pepper. More salt may be needed. Roll the bread dough ¼ inch thick on a lightly floured surface. Cut into squares measuring 3×4 inches or more. Place a scoop of the cabbage mixture in the center of each square and bring the corners up to enclose the filling; pinch to seal. Place on a baking sheet. Bake at 400 degrees for 20 minutes or until golden brown.

Note: It is important to use a generous amount of salt in this recipe.

RUNZA BREAD

1 package (2½ teaspoons) active dry yeast

1¼ cups warm water

2 tablespoons shortening

2 tablespoons sugar

2 tablespoons salt

3 cups flour

Dissolve the package of dry active yeast in the water. Add shortening, sugar and salt and mix well. Add 2 cups flour and mix well. Add the remaining cup of flour and mix until stiff. Turn onto a well floured surface and knead 4 to 5 minutes or until smooth and elastic. Cover and let rise for 15 minutes. Roll dough out and use with Kraut Runza recipe.

First Impressions
Junior League of Waterloo-
Cedar Falls, Iowa

The first of four cookbooks from the Junior League of Baton Rouge, *River Road Recipes* has sold over 1.3 million copies since 1959 and is considered by most to be the textbook of Creole cooking. In fact, *The New York Times* said, "If there were community cookbook awards, the Oscar for best performance would go hands down to RIVER ROAD RECIPES."

LuLu Paste

MAKES ABOUT 3 CUPS

4 cups shredded Cheddar cheese (1 pound)

½ cup catsup

½ cup mayonnaise or salad dressing

¼ cup chopped onion

1 (2-ounce) jar pimientos, drained

¼ cup chopped pecans (optional)

¼ cup chopped dill pickle (optional)

In a blender or food processer, combine cheese, catsup, mayonnaise, onion, pimentos, and, if desired, pecans and dill pickle. Cover and blend or process until well combined. Add additional catsup and mayonnaise, if necessary, to reach desired consistency.

Note: Use as a delicious sandwich spread, or all by itself as a sandwich filling or on crackers.

Heart & Soul
Junior League of Memphis, Tennessee

Chicken Croissants

SERVES 8

4 or 5 chicken breasts, cooked, shredded

8 ounces mushrooms, drained, coarsely chopped

8 ounces chive and onion cream cheese, softened

6 tablespoons margarine, melted

Salt and pepper to taste

2 (8-count) cans crescent rolls

1 can Italian-style bread crumbs

Combine the chicken, mushrooms, cream cheese, margarine, salt and pepper in a bowl and mix well. Drop the chicken mixture into eight ¾-cup mounds on a baking sheet. Chill, covered, for 8 to 12 hours or freeze until firm.

Separate the crescent roll dough into 8 rectangles, pressing the perforations together to seal. Place 1 mound of the chicken mixture on each rectangle. Wrap the crescent roll dough around the mound, forming a ball. Roll in bread crumbs and place on a baking sheet. Bake at 350 degrees for 25 minutes or until golden brown.

Note: Double the amount of cream cheese if a creamier texture is desired. May make the chicken mixture ahead and store the mounds in the freezer. Thaw before using.

One Upon a Time
Junior League of Evansville, Indiana

Chipotle Chicken Salad Wraps

2 pounds shredded cooked chicken

4 ribs celery, chopped

6 tablespoons low-fat mayonnaise

⅓ cup sour cream

1 pinch of celery seeds, or to taste

Salt and pepper to taste

1 to 3 tablespoons chipotle salsa

Shredded lettuce

6 flour tortillas

In a blender or food processer, combine cheese, catsup, mayonnaise, onion, pimento, and, if desired, pecans and dill pickle. Cover and blend or process until well combined. Add additional catsup and mayonnaise, if necessary, to reach desired consistency.

Note: Use as a delicious sandwich spread, or all by itself as a sandwich filling or on crackers.

Be Present at Our Table
Germantown United Methodist Women

Toasted Brie Chicken Tea Sandwiches

2 pounds boneless skinless chicken
  breasts, cubed

2 cups chicken broth

1 cup mayonnaise

1 cup red grapes, sliced

3 stalks celery, finely chopped

2 teaspoons Italian herbs

2 teaspoons pepper

1 teaspoon onion powder

6 to 12 croissants

2 (8-ounce) wheels Brie cheese, rind removed
  and cheese sliced

Preheat the oven to 375 degrees. Combine the chicken and broth in a roasting pan. Roast for 12 to 18 minutes or until cooked through. Do not allow the chicken to brown. Drain and discard the broth. Place the chicken in a large bowl and let stand until cool. Mix the mayonnaise, grapes, celery, Italian herbs, pepper and onion powder in a bowl. Stir in the chicken. Cut each croissant into halves crosswise and cut each half into halves horizontally. Toast the croissants. Place a slice of brie on half of the croissant pieces. Top with the chicken mixture and the remaining croissant pieces.

Savor the Seasons, Vol. 3, The Culinary Collection
Junior League of Tampa, Florida

CILANTRO CHICKEN SANDWICHES

SERVES 4

CILANTRO DRESSING

½ cup fresh cilantro leaves

5 tablespoons olive oil

¼ teaspoon kosher salt

To prepare the dressing, process the cilantro, olive oil and kosher salt in a food processor until smooth.

SANDWICHES

1 long loaf fresh French bread, cut into halves lengthwise

2 large tomatoes, sliced

4 chicken breasts, grilled

2 cups grilled chopped vegetables (such as onions, mushrooms and squash)

To prepare the sandwiches, drizzle each side of the bread halves with a small amount of the cilantro dressing. Layer the sliced tomatoes, chicken and vegetables on the bottom half of the bread. Top with the remaining half of the bread and cut into four equal portions.

A Thyme to Entertain, Menus & Traditions of Annapolis
Junior League of Annapolis, Maryland

HOT BROWN

SERVES 6

12 slices white bread toast, crust removed

12 to 18 slices cooked chicken

⅓ cup butter

⅓ cup flour

3 cups milk

1 teaspoon salt

2 egg yolks, beaten

½ cup freshly grated Parmesan cheese

1 tablespoon butter

12 slices bacon, cooked and drained

In each of 6 individual baking dishes, place 1 slice toast. Top with 2 to 3 chicken slices. Melt ⅓ cup butter in a saucepan and blend in flour. Add milk and salt and stir constantly until thick and smooth. Blend in yolks, then Parmesan and 1 tablespoon butter. Pour ½ cup sauce over each sandwich. Crisscross 2 slices bacon over each and place diagonal halves of toast at the ends of each dish. Sprinkle additional Parmesan over all, run under broiler and serve when golden brown.

Note: A similar recipe was made famous by Louisville's Brown Hotel. Sliced tomatoes, mushrooms, or asparagus may be added.

Cordon Bluegrass
Junior League of Louisville, Kentucky

Dungeness Hot Crab Sandwiches

SERVES 8

1 cup cooked Dungeness crab meat
1 (4¼-ounce) can chopped black olives
1½ cups shredded Swiss chese
3 green onions, finely chopped

⅓ cup mayonnaise
Salt and pepper to taste
8 kaiser rolls, halved crosswise

Mix the crab meat, black olives, Swiss cheese, green onions and mayonnaise in a bowl. Season with salt and pepper. Spread the mixture evenly on the rolls. Wrap each roll in foil and place on a baking sheet. Bake at 375 degrees for 20 minutes.

Cooking from the Coast to the Cascades
Junior League of Eugene, Oregon

Tidewater Crab Rolls

SERVES 4

Rolls

1 (8-count) can refrigerated crescent rolls
4 slices natural Swiss cheese
8 ounces backfin crabmeat

2 tablespoons mayonnaise
1 tablespoon finely chopped green pepper
¼ teaspoon salt

Preheat oven to 375 degrees. Separate crescent rolls into 8 triangles. Place ½ slice of cheese on each roll. Combine remaining ingredients and spoon onto dough. Roll up. Bake at 375 degrees for 18 minutes or until rolls are brown.

Sauce

1 tablespoon butter
1 cup sour cream

1 teaspoon curry powder
Salt and pepper to taste

Melt butter and add remaining ingredients. Heat but do not boil. Spoon over crab rolls.

Tidewater on the Half Shell
Junior League of Norfolk-Virginia Beach, Virginia

Sunday Night Sandwich

1 pound white crab meat
2 to 3 tablespoons (or more) mayonnaise
Juice of ½ lemon, or more to taste
½ teaspoon dry mustard
Dash of Tabasco sauce
Dash of Worcestershire sauce

6 slices bread, lightly toasted
½ cup (2 ounces) shredded sharp Cheddar
  cheese
1 tomato, sliced
6 slices bacon, crisp-cooked and cut into
  halves

Combine the crab meat, mayonnaise, lemon juice, dry mustard, Tabasco sauce and Worcestershire sauce in a small bowl and mix. Adjust the seasonings to taste and add additional mayonnaise and lemon juice if needed. Spread thickly over the toasted bread. Cover each with the cheese, a slice of tomato and two half-slices of bacon. Place on a baking sheet. Broil until the cheese melts.

Pull Up A Chair
Junior League of Columbus, Georgia

The Best Cucumber Sandwiches

1 medium cucumber
½ cup cider vinegar
1 cup water
1 (8-ounce) package cream cheese, softened
¼ cup mayonnaise or mayonnaise-type
  salad dressing

¼ teaspoon garlic powder
¼ teaspoon onion salt
Dash of Worcestershire sauce
1 loaf sliced firm bread
Thinly sliced pimiento-stuffed olives and
  paprika for garnish

Score cucumber lengthwise with a fork, then cut crosswise into thin slices. In a medium bowl, combine vinegar and water. Add cucumber slices and let stand at room temperature for at least 30 minutes. Drain well. Meanwhile, combine cream cheese, mayonnaise, garlic powder, onion salt and Worcestershire sauce. Use a 2-inch cutter to cut circles out of each slice of bread. Spread circles lightly with cream cheese mixture. Just before serving, top each circle with a cucumber slice. Garnish with an olive slice or sprinkle with paprika, or both.

Key Ingredients
Le Bonheur Club, Memphis, Tennessee

EGGPLANT PARMESAN SANDWICHES

1 eggplant, cut into ½-inch slices
Salt and pepper to taste
1 cup panko
½ cup (2 ounces) grated Parmesan cheese
1 tablespoon Italian seasoning
2 eggs, lightly beaten

Vegetable oil for frying
1 loaf crusty French bread, split lengthwise
    into halves
2 cups spaghetti sauce
1½ cups (6 ounces) shredded
    mozzarella cheese

Sprinkle both sides of the eggplant slices with salt and pepper. Mix the bread crumbs, Parmesan cheese and Italian seasoning in a shallow dish. Dip the eggplant in the eggs and coat with the bread crumb mixture. Fry the coated eggplant in oil in a large skillet over medium-high heat until golden brown on each side; drain.

Spread the cut sides of the bread loaf heavily with the sauce. Arrange the eggplant on the bottom half and sprinkle with the cheese. Keeping the sandwich open-face, arrange the bread halves on a baking sheet and broil until the cheese melts. Replace the top bread half and cut into six equal portions.

Starfish Café
Union Mission, Savannah, Georgia

FIG AND PROSCIUTTO SANDWICHES WITH RICOTTA

10 slices crusty fresh bread
1¼ cups fresh ricotta cheese
4 teaspoons chopped fresh thyme
Salt and pepper to taste

10 slices prosciutto
10 fresh green or red figs, cut into
    ¼-inch-thick wedges
2 tablespoons (or more) honey

Spread each bread slice with the ricotta cheese and sprinkle with the thyme, salt and pepper. Place 1 slice of prosciutto on each bread slice. Arrange the figs on top of the prosciutto, dividing evenly among each sandwich. Drizzle the honey over the top of each. Serve sandwiches as open-face.

Main Line Entertains
The Saturday Club of Wayne, Pennsylvania

Greek Pita Pockets

8 ounces feta cheese, cubed

2 medium tomatoes, chopped

1 large cucumber, peeled, chopped

1 small red onion, thinly sliced

1/4 cup sliced black olives (optional)

3 tablespoons vegetable oil

1 tablespoon fresh lemon juice

1 teaspoon oregano

Salt and pepper to taste

4 pita bread rounds

8 lettuce leaves

Alfalfa sprouts (optional)

Combine the cheese, tomatoes, cucumber, onion and olives in a large bowl and toss lightly to mix. Whisk the oil, lemon juice, oregano, salt and pepper in a bowl until well blended. Add to the cheese mixture and toss lightly. Cut the pita rounds crosswise into halves and open to form pockets. Place a lettuce leaf in each pita pocket. Fill with the salad. Add alfalfa sprouts.

In Good Company
Junior League of Lynchburg, Virginia

Fried Green Tomato and Ham Sandwich

3 green tomatoes, cut into 1/4-inch-thick slices

1 cup cornmeal

1/4 teaspoon salt

1/4 teaspoon black pepper

1/8 teaspoon red pepper

Vegetable oil for frying

8 slices French or sourdough bread, toasted

Mayonnaise to taste

8 ounces ham, thinly sliced

Salt and pepper to taste

Coat the tomato slices with a mixture of cornmeal, salt, black pepper and red pepper. Heat 1 inch of vegetable oil in a large skillet. Add the tomato slices in a single layer to the skillet. Fry until golden brown, turning only once. Remove to paper towels to drain.

Spread each toasted bread slice with mayonnaise. Layer ham and hot fried green tomatoes on 1/2 of the bread. Sprinkle with salt and pepper to taste. Top with the remaining bread. Cut into halves. Serve immediately.

Bay Tables, Savor the Abundance
Junior League of Mobile, Alabama

CUBAN SANDWICH

1½ loaves Cuban bread

Mustard to taste

Butter to taste

¾ pound baked ham, thinly sliced

½ pound roast pork

¼ pound thinly sliced Swiss cheese

¼ pound Italian salami, thinly sliced

Lengthwise slices of dill pickle

Cut Cuban bread in 6 pieces 8 inches long. Split lengthwise and spread mustard on 1 piece and butter on the other. Divide ham, pork, Swiss cheese, salami and pickle among the 6 sandwiches, arranging in layers on the bread. Wrap each sandwich in a paper napkin and secure with a toothpick. Flavor is improved by warming in the oven before serving.

The Gasparilla Cookbook
Recipe orginally submitted by The Silver Ring Café, Tampa
Junior League of Tampa, Florida

OPEN-FACE COUGAR CHEESE SANDWICH

VARIABLE SERVINGS

1 loaf French, Italian or sourdough bread,
   cut into 1-inch slices

Bleu cheese salad dressing

Ham slices

Tomato slices

Asparagus spears

Cougar Gold Cheese slices

Spread each slice of bread with the dressing. Layer the ham, tomato and asparagus. Top with cheese slices. Arrange on a baking sheet. Place under the broiler and toast until the cheese is melted.

Fresh from the Valley
Junior League of Yakima,
Washington

Cougar Gold® cheese, a rich, white Cheddar with a smooth, firm texture, is Washington State University's most famous and popular cheese. You can substitute an extra sharp white Cheddar for the Cougar Gold®.

PORTOBELLO BURGERS WITH BASIL MUSTARD SAUCE

SERVES 6

BASIL MUSTARD SAUCE

1 cup mayonnaise

1/3 cup chopped fresh basil

2 tablespoons Dijon mustard

1 teaspoon fresh lemon juice

Salt and pepper to taste

To prepare the sauce, combine the mayonnaise, basil, Dijon mustard and lemon juice in a small bowl and mix well. Season with salt and pepper and chill, covered, until ready to serve.

BURGERS

1/3 cup olive oil

1 tablespoon minced garlic

6 (4- to 5-inch-diameter) portobello mushroom caps

Salt and pepper to taste

6 (3- to 4-inch-diameter) whole grain hamburger buns, split

6 large romaine leaves

6 large tomato slices

To prepare the burgers, whisk the olive oil and garlic in a small bowl. Brush the mushroom caps on both sides with the garlic mixture and season with salt and pepper.

Grill the mushrooms for 4 minutes per side or until tender and golden brown. Remove to a platter and cover with foil to keep warm. Grill the hamburger buns cut sides down for 2 minutes or until light golden brown.

To serve, layer the bottom half of each hamburger bun with 1 mushroom, 1 lettuce leaf and 1 tomato slice. Spread some of the Basil Mustard Sauce over the tomatoes and top with the remaining halves of the hamburger buns. Serve with the remaining sauce.

Note: For additional flavor when grilling Portobello burgers or other burgers, soak 1 1/2 cups mesquite chips in cold water for 1 hour before adding to the hot coals. When the wood chips begin to smoke, add the burgers.

Oil & Vinegar
Junior League of Tulsa, Oklahoma

ENGLISH TEA SANDWICHES

4 slices white bread

4 slices whole wheat bread

1 stick softened butter

2 hard-cooked eggs, finely chopped

Mayonnaise

1 English cucumber, peeled

Smoked salmon

Shredded Cheddar cheese

English watercress or alfalfa sprouts

Cut the crusts from the bread and spread the slices thinly with butter. Spread 1 of the fillings over half the bread slices and top with the remaining bread. Cut each sandwich into 3 fingers. For an egg tea sandwich, combine the egg with enough mayonnaise to bind in a bowl. Proceed as above using white bread.

For a cucumber tea sandwich, slice the English cucumber and smoked salmon very thin and proceed as above using whole wheat bread.

For a watercress sandwich, proceed as above, sprinkling whole wheat bread with shredded Cheddar chese and English watercress.

Island Thyme
Bermuda Junior Service League, Bermuda

WHITLOCK WEDGES

1 cup mayonnaise

¼ cup whole cranberry sauce

1 loaf pumpernickel bread, crusts trimmed

16 ounces smoked turkey, shaved

1 package bean sprouts

Mix the mayonnaise and cranberry sauce in a bowl. Store, covered in the refrigerator until serving time. Spread the mayonnaise mixture over one side of each slice of bread. Layer half the slices with turkey and bean sprouts. Top with the remaining bread slices. Cut each sandwich into fourths (wedges).

Southern On Occasion
Junior League of Cobb-Marietta, Georgia

THINKING OUTSIDE THE BOX FOR MARKETING

Anyone familiar with cookbooks knows *Charleston Receipts,* published in 1950 by the Junior League of Charleston, South Carolina, and the tried-and-true source for Lowcountry recipes. The league has also published *Charleston Receipts Repeats* and *Party Receipts,* an appetizer cookbook. In 2007 they produced *Charleston Receipts Album,* a book for home cooks to store their "loose" recipe collections, such as index cards.

Mollie Grant, product chairperson for the league, finds that just marketing these books takes a tremendous amount of time. "I joke that I live at the league; it's almost a full-time job for me." Mollie and her committee do monthly press releases on each book that are sent to top press venues.

In addition, with the celebration of *Charleston Receipts'* 60th anniversary, the committee launched a new Web site (www.cookinginthesouth.com) that highlights just the cookbooks and has in-depth blogs about the recipes. The group has also encouraged league members to host 60th anniversary parties in their homes using recipes from the book and asking attendees to donate to the Junior League for some of their important projects. This year the giving is focusing on hunger and homelessness.

The cookbooks have taken on another life as well. The league contracted with a local bakery to make some of the items from the books. They then sell the goodies along with the cookbooks.

"This has been great for us because of all the tourism in Charleston, but any group could do this," Mollie said. "Even if you only make 10 cents on each item, it can add up to thousands of extra dollars a month. Hotels especially often like to give their guests little gifts, so we just make custom labels to put on their products. We also do gift bags for VIP visitors and include the food item, a cookbook, and additional city souvenirs."

Mollie said whatever marketing ideas a group decides to use, they just have to stick with it and think outside the box.

CHARLESTON RECEIPTS
JUNIOR LEAGUE OF CHARLESTON

Lowcountry Cooking Benefits the Less Fortunate of Charleston

RAVO BRISKET

1 (7- to 9-pound) brisket

Salt and pepper

¼ cup Worcestshire sauce

¼ cup bottled green jalapeño sauce

1 large onion, cubed

4 cloves garlic, minced

6 cloves garlic, whole

¼ cup soy sauce

¼ cup Louisiana-style hot sauce

2 tablespoons ketchup

2 tablespoons cornstarch

¼ cup lemon juice

Place brisket, fat side down, on a large sheet of heavy-duty foil. Rub salt and pepper over brisket. Pour Worcestshire and green sauce over meat. Top with onion and garlic. Wrap securely in foil and grill over medium coals for 3 to 4 hours. Remove brisket from foil, reserving juices in bowl. Skim excess grease, leaving 1 cup of juice. Heat juice in saucepan with soy sauce, hot sauce, and ketchup. Dissolve cornstarch in lemon juice and add to sauce. Bring sauce to boil and cook until slightly thick. Pour over sliced brisket or serve on the side.

Viva Tradicions!
Junior League of Corpus Christi, Texas

BOURBON-MARINATED BEEF TENDERLOIN

1 (5- to 8-pound) beef tenderloin, trimmed

Lemon pepper to taste

2 cups reduced-sodium soy sauce

½ cup bourbon

2 cloves garlic, crushed

3 slices bacon

1 onion, sliced

Sprinkle the tenderloin with lemon pepper and place in a large sealable plastic bag. Whisk the soy sauce, bourbon and garlic in a bowl and pour over the tenderloin. Seal tightly and turn to coat. Marinate the tenderloin in the refrigerator for 2 to 10 hours, turning occasionally. Bring to room temperature and drain, reserving the marinade. Place the tenderloin on a rack in a shallow roasting pan. Lay the bacon on top of the tenderloin and arrange the onion over the bacon. Place the roasting pan in a preheated 450-degree oven. Reduce the oven temperature to 400 degrees and roast for 40 to 45 minutes for medium-rare or to the desired degree of doneness. Bring the reserved marinade to a boil in a saucepan while the tenderloin is roasting. Reduce the heat and simmer until reduced by one-half or more, stirring occasionally. Discard the bacon and onion and allow the tenderloin to stand for 15 minutes before slicing. Serve with the reduced marinade on the side.

Excellent Courses, A Culinary Legacy of Ravenscroft
Ravenscroft School, Raleigh, North Carolina

Beef Tenderloin

1 beef tenderloin, room temperature
Salt and pepper
Butter or margarine

Trim tenderloin of excess fat and place on a rack in pan. Season with salt and pepper. Bake tenderloin uncovered in a preheated 450-degree oven for 20 minutes. Reduce heat to 350 degrees and bake an additional 15 minutes. Remove tenderloin from oven and spread butter over top and cover with foil. Allow to stand 10 to 15 minutes before slicing.

A Southern Collection—Then and Now
Junior League of Columbus, Georgia

Beef Tenderloin en Croûte

1 tablespoon vegetable oil
4 (6-ounce, 1-inch-thick) beef tenderloin filets
1/4 cup pesto
1 sheet frozen puff pastry, thawed
4 long green onion strips (optional)

Heat the oil in a skillet over medium-high heat. Add the filets and cook for 1 minute per side or until brown. Remove the filets to paper towels to drain and let cool slightly. Spread 1 tablespoon pesto over the top of each filet. Roll out the pastry on a floured work surface to a 12-inch square. Cut the pastry into four 6-inch squares. Place one pastry square over each filet and gently tuck the edges of the pastry under the filet. Arrange the filets, pastry side up, on a rack in a roasting pan lined with foil. Bake in a preheated 450-degree oven for 12 to 15 minutes or until the pastry is golden brown and the beef is medium-rare. Wrap green onion strips around each filet and tie to resemble a package. Serve immediately.

Marshes to Mansions
Junior League of Lake Charles, Louisiana

Sirloin Roast with Ancho Chile Sauce

Ancho Chile Sauce

3 ancho chiles
1 onion, chopped
2 shallots, chopped
3 garlic cloves, chopped
2 tablespoons vegetable oil
2 cups chicken stock

3 tomatoes, chopped
2 jalapeños, seeded, chopped
2 tablespoons sugar
Salt to taste
1 cup chopped fresh cilantro

Remove the stems and seeds from the chiles. Toast the chiles in a hot skillet for a few seconds. Soak the chiles in warm water to cover in a bowl for 1 hour or until rehydrated. Process the chiles and some of the liquid in a blender until puréed. Sauté the onion, shallots and garlic in the oil in a saucepan for a few seconds. Add the stock, tomatoes, jalapeños and chile purée. Bring to a boil; reduce heat. Simmer for a few minutes, stirring occasionally. Stir in the sugar and salt. Process in a blender until puréed. Add the cilantro. Process until puréed. Season with salt.

Roast

1 (5-pound) beef sirloin roast, trimmed
2 tablespoons garlic powder

2 teaspoons salt
Sprigs of fresh cilantro

Rub the roast with a mixture of the garlic powder and salt. Place in a roasting pan. Bake at 350 degrees for 1½ hours or to 140 degrees on a meat thermometer for rare, 160 degrees for medium or 170 degrees for well done. Let stand for 20 minutes before carving. Top each serving with some of the ancho chile sauce and fresh cilantro sprigs.

Landmark Entertains
Junior League of Abilene, Texas

Until very recently, it was believed that the first Junior League cookbook was published by the Junior League of Minneapolis in 1943–1944. Recent discoveries have found two earlier publications: *The Old North State Cookbook*, published by the Junior League of Charlotte in 1942–1943; and now the prestigious title of first Junior League cookbook goes to Augusta, who published *Recipes from Southern Kitchens* in 1940.

CABERNET SIRLOIN WITH GARLIC

1 small onion, minced

3 large garlic cloves, crushed

1 tablespoon fresh grated or
   prepared horseradish

1¼ cups cabernet sauvignon

Freshly ground black pepper to taste

4 pounds sirloin steak, trimmed of excess fat

1 tablespoon light olive oil

Combine onion, garlic, horseradish and wine in a large, shallow glass dish which is large enough to hold the steak. Grind black pepper over steak to taste. Place the steak in marinade and cover. Marinate in refrigerator 3 to 4 hours. Turn occasionally. Remove steak from marinade, pat dry and brush with olive oil on both sides. Place steak on broiler pan and cook in preheated broiler about 5 inches from heat source to rare (about 8 minutes per side for 1-inch thick steak. For each additional ½-inch thickness, add 2 to 3 minutes cooking time on each side. For medium doneness, add 2 to 3 minutes to time for 1-inch steak.) Steaks should be turned only once.

A Southern Collection—Then and Now
Junior League of Columbus, Georgia

CHICKEN-FRIED STEAK— A HEALTHIER VERSION

1 pound lean beef round steak, trimmed

¼ teaspoon pepper

¼ teaspoon garlic powder

2 egg whites, lightly beaten

3 tablespoons buttermilk

¼ cup self-rising flour

¾ cup mixture of half whole wheat flour and
   half all-purpose flour

Preheat the oven to 400 degrees. Pound the steak to tenderize or ask the butcher to pass the steak through a tenderizer machine. Sprinkle with pepper and garlic powder. Cut the steak into 4-ounce portions. Combine the egg whites and buttermilk in a container large enough to accommodate a steak portion and mix well. Sift the self-rising flour and the flour mixture into a container large enough to dredge a steak portion. Dip the steak into the buttermilk mixture and dredge in the flour mixture. Repeat again and set aside on a wire rack. Heat a 10-inch skillet sprayed with nonstick cooking spray. Add the steak and cook for a few minutes until brown on one side. Turn and brown on the other side. Place the steak in a baking pan lined with baking parchment. Bake for 20 minutes or until cooked through. Serve hot.

Living Well, More Than a Cookbook
National Extension Association of Family and Consumer Sciences, Dallas, Texas

CUCUMBER RANCH STEAKS

½ cup finely chopped seeded cucumber
¼ cup prepared ranch salad dressing
1 tablespoon garlic pepper seasoning
4 pieces beef shoulder steaks or ranch steak, cut ¾ inch think
1 small tomato, seeded and chopped for garnish

Preheat a charcoal grill to medium, ash-covered coals. Combine the cucumber and salad dressing in a small bowl. Press the garlic pepper seasoning evenly onto the steaks. Place on a grill rack. Grill, covered, for 9 to 11 minutes for medium-rare to medium doneness, turning once. Garnish with tomato. Serve with cucumber sauce.

Living Well, More than a Cookbook
National Extension Association of Family and Consumer Sciences, Dallas, Texas

GRILLED FLANK STEAK

SERVES 4

¼ cup soy sauce
2 tablespoons honey
2 tablespoons white wine vinegar
½ teaspoon ground ginger
¼ teaspoon garlic powder
3 garlic cloves
¼ cup vegetable oil
1 (1½- to 2-pound) flank steak

Whisk the soy sauce, honey, vinegar, ginger, garlic powder, garlic and oil in a bowl until smooth. Place the beef in a sealable plastic bag. Pour the marinade over the beef and seal the bag. Marinate in the refrigerator for 5 to 12 hours.

Drain the beef, discarding the marinade. Place the beef on a grill rack. Grill to the desired degree of doneness. Serve with hot cooked noodles and peas for a perfect weeknight dinner.

Dining Without Reservations
Junior League of Beaumont, Texas

STUFFED FLANK STEAK

1 (2- to 2¼-pound) untrimmed flank steak
1 cup soy sauce
1 tablespoon meat tenderizer
1 to 2 teaspoons brandy
1 small onion, chopped
½ cup chopped green bell pepper
1 carrot, peeled and chopped
1 cup sliced mushrooms
2 cloves garlic, finely chopped
3 tablespoons butter
1 tablespoon chopped fresh cilantro
½ teaspoon pepper
2 or 3 tablespoons bread crumbs
2 to 4 slices provolone cheese
Pepper to taste

Pound the steak as thin as possible and place in a sealable plastic bag. Mix the soy sauce, meat tenderizer and brandy in a small bowl. Pour over the steak and seal the bag, turning to coat. Marinate in the refrigerator for 2 hours or longer.

Sauté the onion, bell pepper, carrot, mushrooms and garlic in the butter in a skillet until tender. Add the cilantro and ½ teaspoon pepper and mix well. Stir enough of the bread crumbs to blend the mixture together.

Drain the steak, reserving marinade. Layer the provolone cheese over the steak and top with sautéed vegetables. Roll up tightly to enclose the filling and place seam side down in a roasting pan. Pour the reserved marinade over the top and season with pepper to taste. Bake at 350 degrees for 1 hour. Let stand for 5 minutes before slicing to serve.

Note: Can use 1 (2- to 2¼-pound) untrimmed flank steak or 1 (1¾-pound) trimmed flank steak

Now Serving
Junior League of Wichita Falls, Texas

Fajita Marinade for Flank Steaks

Juice of 2 limes

½ can beer

½ cup Worcestershire sauce

½ cup soy sauce

1 medium onion, chopped

8 garlic cloves, chopped

2 tablespoons paprika

1 teaspoon dried basil

½ cup Italian salad dressing

1 tablespoon chopped fresh parsley

1 teaspoon cayenne pepper

3 flank steaks

Combine the lime juice, beer, Worcestershire sauce, soy sauce, onion, garlic, paprika, basil, salad dressing, parsley and cayenne pepper in a 1-gallon sealable plastic bag and shake to mix well. Add the beef and seal the bag. Marinate in the refrigerator for 1 to 2 hours. Drain the beef, discarding the marinade. Grill or cook the beef to the desired degree of doneness.

Dining Without Reservations
Junior League of Beaumont, Texas

Helma's Stuffed Peppers

Variable servings

1 pound ground beef

¾ cup chopped onion

Dash of pepper

½ small bay leaf

1 (1-pound) can tomatoes

1 cup regular rice

1 teaspoon cooking oil

1½ teaspoons salt

⅛ teaspoon garlic

⅛ teaspoon thyme

⅛ teaspoon oregano

1 can cream of mushroom soup

Green bell peppers

Brown meat in oil; add onion. Cook until tender. Stir in other ingredients in given order except bell peppers; bring to boil. Reduce heat; simmer 5 minutes, stirring occasionally. Spoon in green peppers that have been parboiled for 2 minutes. Bake 45 minutes at 350 degrees. Freezes well.

Top with grated cheese the last few minutes. If freezing, do not top with cheese until reheating.

Dining with Pioneers, Volume 1
AT & T Pioneers, Tennessee Chapter 21

MEAT LOAF WITH RED WINE GLAZE

2 eggs, beaten
1/2 cup dry bread crumbs
1/2 cup ketchup
1 sweet onion, finely chopped
1 tablespoon horseradish
2 teaspoons Worcestershire sauce
1/2 teaspoon salt
1/2 teaspoon pepper
1/2 teaspoon dry mustard
1/2 teaspoon garlic powder

1 tablespoon dried parsley
1 cup (4 ounces) shredded Pepper
    Jack cheese
1 1/2 pounds ground beef
8 ounces hot bulk pork sausage
1/2 cup ketchup
2 tablespoons spicy brown mustard
1/4 cup packed brown sugar
1/4 cup Duplin Burgundy or other dry
    red wine

Combine the eggs, bread crumbs, 1/2 cup ketchup, the onion, horseradish, Worcestershire sauce, salt, pepper, dry mustard, garlic powder, parsley and cheese in a bowl and mix well. Add the ground beef and sausage and mix well. Shape into a loaf in a 5×9-inch loaf pan or 8×8 baking pan. Mix 1/2 cup ketchup, the spicy brown mustard, brown sugar and wine in a bowl and spread over the meat loaf. Bake at 350 degrees for 60 to 75 minutes or to 160 degrees on a meat thermometer; drain. Let stand for 10 minutes before slicing.

Note: If you want to sneak some veggies past the kids, you can add one zucchini, grated and one-half cup grated carrot to the meat loaf. They will never know.

Five Forks
Kerr-Vance Academy, Henderson, North Carolina

Our wonderful upper school secretary, who is a self-proclaimed non-cook, purchased a cookbook in support of our school. She sat down at home with the cookbook just to look at it and read it. "The recipes sounded so good" that she ended up giving a few a try. She now is cooking up a storm and makes the Meat Loaf with Red Wine Glaze recipe for her family "at least twice a week!" She is our best spokesperson—telling everyone how easy the recipes are to follow and make and how delicious they are. She even brings samples and gets people to try them. *Five Forks* has made a cook out of a cookbook collector!

OLD WORLD ITALIAN MEATBALLS AND SAUCE

SAUCE

2 (28-ounce) cans Italian plum tomatoes
1 (6-ounce) can tomato paste
2 garlic cloves, minced
1 teaspoon dried basil

1 bay leaf
Salt and pepper to taste
1 pound Italian sausage
Vegetable oil

For the sauce, purée the tomatoes in a blender until smooth. Pour into a large pot. Add the tomato paste, garlic, basil, bay leaf, salt and pepper and mix well. Bring to a boil over medium heat. Reduce the heat and simmer. Sauté the sausage in a small amount of oil in a skillet for 20 minutes or until cooked through. Cut into 2-inch pieces and set into the sauce.

MEATBALLS

4 or 5 bread slices
1 pound ground round
1 garlic clove, minced
½ cup grated Romano cheese

1 tablespoon minced parsley
½ teaspoon salt
¼ teaspoon pepper
4 eggs

For the meatballs, pulse the bread in a food processor until crumbly. Combine the ground round, garlic, cheese, parsley, salt and pepper in a bowl and mix well. Add the eggs and half the bread crumbs. Add additional crumbs until the mixture forms a ball. Shape into nine large meatballs with wet hands. Place the meatballs in a baking pan coated with oil. Bake at 350 degrees for 20 minutes or until cooked through; drain.

Add the meatballs to the sauce. Simmer, partially covered, for 1 hour, stirring frequently and being careful not to break the meatballs. Remove and discard the bay leaf.

Life is Delicious
Hinsdale Junior Woman's Club, Illinois

LASAGNA

RAGU ALLA BOLOGNESE

5 tablespoons extra-virgin olive oil

½ stick butter

1 onion, chopped

1 carrot, finely chopped

1 rib celery, finely chopped

1 clove garlic, sliced

1 pound ground beef

1 pound ground pork

4 ounces pancetta or slab of bacon, ground

1 (6-ounce) can tomato paste or homemade tomato sauce

1 cup milk

1 cup red wine

Freshly ground pepper to taste

Salt to taste

Red pepper to taste

Rosemary to taste

3 or 4 bay leaves

To prepare the ragu alla bolognese, heat the olive oil and butter in a 6- to 8-quart heavy-bottomed saucepan over medium heat. Add the onion, carrot, celery and garlic and sweat for 10 minutes or until the vegetables are translucent and soft but not brown. Add the ground beef, ground pork and pancetta and stir to mix. Brown over high heat, stirring until crumbly. Add the tomato paste, milk and wine. Simmer over medium-low heat for at least 2 hours. Season with remaining ingredients. Cook over medium heat until of the desired consistency, stirring occasionally. Remove the bay leaves.

BÉCHAMEL SAUCE

1 stick unsalted butter

½ cup all-purpose flour

2 tablespoons all-purpose flour

1 quart milk, at room temperature

1 pinch freshly grated nutmeg

Sea salt to taste

White pepper to taste

To prepare the béchamel sauce, melt the butter in a 2-quart saucepan over medium heat. Whisk in the flour. Cook for 2 minutes or until smooth, whisking constantly. Whisk in the milk gradually. Cook until the sauce is smooth and creamy, whisking constantly. Simmer for 10 minutes or until the sauce is thick enough to coat the back of a spoon. Remove from the heat. Stir in the nutmeg, sea salt and white pepper.

ASSEMBLY

1 package ready-to-bake lasagna pasta

Freshly grated Parmigiano-Reggiano

To assemble the lasagna, layer one-half of the béchamel sauce, the lasagna pasta, the remaining béchamel sauce, the ragu alla bolognese and the Parmigiano¬Reggiano cheese in a large baking dish. Bake at 375 degrees for 30 minutes.

Now Serving
Junior League of Wichita Falls, Texas

Miss Frontier's White Lasagna

1 (8-ounce) package lasagna noodles
1½ pounds ground beef
1 cup finely chopped celery
¾ cup finely chopped onion
1 clove of garlic, minced
2 teaspoons crushed dried basil
1 teaspoon crushed dried oregano
¾ teaspoon salt
½ teaspoon pepper
½ teaspoon Italian herb seasonings

1 cup half and half
3 ounces cream cheese, cubed
½ cup dry white wine
2 cups shredded Cheddar cheese
1½ cups Gouda cheese
1 (12-ounce) carton cream-style
  cottage cheese
1 egg, slightly beaten
12 ounces shredded mozzarella cheese

Preheat oven to 350 degrees. Cook noodles according to package directions; drain. Brown ground beef, celery, onion and garlic in skillet; drain. Stir in basil, oregano, salt, pepper and Italian seasoning. Add half-and-half and cream cheese. Cook over low heat until cheese is melted, stirring constantly. Add wine. Add Cheddar and Gouda cheeses gradually, stirring until cheese is almost melted. Remove from heat. Stir cottage cheese and egg together in bowl. Layer half the noodles in greased 9×13-inch baking dish. Top with ½ the meat sauce, ½ the cottage cheese mixture and ½ the mozzarella cheese. Repeat layers. Bake for 30 to 35 minutes. Let stand for 10 minutes before serving.

Cheyenne Frontier Days
Cheyenne Frontier Days, Wyoming

Nacho Supreme

1½ pounds ground chuck
1 medium onion (optional)
32 ounces refried beans
3 cups grated Monterey Jack and
  Cheddar cheese

4 ounces chopped green chilies
1 large jar taco sauce (hot or medium)
1 cup sour cream

Brown meat and onion. Layer beans in bottom of 9×13 casserole dish. Add a layer of meat, cheese and green chilies. Add taco sauce. Bake 30 minutes at 350 degrees. Top with sour cream and serve with tortilla chips.

100 Years of Cooking
The Ladies Ministry of The Hendersonville Church of Christ, Tennessee

NATCHITOCHES MEAT PIES

FILLING

1½ pounds ground beef

1½ pounds ground pork

1 cup chopped green onions with tops

1 tablespoon salt

1 teaspoon coarsely ground black pepper

1 teaspoon coarsely ground red pepper

½ teaspoon cayenne pepper

¼ cup all-purpose flour

Prepare filling: Combine beef, pork, green onions, salt, black pepper, red pepper and cayenne pepper in Dutch oven. Cook over medium heat; stirring often, until meat is no longer red; do not overcook. Sift flour over meat mixture and stir to mix well. Remove from heat, place in colander to drain excess grease and juice and let stand until room temperature.

CRUST

½ mounded cup vegetable shortening

2 cups self-rising flour, sifted

1 egg, beaten

¾ cup milk

Prepare crust: Cut shortening into flour. Add egg and milk, mixing to form dough. Shape dough into a ball. Using about ⅓ of dough at a time, roll on lightly floured surface. Cut into 5- to 5½-inch circles. Stack circles on baking sheet, separating with wax paper. Assemble meat pies by placing a rounded tablespoon of meat filling at 1 side of pastry circle. Using fingertips dipped in water, moisten edge of circle, fold top over meat and crimp to seal with fork tines dipped in water. Pierce upper surface twice with fork tines. Assembled pies can be frozen.

To cook: Deep-fry meat pies in oil heated to 350 degrees until golden brown. If using frozen pies, do not thaw before frying. For cocktail meat pies, use cutter and 1 teaspoon filling.

Louisiana Living
Junior Service League of Natchitoches, Louisiana

RAVIOLI WITH TOMATO GRAVY

SERVES 15 TO 20

TOMATO GRAVY

1½ cups olive oil

5 pounds pork neck bones

3 pounds or 5 large onions

2 whole pods of garlic

1 small rib celery with leaves

2 (28-ounce) cans tomatoes

3 tablespoons oregano leaves

4 tablespoons basil leaves

5 tablespoons parsley flakes

1 (4-ounce) bottle Kitchen Bouquet browning
   and sweetening sauce and gravy aid

1 (12-ounce) can tomato paste

20 (15-ounce) cans tomato sauce

Salt and pepper

Put olive oil in large kettle to heat. Add neck bones to brown. Add onions, garlic and celery to sauté. Mash tomatoes with hands. Add to kettle; then add seasonings, Kitchen Bouquet, tomato paste and tomato sauce. Rinse cans and add water, not to exceed 2 sauce cans full. Salt and pepper to taste and let simmer for 5 to 6 hours. Recipe makes 12 quarts.

RAVIOLI FILLING

6 pounds pork butt, ground

2 tablespoons salt

Pepper to taste

1 clove garlic

10 eggs, beaten

1½ cups olive oil

5 (6-ounce) packages Romano cheese

½ pound crackers, finely crushed

6 (10-ounce) packages chopped frozen
   spinach, cooked and squeezed

3 tablespoons parsley flakes

Brown pork with salt and pepper. Add garlic while cooking gently over low heat. Beat eggs in large container. Add olive oil, cheese and crackers, blending well. Add spinach and blend. Put meat mixture into egg mixture. Add parsley. Mix well with hands. Refrigerate overnight.

RAVIOLI DOUGH

3 cups flour, sifted

2 tablespoons salt

1 egg

1 cup water

Sift together flour and salt. Make a little well and put egg in with a little water. With your hand, begin to mix adding a little water at a time. When thoroughly mixed, put on smooth surface and knead until dough is smooth, easy to handle and quite elastic. With a rolling pin or dough stick roll out very, very thin. This takes time and flour must be added as rolled to keep dough from sticking. When dough feels like a chamois, place balls of filling (about 1 tablespoon) onto the dough about 1 inch apart. Roll dough over filling and seal by pressing dough with fingers. Press firmly between balls of filling with side of hand, making sure all air is out of ravioli pocket. Cut into squares with

146   MORE RECIPES WORTH SHARING

serrated wheel. Dust with flour. Seal individually in foil to freeze. To serve, drop ravioli in boiling salted water to which a few drops of oil have been added. Let cook at a slow boil for 12 to 15 minutes and lift out gently with a slotted spoon. Pour small amount of sauce on plate. Place 2 to 4 ravioli on plate and top with additional sauce. Sprinkle generously with Romano cheese.

Vintage Vicksburg
Junior Auxiliary of Vicksburg, Mississippi

 # INSIDE-OUT RAVIOLI   SERVES 6 TO 8

1½ pounds ground beef
1 medium onion, chopped
1 clove garlic minced, or garlic powder or
    garlic salt
1 tablespoon oil
1 (10-ounce) package frozen chopped spinach
1 (15½-ounce) jar spaghetti sauce
    with mushrooms
1 (8-ounce) can tomato sauce

1 (6-ounce) can tomato paste
½ teaspoon salt
½ teaspoon pepper
1 (8-ounce) package shell macaroni, cooked
1 cup shredded sharp Cheddar cheese
½ cup soft bread crumbs
2 well beaten eggs
¼ cup salad oil

Brown first 3 ingredients in oil. Cook spinach according to package directions. Drain spinach and set aside. Reserve liquid. Add water to make 1 cup. Stir spinach liquid and next 5 ingredients into meat mixture. Simmer 10 minutes. Combine spinach with remaining ingredients. Spread in 13×9×2-inch baking dish. Top with meat sauce and little more shredded cheese if desired. Bake at 350 degrees for 30 minutes.

Well Seasoned
Les Passees, Memphis, Tennessee

4 ounces pancetta

8 ounces cream cheese, softened

10 ounces boursin cheese with fines herbes
   and pepper

1/4 teaspoon salt

1/4 teaspoon pepper

1/4 bunch green onions, chopped

4 bone-in veal chops, frenched

2 tablespoons olive oil

2 cloves garlic, minced

2 tablespoons chopped flat-leaf parsley

2 teaspoons kosher salt

1 teaspoon pepper

Olive oil for searing

1 cup red wine

1 1/4 to 1 1/2 cups beef stock

1 tablespoon cornstarch

This recipe requires 2 hours of refrigeration. Preheat the oven to 375 degrees.

Bake the pancetta in a baking pan for 10 minutes or until brown and crisp; drain. Let stand until cool and then crumble. Process the pancetta, cream cheese, boursin cheese, 1/4 teaspoon salt and 1/4 teaspoon pepper in a food processor until combined. Stir in the green onions. Spoon the boursin mixture into a pastry bag.

Make a small hole in one of the veal chops directly above the bone using a boning knife. Stick the tip of the knife in the hole and rotate the knife 180 degrees to form a small pocket. Stick the tip of the pastry bag as far inside the chop as possible and fill with the boursin mixture. Repeat the process with the remaining chops and remaining boursin mixture.

Mix 2 tablespoons olive oil, the garlic, parsley, 2 teaspoons salt and 1 teaspoon pepper in a shallow dish. Add the chops and turn to coat. Marinate, covered, in the refrigerator for 2 to 12 hours. Bring to room temperature before proceeding with the recipe.

Sear the chops on both sides in olive oil in a skillet for about 3 minutes. Remove the chops to a baking pan lined with baking parchment, reserving the pan drippings. Bake the chops for 15 to 25 minutes or until firm to the touch and the juices run clear.

Deglaze the skillet with the wine, stirring with a wooden spoon to dislodge any browned bits. Stir in the stock and simmer until the mixture is reduced by half. Mix the cornstarch with several ounces of water in a bowl until smooth and add to the wine sauce. Cook until thickened and of a sauce consistency, stirring constantly. Adjust the seasonings as desired.

Drizzle with the wine sauce.

Texas Tables
Junior League of North Harris and South Montgomery Counties, Texas

CALIFORNIA-STYLE VEAL PICCATA

1 egg
2 teaspoons water
2 pounds veal scallops, 1/8 inch thick
1/4 cup all-purpose flour
1/2 teaspoon oregano
1 teaspoon salt
1/2 teaspoon pepper
2 tablespoons (or more) butter
2 tablespoons (or more) olive oil
2 tablespoons minced shallot or other
   mild onion

1/3 cup dry vermouth or other dry white wine
3/4 cup chicken broth
2 tablespoons fresh lemon juice
Salt and pepper to taste
2 tablespoons capers (optional)
Chopped fresh parsley (optional)
1 avocado, cut into 8 slices
1 tablespoon fresh lemon juice
Thin lemon slices

Beat the egg with the water in a shallow dish. Add the veal slices and let stand in the refrigerator for 1 hour or longer. Mix the flour, oregano, 1 teaspoon salt and 1/2 teaspoon pepper in a shallow dish. Remove the veal slices from the egg mixture and coat with the flour mixture, shaking to discard any excess flour. Place on a plate lined with waxed paper or baking parchment. Melt the butter with the olive oil in a 10- to 12-inch covered skillet over medium heat. Add the veal in two or three batches and sauté for 3 minutes on each side or until light brown, adding additional olive oil or butter if necessary. Remove the veal to a plate. Add the shallot to the drippings in the skillet and sauté over medium heat just until translucent. Stir in the vermouth, broth and 2 tablespoons lemon juice; season with salt and pepper to taste. Cook until the mixture is reduced to a slightly thickened and creamy consistency. Return the veal to the skillet and add the capers. Reduce the heat and simmer for 10 minutes, adding parsley during the last 4 to 5 minutes. Preheat the oven to 300 degrees. Sprinkle the avocado with 1 tablespoon lemon juice and place in a small baking dish. Bake for 5 minutes. Remove the veal to a serving plate and arrange the avocado slices and lemon slices around the veal. Spoon the sauce over the top and serve hot.

The Bells Are Ringing
Mission San Juan Capistrano Women's Guild, California

YAKIMA SPRING RACK OF LAMB

SERVES 2

⅓ cup Yakima Valley Red Wine (cabernet or merlot)

2 tablespoons chopped fresh rosemary, or 1 tablespoon dried rosemary

2 to 3 tablespoons lemon juice

2 cloves garlic, minced

¼ teaspoon freshly ground black pepper

½ teaspoon dry mustard

2 tablespoons Worcestershire sauce

2 tablespoons olive oil

Dash of soy sauce

1 (8-rib) rack of lamb

Combine the wine, rosemary, lemon juice, garlic, pepper, dry mustard, Worcestershire sauce, olive oil and soy sauce in a bowl and mix well. Place the lamb in a large sealable plastic bag. Pour the wine mixture over the lamb and seal the bag. Marinade in the refrigerator for 8 to 10 hours. Drain the lamb, discarding the marinade. Place the lamb on a grill rack. Grill over hot coals to the desired degree of doneness. Let stand for 10 minutes before serving.

Note: You may place the lamb on a rack in a roasting pan and bake at 350 degrees for 1 hour.

Fresh From The Valley, A Harvest of Recipes From The Junior League of Yakima
Junior League of Yakima, Washington

PULLED PARTY PORK

SERVES 8 TO 10

3 pounds pork tenderloin or Boston butt roast

1 cup water

18 ounces prepared barbecue sauce

¼ cup packed brown sugar

2 tablespoons Worcestershire sauce

1 teaspoon each, salt and pepper

Combine the pork and water in a slow cooker. Cook on high for 7 hours. Drain, reserving 1 cup liquid. Shred the roast in the slow cooker with a fork. Add the remaining ingredients. Add the reserved cooking liquid if necessary. Cook on low for 1 hour. Serve on rolls for sandwiches if desired.

The Life of the Party, Vol. 1, The Culinary Collection
Junior League of Tampa, Florida

Pork Tenderloin with Comeback Sauce

Comeback Sauce

1 onion, minced	2 tablespoons water
2 cloves garlic, minced	4 teaspoons Worcestershire sauce
1 cup mayonnaise	4 teaspoons mustard
½ cup olive oil	2 teaspoons coarsely ground pepper
⅓ cup chili sauce	¼ teaspoon hot red pepper sauce
¼ cup ketchup	⅛ teaspoon paprika

To prepare the sauce, whisk the onion, garlic, mayonnaise, olive oil, chili sauce, ketchup, water, Worcestershire sauce, mustard, pepper, hot sauce and paprika in a bowl until well blended. Chill, covered, until serving time.

Pork Tenderloin

½ cup olive oil	2 teaspoons salt
8 sprigs fresh thyme	2 teaspoons pepper
2 green onions, chopped	1 (2-pound) pork tenderloin
2 tablespoons horseradish	

To prepare the pork tenderloin, mix the olive oil, thyme, green onions, horseradish, salt and pepper in a sealable plastic bag. Add the pork and turn until coated. Seal tightly and chill for 8 to 10 hours, turning occasionally. Drain, discarding the marinade. Place the pork on a rimmed baking sheet. Broil 6 inches from the heat source for 5 minutes. Bake at 425 degrees for 20 minutes or until cooked through. Serve with the sauce.

Silver Spoons, Blueberry Afternoons
National Association of Junior Auxiliaries, Greenville, Mississippi

$\mathscr{P}$ORK TENDERLOIN
WITH NINE-HERB GREEN SAUCE

SERVES 4 TO 6

PORK

1 (1½ - to 2-pound) pork tenderloin,
   silver skin removed

Olive oil for rubbing
Coarse salt and freshly ground pepper to taste

To prepare the pork, preheat an outdoor grill. Rub the pork with olive oil and sprinkle with salt and pepper. Place on the grill rack. Grill to 160 degrees on a meat thermometer. Place on a warm platter and cover loosely with foil. Let stand for 10 minutes.

NINE-HERB GREEN SAUCE

2 hard-cooked eggs
3 tablespoons vegetable oil
⅔ cup yogurt
⅔ cup sour cream
1 shallot, minced
1 garlic clove, pressed
1 cornichon (gherkin pickle), minced
Juice of ½ lemon

1 teaspoon German-style prepared mustard
1 pinch sugar
Choice of 9 fresh herbs such as borage,
   chervil, chives, dandelion leaves, dill,
   lemon balm, lovage, parsley, salad burnett,
   sorrel, spinach, tarragon and/or watercress
Salt and freshly ground pepper to taste

To prepare the sauce, cut the eggs into halves. Place the egg yolks in a small bowl and mash until smooth, reserving the egg whites. Add the oil and mix to form a smooth paste. Stir in the yogurt and sour cream. Add the shallot, garlic, pickle, lemon juice, mustard and sugar. Chop nine herbs of choice to taste. Add to the sauce. Mince the egg whites. Add to the sauce and mix well. Season with salt and pepper.

To serve, carve the pork into slices and serve with the sauce.

Note: Make this green sauce when your herb garden is at its peak. Choose nine herbs and use as much or as little of them as you like. The sauce is also good served with beef, boiled potatoes, or omelets.

Herbal Cookery
The St. Louis Herb Society, Missouri

Roasted Dijon Pork Tenderloin

4 large garlic cloves, minced
8 teaspoons chopped fresh rosemary
½ teaspoon salt
½ teaspoon black pepper
6 tablespoons olive oil

4 tablespoons Dijon mustard
4 tablespoons fresh lemon juice
3 to 4 pork tenderloins
2 pounds fresh asparagus

Preheat oven to 400 degrees. Combine garlic and next 6 ingredients in small bowl, blending well. Spread half of mixture over pork. Set aside remaining mixture. Place pork on wire rack in roasting pan. Transfer to oven and reduce heat to 325 degrees. Cook uncovered 35 to 45 minutes or until meat thermometer inserted in thickest portion registers 155 degrees. Steam asparagus until crisp-tender and toss with remaining mustard mixture.

Full Moon—High Tide
Beaufort Academy, South Carolina

Sweet Bacon Pork Tenderloin

Olive oil for greasing
2 (1½-pound) pork tenderloins
Salt and pepper to taste
1 pound sliced bacon
⅔ cup packed dark brown sugar

Preheat the oven to 350 degrees. Grease a large cast-iron skillet lightly with olive oil. Sprinkle each pork tenderloin with salt and pepper. Wrap each with bacon continuously from end to end until covered. Sprinkle with the brown sugar on each side and pat into the bacon. Place in the prepared skillet. Bake for 35 to 40 minutes or until cooked through. Serve with horseradish sauce.

Note: Using a cast-iron skillet is the key in this recipe—it crisps the bacon.

My Mama Made That
Junior League of Hampton Roads, Newport News, Virginia

THE KING'S GRILLED TENDERS

1½ cups cooking oil

½ cup soy sauce

½ cup red wine vinegar

½ cup fresh lemon juice

¼ cup Worcestershire sauce

2 tablespoons dry mustard

2 tablespoons snipped parsley

1 tablespoon pepper

2 cloves garlic, minced

3 (1-pound) pork tenderloins

For marinade, combine oil, soy sauce, vinegar, lemon juice, Worcestershire sauce, dry mustard, parsley, pepper, and garlic. Cover and refrigerate for 3 hours. Place tenderloins in a plastic bag set into a shallow dish. Pour marinade over meat. Close bag. Marinate in the refrigerator overnight, turning bag occasionally to distribute marinade. Drain tenderloins. Place tenderloins on cooking grid. Grill, covered, directly over medium coals for 14 to 20 minutes or until no pink remains. Slice to serve.

Heart & Soul
Junior League of Memphis, Tennessee

CURRY-CRANBERRY PORK CHOPS

2 teaspoons curry powder

¼ teaspoon ground ginger

6 pork chops

All-purpose flour

1 tablespoon shortening

1 (16-ounce) can whole cranberry sauce

¼ cup dry white wine

½ teaspoon salt

½ teaspoon pepper

½ teaspoon grated lemon zest

Preheat oven to 350 degrees. Combine the curry powder and ginger and rub over both sides of the pork chops. Coat the chops with flour. Heat the shortening in a large skillet. Add the chops and brown on both sides. Remove the chops to a shallow baking dish. Drain the fat from the skillet and add the cranberry sauce, wine, salt, pepper and lemon zest. Bring to a boil, stirring constantly. Pour over the chops. Bake, uncovered, for 45 minutes or until the chops are tender.

Furniture City Feasts
Junior League of Highpoint, North Carolina

Black Forest Pork Chops

4 (1½-inch-thick) pork loin chops,
Salt and pepper
2 tablespoons oil
1 ounce heated Kirsch
¼ cup beef stock
1 pound can pitted dark sweet cherries
½ teaspoon nutmeg

½ teaspoon cloves
½ teaspoon marjoram
½ teaspoon grated lemon zest
2 tablespoons lemon juice
2 teaspoons cornstarch
1 teaspoon Bovril beef extract (optional)
½ cup chopped walnuts

Trim excess fat from chops. Salt and pepper the chops. Heat oil in skillet over medium heat. Add chops and brown on both sides. Drain fat. Flambé chops with heated kirsch. Pour in stock, cover and simmer for 45 minutes to 1 hour. Drain syrup from cherries (set cherries aside). Add seasonings and lemon juice to syrup. Slowly stir in cornstarch. Cook over low heat until sauce is thick and glossy. Stir in Bovril (optional). After chops have cooked 45 minutes, pour syrup over chops and cook about 15 minutes more, just before serving, add cherries and walnuts.

America Discovers Columbus
Junior League of Columbus, Ohio

Asian Sesame Baby Back Ribs

2 tablespoons paprika
1½ teaspoons cayenne pepper
1 tablespoon salt
1 tablespoon black pepper
2 racks baby back pork ribs
3 tablespoons vegetable oil

12 ounces orange marmalade
6 tablespoons balsamic vinegar
¼ cup plus 1 tablespoon light brown sugar
6 dashes soy sauce
2 tablespoons sesame seeds

Combine the paprika, cayenne pepper, salt and black pepper in a small bowl and mix well. Brush both sides of the ribs with the oil. Season both sides with the spice mixture. Place bone side up on one large or two small foil-lined rimmed baking sheets. Bake at 350 degrees for one hour. Turn and bake for 45 minutes. Process the marmalade, vinegar, brown sugar and soy sauce in a food processor until smooth. Brush one-fourth of the marmalade mixture on each side of the ribs. Bake for 15 minutes longer. Remove the ribs to a platter and let stand until cool. Cut into individual ribs. Brush each with the remaining marmalade mixture. Return the ribs to the baking sheet and sprinkle with the sesame seeds. Bake for 10 minutes.

Silver Spoons, Blueberry Afternoons
National Association of Junior Auxiliaries, Greenville, Mississippi

BARBEQUED SPARERIBS

1 medium onion, chopped

⅓ cup vegetable oil

6 dried red New Mexican chiles,
   stems removed

6 dried Chiltepins or other small hot chiles

1 cup tomato sauce

2 cups beef broth

⅓ cup cider vinegar

2 tablespoons dry mustard

2 tablespoons brown sugar

3 pounds pork spareribs

Sauté onion in oil in skillet until tender. Add chiles. Sauté until tender. Process onion mixture in blender until puréed. Return puréed mixture to skillet. Add tomato sauce, broth, vinegar, dry mustard and brown sugar; mix well. Bring to a boil; reduce heat. Simmer until thickened, stirring frequently. Grill spareribs 6 inches above hot coals for 30 to 45 minutes or until brown; baste with tomato sauce mixture. Grill for 30 minutes longer, basting with tomato sauce mixture every 5 minutes. May omit Chiltepins to reduce heat.

The Kansas City Barbeque Society Cookbook
Kansas City Barbeque Society, Kansas

BOURBON-MARINATED RIBS

SERVES 12 TO 15

RIBS

1 (6- to 8-pound) rack country-cut pork ribs

Pour marinade over ribs and chill overnight in covered pan, turning once. Remove from refrigerator 4 hours before grilling. Cook ribs on charcoal grill for 1 hour, turning and basting with marinade. Place ribs in roaster, add any remaining marinade, and cover. Bake at 250 degrees for 1½ to 2 hours until tender and succulent.

BOURBON MARINADE

1 large onion, minced

⅓ cup bourbon whiskey

⅓ cup cider vinegar

¼ cup soy sauce

¼ cup light brown sugar

2 tablespoons Dijon mustard

1 tablespoon lemon juice

1 tablespoon Worcestershire sauce

Combine all ingredients and mix well.

Gracious Goodness, The Taste of Memphis
The Memphis Symphony League, Tennessee

DALLAS CHALUPAS

1 (16-ounce) package dried pinto beans

1 (2½- to 2¾-pound) pork butt, trimmed

3 garlic cloves, minced

3 tablespoons chili powder

1 tablespoon dried oregano

1 tablespoon ground cumin

1 tablespoon plus 2 teaspoons salt

2 bay leaves

Corn chips

Shredded Cheddar cheese

Chopped green onions

Chopped tomatoes

Shredded iceberg lettuce

Chopped avocados

Hot sauce

Sour cream

Sort and rinse the beans. Generously cover the beans with water in a bowl and let stand for 8 to 10 hours; drain and rinse. Combine the beans and pork in a slow cooker or large Dutch oven. Add enough water to cover the beans and ¾ of the pork. Stir in the garlic, chili powder, oregano, cumin, salt and bay leaves. Cook; covered, on Low for 6 to 8 hours, stirring occasionally.

Remove the pork to a platter and cool slightly. Remove the meat from the bones and shred. Return the pork to the slow cooker and cook for 30 minutes or to the desired consistency, adding water as needed. Serve with shredded cheese, chopped green onions, chopped tomatoes, shredded lettuce, chopped avocados, hot sauce and/or sour cream.

Dallas Dish
Junior League of Dallas, Texas

> "I was so surprised how well the league embraced working on *You're Invited Back*. We received about 1,200 recipe submissions and narrowed it to about 200 for the book. We involved the whole membership and made personal phone calls to all the sustainers to get them to help submit and test recipes."
>
> MEG TATE ERGENZINGER
> JUNIOR LEAGUE OF RALEIGH, NORTH CAROLINA

PENNE WITH BROCCOLI RABE AND SAUSAGE

SERVES 6

2 bunches broccoli rabe
2 pounds sweet Italian sausage
2 tablespoons olive oil
3 cloves garlic, crushed
1/4 teaspoon crushed red pepper flakes
1/2 teaspoon salt

1/2 teaspoon black pepper
1 (14-ounce) can chicken broth
16 ounces penne, cooked al dente
1/2 cup half-and-half (optional)
Grated Parmesan cheese to taste
1/2 cup pine nuts, toasted

Rinse the broccoli rabe and pat dry. Cut into pieces. Cook the sausage in the casings in a skillet until cooked through. Cut the sausage into small pieces. Heat the olive oil in a large skillet. Add the garlic and cook until golden brown. Add the red pepper flakes, salt, black pepper and broccoli rabe to the skillet. Cover and steam for 5 minutes or until the broccoli rabe cooks down. Stir in the broth and sausage. Cook over high heat for 3 minutes or until the sauce reduces slightly. Add the cooked pasta and half-and-half and toss gently. Cook until heated through. Add Parmesan cheese and toss to coat. Add the pine nuts and serve immediately.

A Savory Place, Culinary Favorites of Amelia Island
Micah's Place, Amelia Island, Florida

LEMON ROSEMARY CHICKEN

SERVES 6

1 whole chicken
3 lemons
1/4 to 1/2 cup (1/2 to 1 stick) butter (optional)
2 sprigs fresh rosemary
1/2 medium onion, cut into wedges

1 tablespoon olive oil
1 sprig finely chopped leaves or 1 sprig of
  fresh rosemary

Preheat the oven to 375 degrees. Rinse the chicken inside and out; pat dry. Grate the zest of one of the lemons. Cut the lemons into quarters. Place the butter inside the cavity of the chicken. Add the rosemary sprigs, lemon quarters and onion.

Rub the outside of the chicken with the olive oil. Rub with a mixture of the rosemary leaves and lemon zest. Place the breast side up in a large roasting pan. Roast for 1 1/2 hours or until a meat thermometer inserted into the thigh reaches 180 degrees.

Treasures from the Bend, Rich in History and Flavor
Fort Bend Junior Service League, Sugar Land, Texas

CHICKEN AGRODOLCE

1 red bell pepper
1 tablespoon butter
1 tablespoon (or more) olive oil
1 red onion, sliced
8 ounces fresh oyster mushrooms (if large, tear in half)
2 garlic cloves, minced
1 teaspoon minced fresh rosemary leaves
Salt and freshly ground pepper to taste
4 chicken breasts (whole or fillets)
1/4 cup sweet vermouth
1/2 cup balsamic vinegar
2 tablespoons golden raisins
2 tablespoons toasted pine nuts

Roast the bell pepper on top of the stove or grill until completely blackened. Place in a sealable plastic bag to steam. Let stand until cool. Peel off the blackened skin and discard. Cut the bell pepper into strips.

Melt the butter with the olive oil in a large skillet over medium-high heat. Sauté the onion for 5 minutes or until soft. Add the bell pepper strips and mushrooms. Cook for 5 minutes or until the vegetables are soft. Add the garlic, rosemary, salt and pepper. Remove from the skillet using a slotted spoon and set aside.

Sprinkle the chicken with salt and pepper. Add olive oil to the drippings in the skillet if needed. Add the chicken and cook until brown on both sides. Add the vermouth, stirring to deglaze the skillet by scraping up the browned bits. Reduce the heat. Simmer, covered, for 10 minutes or until the chicken is cooked through. Add the vinegar. Cook until the sauce is syrupy and reduced by half, watching carefully to prevent burning. Return the vegetables to the skillet. Add the raisins and pine nuts. Sprinkle with salt and pepper.

Note: "Agrodolce" is the Italian term for sweet-and-sour sauce. It is thought to have been brought to Sicily by the Arabs.

Herbal Cookery
The St. Louis Herb Society, Missouri

CLASSIC CHICKEN PICCATA

1 teaspoon paprika
1/3 cup flour
4 boneless skinless chicken breasts
1 tablespoon olive oil
1/4 cup water
1/4 cup lemon juice
1 tablespoon instant chicken bouillon
1 tablespoon lemon juice

1 tablespoon grated lemon peel
1/4 cup milk
1/4 cup water
1 tablespoon flour
1/4 teaspoon garlic powder
1 tablespoon capers
1/2 cup shredded Swiss cheese

Mix the paprika and 1/3 cup flour in a plastic bag. Add the chicken 1 or 2 pieces at a time and shake to coat lightly.

Brown the chicken on both sides in the olive oil in a large skillet. Add 1/4 cup water and 1/4 cup lemon juice. Reduce heat and simmer, covered, for 10 minutes or until tender. Remove to a baking dish, reserving the pan juices in the skillet.

Combine the chicken bouillon, 1 tablespoon lemon juice, lemon peel, milk, 1/4 cup water, 1 tablespoon flour and garlic powder in a bowl and mix well. Pour into the skillet. Bring just to the simmering point over medium heat; do not boil. Stir in the capers. Pour over the chicken.

Bake the chicken, covered, at 350 degrees for 15 minutes. Sprinkle with the cheese. Bake, uncovered, for 2 to 3 minutes longer or until the cheese melts.

Always in Season
Junior League of
Salt Lake City, Utah

Classic Chicken Piccata is a very flexible recipe that can be easily adjusted. Add more or less lemon juice or peel, omit capers, or add more cheese—whatever you like. It's also easy to double and makes an excellent dinner party dish with rice pilaf and steamed fresh asparagus.

CHICKEN TORTILLA CASSEROLE

4 or 5 whole chicken breasts
1 dozen corn tortillas
1 can cream of chicken soup
1 can cream of mushroom soup

1 can chili salsa (Old El Paso)
1 onion, grated
½ to ¾ pound Cheddar cheese, grated

Boil chicken until tender. Bone and cut into large pieces. Cut tortillas into 1-inch strips. Mix soups, salsa, and onion together. In a large casserole, layer tortillas, chicken, and soup mixture. Refrigerate for 24 hours. Bake at 300 degrees for 1 to 1½ hours. Top with cheese and return to oven to melt.

Bay Leaves
Junior League of Panama City, Florida

CREAMY BAKED CHICKEN BREASTS

4 medium boneless skinless chicken breasts
4 to 6 slices Swiss cheese
1 (10-ounce) can cream of chicken soup
¾ cup dry white wine
1 cup herb-seasoned stuffing mix or crushed seasoned croutons
¼ cup salted butter or margarine, melted

Preheat the oven to 350 degrees. Arrange the chicken in a lightly greased 9×13-inch baking dish and top with the cheese. Combine the soup and wine in a bowl and mix well. Spoon evenly over the chicken.

Sprinkle the chicken with the stuffing mix and drizzle with the butter. Bake for 45 to 55 minutes or until cooked through.

Creating Comfort
Genesis Women's Shelter, Dallas, Texas

GOAT CHEESE CHICKEN OVER ANGEL HAIR PASTA

CHICKEN AND ANGEL HAIR PASTA

4 chicken breast halves, skinned and boned

½ teaspoon salt

½ teaspoon freshly ground black pepper

8 large fresh basil leaves

3 ounces goat cheese, softened

½ cup chopped fresh basil

8 ounces angel hair pasta, cooked al dente

Tomato-Basil Sauce

Preheat oven to 350 degrees. Place chicken breasts between sheets of heavy-duty plastic wrap. Flatten to ¼-inch thickness. Season with salt and pepper. Place 2 basil leaves and 2 tablespoons cheese in center of each chicken breast. Roll up jelly-roll fashion starting with short end and secure with toothpick. Place rolls seam side down in lightly greased 8-inch square baking dish. Bake for 30 to 35 minutes. Let stand 10 minutes. Cut into ½-inch slices. Toss pasta with half of Tomato-Basil Sauce. Serve chicken over pasta and top with remaining sauce.

TOMATO-BASIL SAUCE

1 small onion, chopped

4 garlic cloves, minced

2 tablespoons olive oil

1 cup dry red wine

½ teaspoon salt

¼ teaspoon freshly ground black pepper

2 (28-ounce) cans diced tomatoes, drained

½ cup fresh shredded basil leaves

Sauté onion and garlic in hot oil in large saucepan until tender. Add wine, salt and pepper. Cook, stirring occasionally, about 5 minutes. Add tomatoes; reduce heat and simmer, stirring often, about 30 minutes. Cool slightly. Process half of tomato mixture in food processor or blender until smooth, stopping once to scrape down sides. Return to saucepan. Repeat process with remaining tomato mixture. Cook over medium heat until sauce is thoroughly heated. Stir in shredded basil. Tomato-Basil Sauce yields 5 cups.

Full Moon—High Tide
Beaufort Academy, South Carolina

GRILLED CHILI LIME CHICKEN WITH STRAWBERRY SALSA

GRILLED CHILI LIME CHICKEN

2 tablespoons lime juice

1 tablespoon grapeseed oil or other mild-flavored vegetable oil

1 tablespoon acacia honey, clover honey or other mild-flavored honey

2 garlic cloves, minced

1 teaspoon chili powder

4 medium (4-ounce) boneless skinless chicken breasts

Combine the lime juice, grapeseed oil, honey, garlic and chili powder in a medium bowl and whisk until smooth. Combine with the chicken in a large sealable plastic bag. Place in a shallow bowl and marinate on the bottom shelf of the refrigerator for 4 to 12 hours, turning the bag occasionally.

Preheat the grill to medium-high heat. Drain the chicken and place on the grill. Grill for 12 minutes or to 170 degrees on a meat thermometer, turning once. Remove to a platter and let stand for 5 minutes before slicing to serve.

STRAWBERRY SALSA

8 large strawberries, chopped

1/3 cup finely chopped white onion

1 tablespoon finely chopped fresh cilantro

1 tablespoon lime juice

1/4 teaspoon chili powder

Salt and freshly ground pepper to taste

Combine the strawberries, onion, cilantro, lime juice and chili powder in a small bowl. Season with salt and pepper. Serve with the chicken.

Orange County Fare; a culinary journey through the California Riviera
Junior League of Orange County, California

"Community cookbooks are a voyeur's treat, a window into the everyday life and foods of a group of churchgoers, a clutch of quilters, or a league of ladies inclined toward service."

JOHN T. EDGE
A GRACIOUS PLENTY

HONEY AND ORANGE CHICKEN

4 chicken breasts with bones and skin

1 tablespoon sunflower oil

4 green onions, chopped

1 clove garlic, crushed

3 tablespoons honey

4 tablespoons orange juice

1 orange, peeled and segmented

2 tablespoons soy sauce

Preheat oven to 375 degrees. Place chicken breasts in a single layer in baking dish. Heat sunflower oil in a small saucepan. Gently cook green onions and garlic until softened but not brown, approximately two minutes. Stir in honey, orange juice, orange segments, and soy sauce; cook until honey has completed dissolved. Pour sauce over chicken. Bake in preheated 375 degree oven for 55 minutes or until chicken is cooked. Baste with sauce every 15 minutes during cooking.

Toast to Tidewater
Junior League of Norfolk-Virginia Beach, Virginia

SOUTHERN HOSPITALITY CHICKEN

1 pound boneless chicken breasts

2 (10-ounce) packages frozen broccoli

1 (10-ounce) can cream of chicken soup

1 cup mayonnaise

2 cups sour cream

1 cup shredded sharp Cheddar cheese

Grated Parmesan cheese

Paprika

Butter

Combine the chicken with enough water to cover in a saucepan. Bring to a boil. Boil until the chicken is cooked through; drain. Cut into bite-size pieces, discarding the skin. Cook the broccoli using the package directions; drain. Combine the soup, mayonnaise, sour cream and Cheddar cheese in a bowl and mix well. Layer the chicken, broccoli and sour cream mixture in a 3-quart baking dish, sprinkling Parmesan cheese generously over each layer. Sprinkle paprika over the top and dot with butter. Bake at 350 degrees for 30 minutes.

Meet Me at the Garden Gate
Junior League of Spartanburg, South Carolina

Tortilla-Crusted Chicken Stuffed with Pepper Jack Cheese and Spinach

Tortilla-Crusted Chicken

4 boneless skinless chicken breasts

4 slices Pepper Jack cheese

1 (10-ounce) package frozen chopped
   spinach, cooked, drained and squeezed dry

1 cup crushed tortilla chips (red, if available)

¼ teaspoon salt

½ teaspoon oregano

¼ teaspoon cumin

¼ teaspoon pepper

1 egg

1 tablespoon vegetable or corn oil

Cilantro Pesto

Make a slit in each chicken breast and stuff with the cheese and spinach. Mix the tortilla chips, salt, oregano, cumin and pepper in a shallow dish. Beat the egg in a shallow dish. Dip the chicken in the egg and coat in the tortilla chip mixture. Heat the oil in an ovenproof skillet over medium-high heat. Add the chicken and brown for 3 minutes per side. Reduce the heat to medium-low and cook for 15 to 18 minutes or until the chicken is cooked through, turning once. Serve with Cilantro Pesto.

Cilantro Pesto

¼ cup extra-virgin olive oil

1 cup loosely packed fresh cilantro

2 tablespoons toasted pine nuts

2 large garlic cloves

1 jalapeño chile, seeded and sliced

⅓ cup grated Romano or Parmesan cheese

Combine the olive oil, cilantro, pine nuts, garlic, jalapeño and cheese in a food processor. Process until smooth. Store in an airtight container in the refrigerator for up to 3 to 4 weeks or in the freezer for up to 6 months. Makes 1 cup.

A League of Our Own
Rockwall Women's League, Texas

Tyson Family Southern Fried Chicken Serves 4 to 6

Chicken Seasoning Mix

1 cup salt

1 cup dried thyme

¼ cup pepper

3½ tablespoons paprika

3 tablespoons garlic powder

2 tablespoons onion powder

Combine the salt, thyme, pepper, paprika, garlic powder and onion powder in a bowl and mix well. Store in an airtight container for up to 6 months.

Chicken

4 eggs, beaten

⅓ cup water

½ cup hot red pepper sauce

2 cups self-rising flour

1 teaspoon coarsely ground pepper

1 (2½-pound) chicken, cut up

Shortening for frying

Combine the eggs, water and hot sauce in a shallow dish and mix well. Mix the flour and pepper in a shallow dish. Spread enough seasoning mix in a shallow dish to coat all of the chicken. Coat the chicken in the seasoning mix. Dip in the egg mixture and then coat in the flour mixture. Heat shortening in a cast-iron skillet until hot. Fry the chicken for 10 to 12 minutes per side or until the chicken is cooked through. Drain on a wire rack; do not drain on paper towels or the chicken will stick.

Add Another Place Setting
Junior League of Northwest Arkansas

> "When you believe in your cookbook, you don't have qualms about approaching people to tell them that this is a really good product and that they will be happy carrying it in their shop or restaurant or to give to their employees, family, or friends."
>
> Ruth McLeod
> Arizona Historical Society Museum

CREOLE CHICKEN CAKES WITH RÉMOULADE SAUCE

CHICKEN CAKES

2 tablespoons butter

½ red bell pepper, chopped

4 green onions, thinly sliced

1 clove garlic, crushed

3 cups chopped cooked chicken

1 cup soft bread crumbs

1 egg, lightly beaten

2 tablespoons mayonnaise

1 tablespoon Creole mustard

2 teaspoons Creole seasoning

¼ cup vegetable oil

To prepare the cakes, melt the butter in a large skillet over medium heat. Add the bell pepper, green onions and garlic and sauté for 3 to 4 minutes or until the vegetables are tender. Combine the bell pepper mixture, chicken, bread crumbs, egg, mayonnaise, Creole mustard and Creole seasoning in a bowl and mix well.

Shape into eight 1-inch cakes to serve as an appetizer, or four 3-inch cakes to serve as an entrée. Fry the chicken cakes in the oil in a large skillet over medium heat for 3 minutes on each side or until golden brown. Drain on paper towels.

RÉMOULADE SAUCE

1 cup mayonnaise

2 tablespoons Creole mustard

1½ tablespoons chili sauce

2 green onions, thinly sliced

2 cloves garlic, crushed

1 tablespoon chopped fresh parsley

¼ teaspoon ground red pepper

To prepare the sauce, combine the mayonnaise, Creole mustard and chili sauce in a bowl and mix well. Stir in the green onions, garlic, parsley and red pepper. Serve with the chicken cakes. Store any leftover sauce in the refrigerator.

Excellent Courses, A Culinary Legacy of Ravenscroft
Ravenscroft School, Raleigh, North Carolina

Weems Creek Apricot Chicken

1 (10-ounce) jar apricot preserves
1 (8-ounce) bottle Russian salad dressing
1 envelope onion soup mix
½ cup (1 stick) margarine, melted
4 boneless skinless chicken breasts
All-purpose flour for dredging

Combine the preserves, salad dressing, soup mix and margarine in a bowl and mix well. Coat the chicken in flour, shaking off any excess. Place the chicken in a baking dish and pour the sauce over the top. Bake at 350 degrees for 40 minutes or until the chicken is cooked through.

Note: You may use Catalina dressing instead of Russian dressing.

A Thyme to Entertain—Menus & Traditions of Annapolis
Junior League of Annapolis, Maryland

Chicken Pesto Pan Pizza

1 can refrigerator pizza dough
1 (10-ounce) package frozen chopped
   spinach, thawed and drained
8 ounces pesto
½ cup ricotta cheese
¼ cup chopped onion

2 cups shredded cooked chicken
Sliced fresh mushrooms
Sliced plum tomatoes
4 ounces shredded Swiss cheese
¼ cup grated Romano cheese

Preheat oven to 425 degrees. Unroll the pizza dough and pat into a rectangle on a 10×15 inch baking sheet, building up the edges slightly to form rim. Pierce with a fork. Bake for 7 minutes or until light brown. Maintain oven temperature.

Press the excess moisture from the spinach. Combine the spinach, pesto, ricotta cheese and onion in a bowl and mix well. Spread the spinach mixture over the baked layer and top with the chicken, mushrooms, tomatoes, Swiss cheese, and Romano cheese. Bake for 7 minutes or until the cheese melts and the crust is golden brown.

Pomegranates & Prickly Pears—flavorful entertaining from the Junior League of Phoenix
Junior League of Phoenix, Arizona

Chicken Tetrazzini

2 large hens or 1 turkey breast	1½ cups Parmesan cheese, divided
Salt	Salt to taste
Celery leaves	Cayenne pepper to taste
Bay leaves	Hot pepper sauce to taste
Onions	3 large onions, sliced
¾ cup butter or margarine	½ cup butter or margarine, separated
¾ cup all-purpose flour	1 pound mushrooms, sliced
3 cups half-and-half	1 (8-ounce) box thin spaghetti
4 cups milk	Sherry to taste (optional)

Boil hen or turkey in water to which salt, celery leaves, bay leaves and chopped onions have been added. After meat has finished cooking, strain broth and set aside. When cool, cut meat into bite-size pieces. Combine butter, flour, half-and-half and milk in a double boiler to make cream sauce. Cook over medium heat, stirring constantly until thickened. Remove cream sauce from heat. Add 1 cup Parmesan cheese and seasonings to taste. Set aside. Sauté onion in four tablespoons of butter until soft. Set aside. Sauté mushrooms in remaining four tablespoons of butter for about five minutes. Cook spaghetti in reserved broth; drain. Combine spaghetti, meat, sauce, onions and mushrooms. Adjust seasonings to taste, add sherry if desired, and put mixture in a 13×9×2-inch baking dish. Sprinkle top with ½ cup Parmesan cheese and bake in a preheated oven at 350 degrees until it bubbles.

A Southern Collection—Then and Now
Junior League of Columbus, Georgia

Easy Chicken and Dressing

1 chicken or at least 2 cups	1 can water
1 can cream of celery soup	1 package Pepperidge Farm corn bread stuffing
1 can cream of chicken soup	½ cup melted butter

Debone chicken; cut up into bite-size pieces. Mix with soups and water. Put in a 9×11-inch or similar size pan (you do not want to use a small deep type bowl). Sprinkle bread stuffing over this mixture; pour butter over it. Bake about 30 minutes at 350 degrees. Stir a little before finished baking. If you don't want it very dry, reduce baking time.

Dining with Pioneers, Volume 1
AT&T Pioneers, Tennessee Chapter 21

CREAMY CHICKEN ENCHILADAS

1 medium onion, chopped

1 tablespoon butter

1 (4-ounce) can chopped green chiles

3½ cups chopped cooked chicken

8 ounces cream cheese, softened

8 (8-inch) medium flour tortillas

4 cups shredded Monterey Jack cheese

2 cups heavy cream

1 (7-ounce) can salsa verde

Sauté the onion in the butter in a large skillet over medium heat for 5 minutes. Add the green chiles and sauté for 1 minute. Stir in the chicken and cream cheese. Cook until the cream cheese melts, stirring constantly.

Arrange the tortillas on a work surface and spoon 2 to 3 tablespoons of the chicken mixture down the center of each tortilla. Roll the tortillas to enclose the filling and arrange seam side down in a lightly greased 9×13-inch baking dish. Sprinkle with the Monterey Jack cheese and drizzle with the cream.

Bake at 350 degrees for 30 to 45 minutes or until bubbly and light brown. Serve with the salsa.

Notably Nashville
Junior League of Nashville, Tennessee

"This has become one of my 'go-to' recipes when having company for dinner. Delicious!"

Jennifer Kennedy
FRP Communications Coordinator

FRP Family Favorites

Green Enchiladas

5 or 6 boneless skinless chicken breasts,
  cooked and chopped

2 cups (8 ounces) shredded Monterey
  Jack cheese

2 cups (8 ounces) shredded Cheddar cheese

1 medium onion, chopped

Vegetable oil

24 corn tortillas

1 (10-ounce) package frozen chopped
  spinach, cooked and drained

3 green onions, chopped

1 (4-ounce) can chopped green chiles

2 jalapeño chiles, seeded and chopped

2 (10-ounce) cans cream of chicken soup

2 cups sour cream

Salt and pepper to taste

1 cup (4 ounces) shredded Cheddar cheese,
  or enough to cover

1 cup (4 ounces) shredded Monterey Jack
  cheese, or enough to cover

Preheat the oven to 350 degrees. Combine the chicken with 2 cups Monterey Jack cheese, 2 cups Cheddar cheese and the onion in a large bowl.

Heat a small amount of oil in a skillet. Add the tortillas one at a time and cook for a few seconds on each side, turning with tongs; remove to a work surface. Spoon the chicken mixture onto the tortillas and roll the tortillas to enclose the filling. Arrange in a large baking dish.

Combine the spinach, green onions, green chiles, jalapeño chiles, soup and sour cream in a bowl and mix well. Season with salt and pepper. Spoon over the enchiladas. Sprinkle with 1 cup Cheddar cheese and 1 cup Monterey Jack cheese. Bake for 20 to 30 minutes or until bubbly.

Treasures from the Bend, Rich in History and Flavor
Fort Bend Junior Service League, Sugar Land, Texas

Salsa Verde Chicken Enchiladas

1 small package white corn tortillas,
  cut into quarters

4 chicken breasts, cooked and chopped

3 (7-ounce) cans salsa verde

2 cups shredded Monterey Jack Cheese

1 pint heavy whipping cream, whipped

Layer the tortilla quarters, chicken, salsa verde, cheese and whipped cream one-half at a time in a greased 9×13-inch baking pan. Cover and bake for 35 minutes. Uncover and bake for 5 to 10 minutes longer or until light brown. Let stand for 5 minutes before serving.

Now Serving
Junior League of Wichita Falls, Texas

Sour Cream Chicken Enchiladas

3 tablespoons butter
1 cup chopped onion
¼ cup flour
1 teaspoon cumin
¾ teaspoon salt
2½ cups chicken broth

1 (4-ounce) can chopped green chiles
1 cup (8 ounces) sour cream
1½ cups shredded Monterey Jack cheese
2 cups chopped cooked chicken
12 medium (6-inch) flour tortillas

Melt the butter in a skillet. Add the onion and sauté until the onion is translucent. Stir in the flour and cook for 1 to 2 minutes or until bubbly. Stir in the cumin and salt. Add the chicken broth gradually and cook until thickened, stirring constantly. Add the green chiles. Remove from the heat and stir in the sour cream and half the Monterey Jack cheese.

Spoon the chicken onto the tortillas and top each with 1 to 2 tablespoons of the sauce. Roll the tortillas to enclose the filling. Place seam side down in a 9×13-inch baking pan.

Spoon the remaining sauce over the rolled tortillas and top with the remaining ¾ cup Monterey Jack cheese. Bake at 350 degrees for 25 minutes or until the cheese melts and the sauce is bubbly.

Note: You may substitute 2 additional cups of cheese for the chicken to prepare meatless enchiladas. Or add additional chicken, omit the tortillas, and serve as a dip.

Lone Star to Five Star
Junior League of Plano, Texas

Quick Chicken and Spinach Tetrazzini

4 ounces spaghetti, broken into 3- to
   4-inch lengths
1½ cups chopped cooked chicken
1 (9-ounce) package frozen creamed low-fat
   spinach, thawed
1 cup ricotta cheese

½ cup drained, oil-packed sun-dried
   tomatoes, chopped
5 tablespoons grated asiago cheese, divided
1 clove garlic, minced
Freshly ground black pepper to taste

Preheat the oven to 500 degrees. Cook the spaghetti in a large pot of boiling, salted water until al dente. Drain, reserving ¼ cup of the cooking liquid. Combine the spaghetti, chicken, spinach, ricotta, tomatoes, 4 tablespoons of the cheese, the garlic, and reserved cooking liquid in a large bowl. Season with pepper. Spread the mixture in a 9-inch pie plate. Sprinkle with the remaining asiago cheese. Bake until hot and bubbly, about 15 to 20 minutes.

Dancing on the Table
Junior League of Wilmington, Delaware

GRILLED BOURBON TURKEY

1 to 2 tablespoons Woodford Reserve Bourbon
1 teaspoon soy sauce
1 tablespoon Worcestershire sauce
1 tablespoon vegetable oil
¼ teaspoon thyme
⅛ teaspoon salt
1 large onion, cut into ¼-inch slices
2 (8-ounce) turkey breast steaks
¾ teaspoon coarse ground pepper

Combine the bourbon, soy sauce, Worcestershire sauce, oil, thyme and salt in a shallow medium bowl and mix well. Add the onion and turkey steaks and turn to coat. Marinate in the refrigerator for 30 minutes or longer. Drain, reserving the turkey and onion slices. Press the coarse ground pepper firmly over both sides of the turkey.

Grill or broil the turkey 5 to 6 inches from the heat source for 3 to 5 minutes on each side or until the juices run clear when the turkey is pierced. Place the reserved onion on the grill just before the turkey is done and grill for 2 to 3 minutes. Serve the onion with the steaks.

Splendor in the Bluegrass
Junior League of Louisville, Kentucky

> "It's not just how many dollars we get for selling cookbooks but what else the cookbook can do. You can use it as a way to promote healthy eating habits or just as a way to promote cooking at home, which helps families and overall health and well being."
>
> HOLLY SIDES
> JUNIOR LEAGUE OF BATON ROUGE, LOUISIANA

Cocoa-Crusted Venison Strip Loin with White Chocolate Chestnut Purée, Brussels Sprouts and a Semisweet Venison Reduction

SERVES 4

Chocolate Chestnut Purée

4 ounces frozen or dried chestnuts
   (soak the dried ones in water until soft)

¼ yellow onion, sliced

1 garlic clove, crushed

Vegetable oil for cooking

½ vanilla bean, scraped

1 cup or more chicken stock, vegetable stock,
   beef stock or water

1 tablespoon cold butter

1 tablespoon crème fraîche or cream

2 ounces white chocolate, chopped

Salt to taste

For the chocolate chestnut purée, sauté the chestnuts, onion and garlic in a little oil in a skillet until the onion is tender. Add the vanilla and chicken stock. Simmer for 20 minutes or until the liquid is reduced by half. Purée in a blender. Add the butter, crème fraîche and white chocolate and purée until smooth, adding more stock if the mixture is too thick. Season with salt. Place in a bowl and cover tightly with plastic wrap to prevent a skin from forming.

Venison Sauce

2 tablespoons vegetable oil

1 pound venison or beef stew meat

¾ yellow onion, sliced

8 garlic cloves, crushed

½ cup (1 stick) butter

8 ounces red wine (such as a southern Rhône,
   preferably a syrah)

4 cups chicken stock

2 ounces semisweet chocolate, chopped

For the venison sauce, heat the oil in a saucepan over high heat until smoking. Add the venison and sauté until brown on all sides. Add the onion, garlic, and butter. Cook for 3 minutes longer. Add the red wine. Cook to deglaze the pan, stirring constantly. Add the chicken stock. Simmer over low heat for 1 hour. Strain the sauce and return to the pan. Cook until reduced to a sauce consistency. Add the chocolate and stir until melted.

Venison

4 (6-ounce) portions of venison

Salt and pepper to taste

½ cup cocoa nibs, pulsed slightly in a
   coffee grinder

Vegetable oil for sautéing

Brussels sprouts

For the venison, season the venison portions with salt and pepper. Coat with the cocoa nibs. Sear the venison on both sides in a little oil in a skillet over medium heat. Place in a roasting pan. Roast in a preheated 400-degree oven for 5 to 10 minutes or to the desired degree of doneness. Let stand at room temperature for 10 minutes before serving. Sauté the brussels sprouts in a little oil in a skillet for 2 minutes. Season with salt and pepper.

To serve, spoon some of the chocolate chestnut purée onto the center of each plate. Add some of the brussels sprouts. Top with a portion of venison. Spoon the venison sauce over the top.

Note: To spice it up a bit, add some chopped toasted hazelnuts and grapes to the brussels sprouts.

Peeling the Wild Onion
Junior League of Chicago, Illinois

SOUTHWESTERN DUCK WITH CHIPOTLE-APRICOT GLAZE
SERVES 4

16 cups (1 gallon) water
3 tablespoons finely chopped cilantro
½ cup plus 2 tablespoons salt
½ cup honey
¼ cup packed dark brown sugar
2 teaspoons onion powder

1 teaspoon garlic powder
1 tablespoon mixed pickling spice
4 boneless skinless teal or wood duck breasts
1 jar apricot jam
1 tablespoon finely chopped seeded chipotle chile packed in adobo sauce

Mix the water, cilantro, salt, honey, brown sugar, onion powder, garlic powder and pickling spice in a large container. Add the duck breasts. Marinate in the refrigerator for 6 hours to overnight. Drain and discard the marinade. Pat the duck dry with paper towels. Mix the jam and chipotle chile in a saucepan. Simmer for 5 minutes, stirring occasionally. Strain through a wire mesh strainer into a bowl.

Grill the duck over high heat to medium-rare, moving infrequently so that grill marks form on the duck. Baste the duck lightly with the apricot glaze just before done. Remove the duck to a cutting board and let stand for a few minutes. Slice the duck diagonally and arrange on serving plates. Drizzle with the remaining apricot glaze and garnish with chopped cilantro or scallions. Serve with wild rice or your favorite side dish.

The Hunter's Table
Joshua Sasser, 1st-place winner
Ducks Unlimited®, FRP.INC

Grilled Mallard Breast with Currant Jelly Sauce

Currant Jelly Sauce

6 to 8 tablespoons butter

1 (12-ounce) jar currant jelly

1 tablespoon finely chopped fresh thyme

1 tablespoon finely chopped fresh rosemary

1 teaspoon finely chopped fresh savory

The Sauce: Melt the butter in a saucepan and add the jelly. Cook until smooth, stirring frequently. Stir in the thyme, rosemary and savory. Keep warm until ready to serve.

Duck

1 package wild rice mix

1 cup olive oil

3 to 4 tablespoons soy sauce

3 to 4 tablespoons lemon juice

2 large mallard breast fillets

Olive oil

Asparagus spears

Butter

Sea salt

The Duck: Prepare the wild rice using the package directions, substituting chicken broth for water. Keep warm until ready to serve. Whisk 1 cup olive oil, the soy sauce and lemon juice in a glass bowl. Add the duck and turn to coat. Marinate in the refrigerator for 20 to 30 minutes. Drain and discard the marinade. Pat the duck dry with paper towels.

Heat the grill to medium-high heat and coat the cooking rack with additional olive oil. Grill the duck for 3 to 4 minutes per side for medium-rare. Remove the duck to a cutting board and slice very thin, but do not shave. Cook the asparagus in a small amount of water in a covered skillet for 3 to 4 minutes or until tender-crisp; drain. Add a small amount of butter and sea salt and cook until the butter is melted.

Arrange the duck slices on serving plates. Spoon the rice and asparagus onto the plates. Pour the sauce over the duck.

The Hunter's Table
Bill Palmer, 2nd-place winner
Ducks Unlimited®, FRP,INC

BUDREAUX'S PECAN PATTIES

2 to 4 cups chopped pecans
1/2 cup finely chopped white onion
1 green onion, finely chopped
1/2 cup finely chopped fresh parsley
1 tablespoon minced garlic
3 tablespoons vegetable oil
4 boneless skinless duck breasts
1/2 teaspoon salt
1 cup seasoned bread crumbs
3 eggs
1/2 cup milk
Vegetable oil for frying

Spread the pecans over a baking sheet. Bake at 350 degrees for 5 to 10 minutes or until toasted. Remove to a shallow dish and let cool.

Sauté the white onion, green onion, parsley and garlic in 3 tablespoons oil until the vegetables are tender. Remove from the heat and let cool.

Grind the duck in a food processor to the consistency of sausage. Remove to a bowl. Add the onion mixture, salt and bread crumbs and mix well. Shape into 2-inch patties, 1/2-inch thick.

Beat the eggs and milk in a bowl. Dip the duck patties in the egg mixture and coat in the pecans. Repeat if a thicker crust is desired.

Heat oil to 350 degrees in a deep skillet. Add the patties and fry until golden brown on both sides and cooked through. Remove to paper towels to drain. Serve with rice and gravy.

The Hunter's Table
Neal Sinclair, 3rd-place winner
Ducks Unlimited®, FRP INC

MORE THAN A PLACE IN THE SUN

Amelia Island, Florida, is known for its beautiful beaches and Fernandina Beach, its colorful seaport village. Tourists flock to this resort island each year to bask in the sunshine, partake of its shrimp, and enjoy the summer festivities.

In addition to the fun and festivities on Amelia Island, a volunteer auxiliary works tirelessly to assist in fund-raising and community education for Micah's Place, a domestic violence shelter and support program for victims of abuse in Nassua County, Florida.

The auxiliary has supported luncheons, galas, home and garden tours, and their latest venture, the publishing of the cookbook *A Savory Place: Culinary Favorites of Amelia Island.*

Iris Jacobsen, auxiliary president during the recipe compilation and production of the cookbook, has other vested interests in the project. With a background in fine arts, she served as art director for the cookbook, and her 1797 historic home, Mount Hope Plantation, is featured on the cover.

"For years our auxiliary members talked about starting a cookbook, and we finally took it to the next level," Iris said. Half of the first printing sold within the first four months of publication.

Besides getting the cookbook in local gift shops to offer it to the thousands of visitors each summer, the auxiliary proudly shows off their cookbook during many of the warm-weather activities on Amelia Island, including the summer shrimp festival.

"Marketing of the cookbook continues as we embark on the '100 Days of Summer' festivities on Amelia Island," Iris said. "Besides selling books at that time to provide funding for Micah's Place, it is also our chance to educate the thousands of visitors about the people on our island and the good they are doing for such a worthy cause."

A SAVORY PLACE
MICAH'S PLACE

Serving Safety, Shelter & Support

GRILLED STUFFED WHOLE GROUPER

1 (10- to 12-pound) black grouper or
    red grouper
1 large onion, chopped
10 to 12 garlic cloves, chopped
2 each yellow squash and zucchini,
    cut into halves and sliced
12 cherry tomatoes, cut into halves
1 pound asparagus, chopped
¼ cup virgin olive oil
2 tablespoons mayonnaise
⅓ cup rum
3 tablespoons Old Bay seasoning

1 teaspoon thyme
1 tablespoon crushed bay leaves
1 tablespoon salt
1½ tablespoons black pepper
1 teaspoon cayenne pepper
1½ pounds blue crab or black fin
    lump crab meat
Olive oil
Kosher salt
Sliced aged Swiss cheese, or other strong-
    flavored cheese

Place a sharp knife on the back of the fish behind the gill plate and cut down the back along 1 side of the backbone, cutting to but not through the skin of the belly. Repeat the process on the other side of the backbone. Remove and discard the backbone, ribs, and entrails, reaching into the throat to remove the liver and heart if possible; leave the head and tail intact. Rinse well.

Combine the onion, garlic, yellow squash, zucchini, cherry tomatoes, and asparagus in a large bowl. Add ¼ cup olive oil, the mayonnaise, rum, Old Bay seasoning, thyme, bay leaves, salt, black pepper and cayenne pepper and mix well.

Spoon the vegetable mixture and crab meat into the cavity of the fish, beginning at the head and pouring any remaining liquid over the stuffing. Sew the cavity closed with baker's twine. Rub the fish with additional olive oil and sprinkle with kosher salt.

Wrap the fish with foil and grill for 1½ to 2 hours or to 160 to 165 degrees internally. Place on a serving platter and remove the twine. Open the fish and layer Swiss cheese over the stuffing. Garnish with Parmesan cheese and chopped parsley.

From Grouper to Grits
Junior League of Clearwater Dunedin, Florida

BAKED HALIBUT

8 (½-inch-thick) halibut fillets

½ teaspoon salt

¼ teaspoon pepper

¼ teaspoon paprika

⅓ cup grated Parmesan cheese

3 ounces cream cheese

1 cup shredded Gruyère cheese

¼ cup sour cream

4 green onions, minced

8 slices prosciutto, finely chopped

1 garlic clove, minced

2 medium shallots, minced

¼ cup butter, melted

4 to 8 ounces sliced mushrooms

¼ cup butter

3 tablespoons all-purpose flour

¾ cup white wine

1 to 3 tablespoons additional grated
    Parmesan cheese

Place the fish in a greased 7×11-inch baking dish. Sprinkle with the salt, pepper and paprika. Combine ⅓ cup Parmesan cheese, the cream cheese, Gruyère cheese, sour cream, green onions, prosciutto and garlic in a bowl and mix well. Spread evenly over the fish. Bake at 350 degrees for 10 to 12 minutes or until the fish begins to flake. Remove from the oven and keep warm. Sauté the shallots in ¼ cup butter in a medium skillet until tender. Add the mushrooms and sauté until tender. Remove the shallots and mushrooms to a bowl using a slotted spoon, reserving the pan drippings. Melt ¼ cup butter in the skillet. Stir in the flour until smooth. Cook over medium heat until brown, stirring constantly. Add the wine gradually, stirring constantly. Cook until thickened and bubbly, stirring constantly. Stir in the mushroom mixture. Pour over the fish. Sprinkle with additional Parmesan cheese. Bake for 5 minutes. Remove the fish and mushrooms to a serving platter using a slotted spoon.

Oh, Shenandoah!
Museum of the
Shenandoah Valley,
Virginia

Community cookbooks seem to be about sharing recipes and sharing the purpose of a project.

THE AMERICAN COOKBOOK

GRILLED HALIBUT
WITH BLUEBERRY MINT SALSA

GRILLED HALIBUT

1½ pounds halibut fillets, cut into 4 servings
Salt and pepper to taste
Blueberry Mint Salsa to taste
4 sprigs fresh mint

Preheat a charcoal grill. Season the halibut with salt and pepper. Place on the grill and sear for 4 to 5 minutes on each side or until opaque, turning once.

Place the Blueberry Salsa in a saucepan and heat over very low heat until heated through. Place the halibut fillets on four serving plates and spoon Blueberry Salsa over the top. Top each serving with a sprig of fresh mint.

BLUEBERRY MINT SALSA

1 cup blueberries
1 cup finely chopped mixed red and yellow bell peppers
2 small green onions, finely chopped
2 tablespoons chopped fresh cilantro
¼ cup chopped fresh mint
1 tablespoon finely chopped poblano chile
1 tablespoon red wine vinegar
Juice of 2 limes to taste
Juice of 1 lemon to taste

Combine the blueberries with the bell peppers, green onions, cilantro, mint, poblano chile, red wine vinegar, lime juice and lemon juice in a small bowl; mix well. Chill for 2 to 3 hours to develop the flavors.

Northwest Inspirations
Junior League of Olympia, Washington

Northwest Cedar-Planked Salmon

SERVES 4

Salmon

1 large or 2 small cedar baking planks

Vegetable oil

1 tablespoon unsalted butter,
    at room temperature

1 tablespoon finely grated lemon zest

½ teaspoon sugar

¼ teaspoon salt

¼ teaspoon freshly ground black pepper

¼ teaspoon powdered mustard

4 salmon fillet pieces (about 8 ounces each),
    skin and pin bones removed

8 large cremini mushrooms, halved

Rub the top of the cedar planks with a little vegetable oil. Put the planks in a cold oven and preheat the oven to 350 degrees for about 15 minutes. Combine the butter, lemon zest, sugar, salt, pepper, and powdered mustard, stirring to make a smooth paste. Rub the seasoning on both sides of the salmon pieces.

Take the planks from the oven and immediately set the salmon on top. Surround the salmon with the mushrooms and return the planks to the oven. Bake until the salmon is just barely translucent in the center, 18 to 20 minutes, depending on the thickness of the fish, turning once halfway through.

To serve, drizzle the sauce over the salmon and mushrooms and sprinkle with parsley.

Spice Wine Sauce

1 cup dry white wine

¼ cup minced shallot

¼ cup freshly squeezed lemon juice

½ cup whipping cream

6 tablespoons unsalted butter, cut into pieces

1 teaspoon hot pepper sauce

Salt and freshly ground black pepper

¼ cup chopped fresh parsley, for garnish

Combine the wine, shallot, and lemon juice in a small saucepan. Bring to a boil over medium-high heat and boil until reduced to ¼ cup, 5 to 8 minutes. Add the cream and simmer until slightly thickened, about 3 minutes. Reduce the heat to medium-low and whisk in the butter, 1 piece at a time, until thoroughly incorporated. Remove the sauce from heat and stir in the pepper sauce with salt and pepper to taste. Keep warm over low heat until ready to serve; do not allow the sauce to boil or it will turn oily.

Celebrate the Rain
Junior League of Seattle, Washington

Salmon and Spinach in Puff Pastry with Lemon-Herb Sauce

SERVES 4 AS A MAIN DISH, 8 AS AN APPETIZER

1 package frozen spinach, thawed
and drained

¼ cup white wine

1 clove crushed garlic

1½ cups cooked white rice

⅓ cup sour cream

⅔ cup mayonnaise

3 tablespoons lemon juice

2 teaspoons dried parsley

1 teaspoon dried dill

½ teaspoon white pepper

2 sheets of puff pastry

2 (10-ounce) salmon fillets

1 egg, beaten

Fresh parsley or dill for garnish

Preheat oven to 400 degrees. Sauté spinach in a frying pan over medium heat with the white wine and garlic until the wine is almost evaporated. Remove from heat and mix with rice, set aside. Mix together the sour cream, mayonnaise, lemon juice, herbs and pepper, and set aside. Unfold the puff pastry. Place on a lightly floured board and gently roll out until approximately 2 inches larger on all edges. Lift off of board and place on a baking sheet. Fill one sheet at a time. Pat salmon fillets dry with a paper towel. Spread one side with the herb mixture. Reserve at least half of the mixture for garniture after baking. Place the fillet face down in the center of the pastry sheet. Place ¾ of a cup of the spinach/rice mixture on top of the fillet. Pinch edges shut and gently reverse pastry package so smooth edge faces up. Repeat with the second fillet. Brush both pastries with the beaten egg. Bake for 45 minutes or until the pastry is golden brown. To serve, cut in 4 or 8 slices and garnish with 1 tablespoon of sauce and a sprig of fresh herb. Can be served hot or cold.

Of Tide and Thyme
Junior League of Annapolis, Maryland

Roasted Sea Bass in Prosciutto

SERVES 4

¼ cup unsalted butter, softened

2 teaspoons dried rosemary leaves, crushed

½ teaspoon dried thyme leaves

1 tablespoon grated lemon zest

½ teaspoon salt

Freshly ground pepper to taste

4 (6-ounce) ½-inch-thick pieces Chilean sea
bass fillet, cod or other firm white fish

4 teaspoons fresh lemon juice

5 or 6 very thin slices prosciutto

Combine the butter, rosemary, thyme, lemon zest, salt and freshly ground pepper in a small nonreactive bowl and mix well. Arrange the fish on a foil-lined baking sheet. Sprinkle with the lemon juice and spread with the butter mixture. Arrange the prosciutto over the fish, covering the tops and sides. Roast at 450 degrees on the middle oven rack for 15 minutes or until the fish is opaque and flakes easily with a fork. Remove to a serving platter and garnish with Parmesan cheese and rosemary sprigs.

Note: The herb butter can be prepared in advance and chilled until needed; let stand at room temperature for 30 minutes before using. The fish can be prepared in advance and stored, wrapped in plastic wrap, in the refrigerator for 1 hour. Let stand at room temperature for 15 minutes before roasting.

Savor the Moment, Entertaining Without Reservations
Junior League of Boca Raton, Florida

GRILLED SWORDFISH WITH AVOCADO BUTTER

SERVES 6 TO 8

SWORDFISH

3 pounds thickly sliced swordfish fillets
Lemon juice to taste
Melted butter to taste

Soy sauce to taste
Avocado Butter

Brush the fish with lemon juice, butter and soy sauce. Arrange on a grill rack. Grill over hot coals until the fish flakes easily, basting frequently with lemon juice, butter and soy sauce. Serve with Avocado Butter.

AVOCADO BUTTER

½ cup (1 stick) butter, softened
¼ cup mashed avocado (seed reserved)
1 tablespoon lemon juice

1 teaspoon Worcestershire sauce
½ teaspoon garlic salt
½ teaspoon barbecue spice

Whip the butter in a small bowl until smooth and creamy. Fold in the avocado, lemon juice, Worcestershire sauce, garlic salt and barbecue spice. Place the reserved avocado seed in the center to prevent turning brown. Chill, covered, until ready to use. Remove the avocado seed before serving. Makes ¾ cup.

Celebrate Highlands
The Laurel Garden Club, Highlands, North Carolina

Swordfish with Mustard Creole Sauce

SERVES 4

Fish

4 swordfish steaks (6 ounces each)

Season steaks with salt and pepper and lightly brush with oil. Broil until fish flakes easily with fork.

Creole Mustard Sauce

1½ tablespoons shallots

1 tablespoon cider vinegar

2 peppercorns

¼ bay leaf

½ cup white wine

⅔ cup heavy cream

½ pound unsalted butter, cut in small pieces

Dijon mustard

Combine shallots, vinegar, peppercorns, bay leaf and white wine in a stainless steel saucepan. Cook until very dry. Add heavy cream and cook to reduce sauce. Add butter and continue to reduce sauce until thick enough to coat steaks. Add Dijon mustard to taste. Remove bay leaf. Position sauce lightly around steaks; do not coat.

Cordon Bluegrass
Junior League of Louisville, Kentucky

Baked Tilapia with Vegetables

SERVES 4

4 (6-ounce) tilapia fillets

1 tablespoon Key lime juice

1 teaspoon dried dill weed, or 2 teaspoons chopped fresh dill weed

1 cup coarsely chopped tomato

½ cup coarsely chopped red bell pepper

½ cup coarsely chopped yellow bell pepper

½ cup coarsely chopped orange bell pepper

¼ teaspoon pepper

½ cup white wine

½ cup to 1 cup (2 to 4 ounces) shredded provolone cheese or Parmesan cheese

Preheat the oven to 400 degrees. Arrange the fillets in a single layer in a 9×13-inch baking dish sprayed with nonstick cooking spray. Drizzle the fillets with the lime juice and sprinkle with the dill weed. Top evenly with the tomato and bell peppers and sprinkle with the pepper.

Pour the wine around the fillets and sprinkle the cheese over the top. Bake for 30 minutes or until the fillets flake easily with a fork. Serve immediately.

Simply Sarasota
Junior League of Sarasota, Florida

1 pound catfish, crappie or salmon fillets

2 tablespoons white cooking wine

¼ teaspoon salt

½ teaspoon pepper

2 tablespoons dried onion flakes

½ cup mayonnaise-type salad dressing

¼ cup fat-free milk

1 tablespoon dried dill weed

1 tablespoon lemon juice

2 teaspoons Dijon mustard

Preheat the oven to 425 degrees. Place the fish in a single layer on a 9×13-inch baking dish coated with nonstick cooking spray. Sprinkle with the wine, salt, pepper and onion flakes. Bake, covered with foil, for 20 to 25 minutes or to 145 degrees on a meat thermometer.

Place the mayonnaise-type salad dressing in a saucepan. Whisk in the milk gradually. Whisk over medium-low heat for 2 minutes or until smooth and heated through but not bubbly. Remove from the heat. Stir in the dill weed, lemon juice and Dijon mustard.

Remove the fish to a serving platter. Pour the drippings from the baking pan into the dill mixture and mix well. Spoon over the fish.

Note: This is a quick and healthier way to cook catfish or crappie. Also, it cooks quickly for a quick weeknight meal.

Living Well More Than a Cookbook
National Extension Association of Family and Consumer Sciences, Dallas, Texas

"From working on this cookbook, I gained an appreciation for anyone who ever did a cookbook without a computer or the internet. *Virginia Hospitality* had 400 triple-tested recipes that were typed on index cards using a typewriter. I have so much respect for them; it was such a labor of love."

SAMANTHA BISHOP
MY MAMA MADE THAT, JUNIOR LEAGUE OF HAMPTON ROADS

Fish Tacos with Cabbage Slaw and Cilantro Aïoli

SERVES 4

Cilantro Aïoli

⅓ cup chopped cilantro

Green tops of 4 scallions, chopped

2 serrano chiles or jalapeño chiles, seeded and chopped

1 teaspoon drained capers

2 teaspoons minced garlic

1 egg

¾ cup (or less) olive oil

Salt and pepper to taste

To prepare the aïoli, combine the cilantro with the scallion tops, serrano chiles, capers and garlic in a food processor and pulse to mix. Add the egg and pulse until smooth. Drizzle in the olive oil very gradually, processing constantly until the mixture emulsifies. Spoon into a bowl and season with salt and pepper. Chill until serving time.

Cabbage Slaw

2 cups finely shredded green cabbage

½ cup thinly sliced red bell pepper

⅓ cup thinly sliced red onion

¼ cup thinly sliced basil

Salt and pepper to taste

To prepare the slaw, combine the cabbage with the bell pepper, onion and basil in a bowl. Toss gently and season with salt and pepper. Chill until serving time.

Tacos

⅓ cup olive oil

1 tablespoon fresh lime juice

1 tablespoon ancho chile powder

Kosher salt and freshly ground pepper to taste

4 (4-ounce) fillets of halibut, grouper, amberjack or sea bass

4 (10-inch) flour or corn tortillas

To prepare the tacos, combine the olive oil, lime juice, chile powder, kosher salt and pepper in a small bowl. Brush generously on the fish fillets. Grill the fish until cooked through. Grill the tortillas briefly until warm. Place 1 tortilla on each plate and top with the slaw and a fish fillet. Drizzle with the aïoli. Fold and roll the tortilla to enclose the filling. Serve immediately.

To avoid the possibility of salmonella from uncooked eggs, you can use an equivalent amount of egg substitute.

Beach Appétit
Junior League of the Emerald Coast, Fort Walton Beach, Florida

E.E. WILKERSON'S CRAB CAKES

4 slices white bread

1 pound crab meat (lump)

½ teaspoon seafood seasoning

Salt to taste

Pepper to taste

1 tablespoon Worcestershire sauce

¼ cup finely chopped onion

¼ cup finely chopped celery

1 stick butter

Run water over bread and squeeze out all water. Add crab meat, seafood seasoning, salt, pepper and Worcestershire sauce. Sauté onion and celery in butter. Add to mixture. Mix well and make into 3-ounce cakes. Place in a frying pan with cooking oil and fry until golden brown.

Share the Vision Cookbook
Dahlgren United Methodist Church, Dahlgren, Virginia

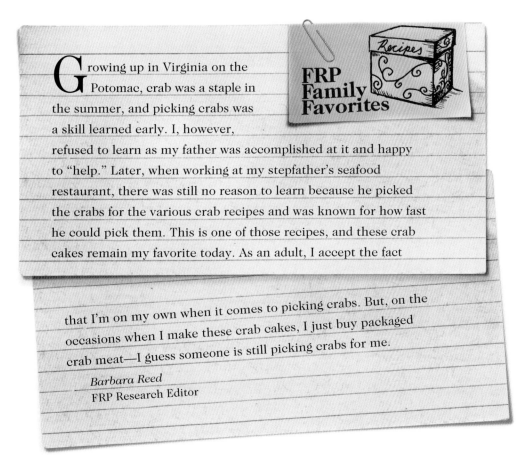

Growing up in Virginia on the Potomac, crab was a staple in the summer, and picking crabs was a skill learned early. I, however, refused to learn as my father was accomplished at it and happy to "help." Later, when working at my stepfather's seafood restaurant, there was still no reason to learn because he picked the crabs for the various crab recipes and was known for how fast he could pick them. This is one of those recipes, and these crab cakes remain my favorite today. As an adult, I accept the fact that I'm on my own when it comes to picking crabs. But, on the occasions when I make these crab cakes, I just buy packaged crab meat—I guess someone is still picking crabs for me.

Barbara Reed
FRP Research Editor

IMPERIAL CRAB

1 pound crab meat (backfin)
¼ cup pimento (chopped)
½ teaspoon seafood seasoning
⅓ cup capers
⅓ cup green pepper (chopped)

¾ teaspoon dry mustard
½ cup mayonnaise
½ teaspoon salt
1 egg
Dash paprika

Mix first 8 ingredients. Beat egg and fold in. Just before baking in a dish or in crab shells, sprinkle with paprika. Bake 20 minutes at 350 degrees.

Sharing the Vision Cookbook
Dahlgren United Methodist Church, Dahlgren, Virginia

CRAWFISH ÉTOUFFÉE—THE TEXAS WAY

½ cup (1 stick) of butter
2 cups chopped onions
1 cup chopped celery
1 cup chopped bell pepper
1 clove garlic, minced
1 pound peeled crawfish tails
2 bay leaves
1 tablespoon all-purpose flour

1 cup cold water
1½ teaspoons Creole seasoning
¼ teaspoon cayenne pepper
1 (10-ounce) can cream of golden
  mushroom soup
3 tablespoons chopped green onions
2 tablespoons chopped parsley
Hot cooked rice

Melt the butter in a large skillet over medium-high heat. Add the onions, celery, bell pepper and garlic and mix well. Sauté for 10 to 12 minutes or until the vegetables are tender and golden brown. Stir in the crawfish and bay leaves. Reduce the heat to medium. Cook for 10 to 12 minutes, stirring occasionally. Dissolve the flour in the cold water in a small bowl and add to the crawfish mixture. Stir in the Creole seasoning and cayenne pepper. Cook for 4 minutes or until thickened. Add the soup, green onions and parsley. Cook for about 2 minutes. Discard the bay leaves and serve over the rice.

Texas Tables
Junior League of North Harris and South Montgomery Counties, Texas

CRAWFISH BOIL FOR A DOZEN

2 (30- to 35-pound) sacks live crawfish
Water
Salt
3 (16-ounce) packages powdered crawfish-
　crab-shrimp seasoning mix, divided

1 (16-ounce) bottle crab boil
4 pounds small new potatoes
16 ears corn on cob
6 small onions, cut into quarters
Cajun seasoning salt

Rinse crawfish in sack with water. If desired, purge crawfish by placing sacks in ice chest; cover with water, add ½ (16-ounce) box salt. Let stand for 5 to 10 minutes; drain and rinse well. Using 15-gallon pot equipped with wire basket, fill about half-full with water. Place on propane jet burner and turn flame to high setting. Add ½ (16-ounce) box salt, 2 packages seasoning mix, liquid crab boil and potatoes to water. Cover and bring to a boil. Add 1 sack crawfish, corn and onion to boiling water. Sprinkle with ½ package seasoning mix. Stir with large utensil such as boat paddle. Bring to a boil. Cook for 3 minutes if crawfish are to be placed in ice chest until served, or cook for 5 minutes if crawfish are to be served immediately. Check potatoes; if not yet tender, retain in pot to cook with second sack of crawfish. Pour crawfish, corn, potatoes (if tender) and onions on table. Sprinkle with Cajun seasoning salt. Repeat procedure for second sack of crawfish. Seasoning amounts will accommodate about 200 pounds of crawfish; add ½ package seasoning mix to each batch as cooked and adjust corn, potato and onion quantities for number of guests to be served.

Louisiana Living
Junior Service League of Natchitoches, Louisiana

BOILED LOBSTER, YORK HARBOR STYLE

1 (12-ounce) bottle of beer at room
　temperature, preferably Samuel Adams or
　Red Stripe
2 (1¼- to 1½-pound) lobsters

½ cup butter
1 clove garlic, minced
½ cup white wine

Fill a large lobster pot with enough water to cover the lobsters. Bring the water to just below a boil. Add the beer. Bring the liquid to a full boil. Add the lobsters claws first. Boil, covered, for 10 to 12 minutes or until the lobsters are uniformly red. Remove from the pot.

Melt ¼ cup of the butter in a small saucepan. Add the garlic. Cook until lightly browned. Add the remaining ¼ cup butter and the wine. Heat until the butter melts, stirring constantly. Divide the butter sauce between two small bowls. Serve with the lobster.

Boston Uncommon
Junior League of Boston, Massachusetts

Florida Lobster with Lemon Basil Butter

SERVES 4

4 ounces butter

1½ teaspoons freshly grated lemon zest

4 (6- to 8-ounce) Florida lobster tails, fresh or frozen and defrosted

½ cup fresh basil leaves, chopped

In a small saucepan over very low heat, melt the butter. Add the lemon zest. Pour into a small bowl.

Using a sharp knife or kitchen shears, split each tail in half lengthwise. Lightly brush exposed meat with the butter. Grill the lobster tails, meat side down, over medium heat until lightly marked, 2 to 3 minutes. Turn the tails over and grill until the meat is white and firm, but not dry, about 5 to 7 more minutes, brushing with more butter if desired.

Remove from grill. Add the basil to the remaining butter and top each tail with the mixture. Serve any extra as a dipping sauce at the table.

Capture the Coast, Vol. 4, The Culinary Collection
Junior League of Tampa, Florida

Sea Scallops with Orange Basil Sauce

SERVES 4

1½ pounds sea scallops

1 tablespoon olive oil

⅔ cup orange juice

2 teaspoons Dijon mustard

¼ teaspoon dried basil leaves

1 tablespoon butter

Pat scallops dry with paper towel. Coat scallops with oil and season both sides with salt and pepper. Set aside.

Whisk together orange juice, mustard, and basil in a small bowl and set aside. Heat skillet to high. Add scallops and sear until they develop a brown crust, about 2 minutes. Turn scallops and continue to cook until remaining side browns, about 2 minutes longer. Remove from pan.

Add orange juice mixture to empty skillet; boil until reduced by half, about a minute. Tilting the skillet so that reduced liquid is at one side of pan, whisk in butter and any accumulated scallop juices. Spoon a little sauce over each portion of scallops and serve immediately.

You're Invited Back—A Second Helping of Raleigh's Favorite Recipes
Junior League of Raleigh, North Carolina

SOUTHERN SCALLOPS
IN LEMON BUTTER SAUCE

SERVES 2 TO 4

1 pound fresh or frozen bay scallops
7 tablespoons unsalted butter, divided
2 teaspoons Cajun Creole seasoning
1 cup sliced fresh mushrooms
¾ cup sliced green onions

½ cup chicken broth
2 tablespoons fresh lemon juice
1 tablespoon snipped parsley
Hot cooked rice or crusty French bread

Thaw scallops, if frozen. In a 12-inch skillet, melt 4 tablespoons of the butter over medium heat. Remove from heat. Add scallops and stir to coat well with the butter. Sprinkle Cajun seasoning over scallops and stir to coat evenly. Return skillet to medium-high heat and cook about 2 minutes or just until scallops are opaque. Remove scallops with a slotted spoon and set aside. Add 1 tablespoon of the remaining butter to skillet and return to medium heat. Add mushrooms and onions. Cook about 4 minutes or until tender. Remove vegetables with a slotted spoon and set aside. Increase heat to high. Stir in chicken broth and lemon juice, scraping up any browned bits from bottom of skillet. Bring to boiling; boil for 3 minutes. Cut remaining 2 tablespoons butter into small pieces; stir a few pieces at a time into skillet until all butter is melted and sauce is smooth, about 1 minute. Stir in parsley, reserved scallops, and reserved vegetables. Return to boiling. Remove from heat immediately. Serve over hot cooked rice or in bowls with crusty French bread for dipping.

Heart & Soul
Junior League of Memphis, Tennessee

COLD CAMERON SHRIMP

SERVES 8

1½ cups vegetable oil
¾ cup cider vinegar
2 teaspoons salt
1 teaspoon Worcestershire sauce
½ teaspoon sugar
¼ teaspoon hot red pepper sauce

2½ to 3 pounds small to medium cooked
   shrimp, peeled
2 cups thinly sliced sweet onions
5 to 7 medium bay leaves
1 bottle capers with liquid
4 or 5 large lemons, thinly sliced

Whisk the oil, vinegar, salt, Worcestershire sauce, sugar and hot sauce in a large bowl. Add the shrimp, onions, bay leaves, capers with liquid and lemons and toss gently to mix. Chill covered, for 8 hours or longer. Remove the bay leaves and serve.

Marshes to Mansions
Junior League of Lake Charles, Louisiana

Rock Shrimp Cakes with Peach and Mint Aïoli

Peach and Mint Aïoli

1/3 cup puréed peaches

1/2 cup mayonnaise

1 teaspoon sugar

1 teaspoon chopped mint leaves

1/2 teaspoon minced garlic

1/2 teaspoon grated fresh gingerroot

Zest and juice of 1 lemon

Coarse salt and freshly ground pepper to taste

To prepare the aïoli, combine the peach purée, mayonnaise, sugar, mint, garlic, gingerroot, lemon zest and lemon juice in a small bowl. Sprinkle with salt and pepper. Chill, covered, until serving time.

Rock Shrimp Cakes

2 pounds rock shrimp or Gulf shrimp, peeled, deveined and chopped

1/4 cup fresh lime juice

2 eggs

2 tablespoons chopped fresh chives

2 tablespoons chopped fresh cilantro

1 tablespoon crab seasoning blend

2 tablespoons Dijon mustard

1/3 cup panko (Japanese bread crumbs) plus more for sprinkling

Butter for frying

To prepare the shrimp cakes, combine the shrimp, lime juice, eggs, chives, cilantro, crab seasoning blend and Dijon mustard in a large bowl and mix well. Stir in 1/3 cup of the panko. Chill, covered, for 1 hour. Preheat the oven to 350 degrees. Shape the shrimp mixture into sixteen patties. Lightly sprinkle the top and bottom of each with additional panko. Cook the patties in melted butter in a large nonstick skillet over medium heat for 1 minute per side or until light brown. Place on a large baking sheet. Bake for 3 to 4 minutes or until cooked through. Serve with the aïoli.

Note: These cakes are easy to make, and leftovers freeze nicely. If fresh peaches are not yet in season, try apricots for a delicious alternative.

Herbal Cookery
The St. Louis Herb Society, Missouri

Texas Shrimp Creole

8 ounces pork and beef sausage

1 medium onion, chopped

1 medium green bell pepper, chopped

2 cloves garlic, minced

2 tablespoons olive oil

2 (10-ounce) cans tomatoes with green chiles

3 tablespoons seasoned tomato paste

3 tablespoons Worcestershire sauce

1 to 2 teaspoons sugar, or to taste

1 or 2 bay leaves

1 pound peeled deveined shrimp
  (about 1⅓ pounds unpeeled shrimp)

1 cup chicken broth

Hot cooked rice

Remove the casing from the sausage and crumble the sausage. Sauté the sausage with the onion, bell pepper and garlic in the olive oil in a skillet. Add the tomatoes with green chiles, tomato paste, Worcestershire sauce, sugar and bay leaves; mix well. Simmer for 15 minutes. Add the shrimp and as much of the chicken broth as needed for desired consistency. Cook for 15 to 20 minutes. Adjust the seasonings and discard the bay leaves. Serve over rice. You can substitute one can of diced tomatoes with Italian seasoning for one can of the tomatoes with green chiles.

Treasures from the Bend, Rich in History and Flavor
Fort Bend Junior Service League, Sugar Land, Texas

Shrimp and Feta Sauce

4 cloves garlic, minced

¼ cup olive oil

1 (28-ounce) can Italian-style peeled
  tomatoes, chopped

¼ cup fresh parsley

1 teaspoon oregano

Pepper to taste

½ cup sliced black olives

1 pound shrimp, peeled and cleaned

5 ounces feta cheese, cubed (or more)

Fettuccini or linguini

Heat garlic in olive oil until it just begins to brown (use large skillet). Add tomatoes, parsley, oregano and pepper. Simmer until sauce is thick. Add olives, shrimp and feta cheese. Cook until shrimp is done, about 15 minutes. Serve with fettuccini or linguini.

Cordon Bluegrass
Junior League of Louisville, Kentucky

Greek Shrimp Sauté

2 pounds large shrimp, peeled, deveined and
   tails removed
1 tablespoon Lawry's garlic salt
1 tablespoon dried oregano
Juice of 1 large lemon

½ cup olive oil
3 tablespoons butter
1 cup flour
Lemon wedges
Hot sauce

Combine the shrimp with the garlic salt, oregano and lemon juice in a medium bowl and toss well to coat. Chill, covered, for 45 minutes. Remove the shrimp from the marinade and discard the marinade. Pat the shrimp dry with paper towels. Heat the olive oil and butter in a cast-iron skillet to bubbling but not smoking over medium to medium-high heat. Combine the shrimp with the flour in a large resealable plastic bag and shake to coat. Shake the excess flour off the shrimp and working in batches, place in the skillet, leaving room between each shrimp. Cook until golden brown on all sides and cooked through, turning once. Drain on paper towels. Serve with lemon wedges and hot sauce.

EveryDay Feasts, Vol. 2, The Culinary Collection
Junior League of Tampa, Florida

Southwest Agave Lime Shrimp

1 pound fresh shrimp, peeled and deveined
1 teaspoon chili powder
4 teaspoons butter
2 garlic cloves, minced
2 tablespoons tequila, 100% agave

Juice of 1 lime
½ teaspoon salt
1 jalapeño chile, seeded and chopped
1 tablespoon chopped cilantro

Mix the shrimp and chili powder in a large bowl. Cook the shrimp with the butter and garlic in a large skillet for 1 minute and then turn the shrimp. Stir in the tequila, lime juice, salt, jalapeño chile and cilantro. Cook until the shrimp turn pink. Garnish with additional cilantro.

Settings Sunrise to Sunset
Assistance League of the Bay Area, Houston, Texas

Spicy Shrimp with Green Sauce

Shrimp

2½ pounds shrimp	1½ teaspoons celery seeds
1 teaspoon salt	2 bay leaves, crumbled
1 tablespoon mustard seeds	¼ cup olive oil
1 tablespoon peppercorns	Juice of 1 lemon
1 tablespoon thyme	½ cup dry white wine
¾ teaspoon red pepper flakes	Green Sauce
¾ teaspoon cayenne pepper	

Toss the unpeeled shrimp with salt, mustard seeds, peppercorns, thyme, red pepper flakes, cayenne pepper, celery seeds and bay leaves in a bowl. Pour enough of the olive oil in a large skillet to cover the bottom. Add the shrimp. Sauté for 6 to 7 minutes or until the shrimp turn pink. Chill in the refrigerator.

To serve, peel the shrimp, leaving the tails intact. Place the shrimp on a serving plate. Serve the Green Sauce in a small serving bowl. Garnish with lemon slices and parsley.

Green Sauce

1 pound tomatillos	1½ teaspoons sugar
¼ cup rice wine vinegar	2 teaspoons mustard seeds, toasted
1 tablespoon (or more) lime juice	1 tablespoon green Tabasco sauce
1 tablespoon minced garlic	1 tablespoon grated horseradish

Remove the husks from the tomatillos and rinse well. Cut the tomatillos into quarters and place in a food processor container. Add the rice wine vinegar, lime juice, garlic, sugar, mustard seeds, green Tabasco sauce and horseradish and process until finely chopped.

Settings on the Dock of the Bay
Assistance League of the Bay Area, Houston, Texas

Shrimp Mezcal

1 pound shrimp, peeled and deveined	Juice of 1 lime
¼ cup (½ stick) butter	1 teaspoon green jalapeño Tabasco sauce
1 ounce mezcal or tequila	2 tomatoes, chopped
1 teaspoon minced garlic	¼ cup chopped fresh cilantro
1 avocado, chopped	

Sauté the shrimp in the butter in a skillet for 1 minute. Add the mezcal and garlic and ignite with a match. As the flame burns down, stir in the avocado, lime juice and jalapeño Tabasco sauce.

Simmer for 3 minutes or until the shrimp turn pink, stirring occasionally. Spoon the shrimp mixture into a bowl and top with the tomatoes and cilantro. Great over rice pilaf or hot cooked pasta.

California Sol Food
Junior League of San Diego, California

Hampton Plantation Shrimp Pilau

4 strips bacon	2 tablespoons chopped bell pepper
1 teaspoon salt	2 cups raw shrimp, peeled
1 cup raw rice	1 teaspoon Worcestershire sauce
3 tablespoons butter	1 tablespoon flour
½ cup celery, chopped fine	Salt and pepper to taste

Fry bacon until crisp. Drain. Add bacon grease and salt to water to cook rice. Cook rice according to package directions. In a large frying pan, melt butter and sauté celery and peppers. Sprinkle shrimp with Worcestershire and dredge in flour. Add shrimp to pan and simmer until flour is cooked. Season with salt and pepper. Add cooked rice and mix well. Stir in crumbled bacon.

Charleston Receipts Repeats
Junior League of Charleston, South Carolina

City Grocery Shrimp and Grits

Grits

1 cup grits	1 teaspoon cayenne pepper
4 tablespoons unsalted butter	1½ tablespoons paprika
¾ cup extra-sharp white Cheddar cheese	1 tablespoon Tabasco sauce
½ cup grated Parmesan cheese	Salt and pepper to taste

Cook grits according to package instructions. Whisk in butter, Cheddar, Parmesan, cayenne, paprika and Tabasco. Mix thoroughly and season with salt and pepper to taste.

Shrimp

2 cups chopped smoked bacon	2 teaspoons minced garlic
3 tablespoons olive oil	3 cups sliced mushrooms
1½ pounds raw (26- to 30-count) shrimp, peeled	2 tablespoons lemon juice
	3 tablespoons white wine
Salt and pepper to taste	2 cups sliced green onions

In a skillet over medium-high heat, cook bacon until it begins to brown. Remove from heat and reserve bacon and drippings. Heat a large skillet until very hot. Add olive oil and 2 tablespoons of reserved bacon grease. As oil begins to smoke, toss in shrimp to cover bottom of pan. Before stirring, season with salt and pepper. Stir until shrimp begin to turn pink all over. Let the pan return to its original hot temperature. Stir in minced garlic and bacon bits. Be careful not to burn the garlic. Toss in mushrooms and quickly coat with oil. Add lemon juice and wine. Stir until everything is well coated, about 30 seconds. Toss in green onions and stir about 20 seconds. Serve over grits.

Square Table
Yoknapatawpha Arts Council, Oxford, Mississippi

# GRITS A YA-YA

SMOKED GOUDA CHEESE GRITS

4 cups chicken stock

2 cups grits

1 cup heavy cream

½ cup (1 stick) butter

1 (14- to 16-ounce) can cream-style corn

8 ounces smoked Gouda cheese, shredded

For the grits, bring the stock to a boil in a saucepan and gradually add the grits, stirring constantly. Reduce the gas heat to low and simmer for 40 minutes, stirring occasionally and adding some of the cream if needed. Stir in the remaining cream, butter and corn. Mix in the cheese. Simmer until the cheese melts and the grits are heated through. Remove from the heat and cover to keep warm.

SHRIMP

8 slices applewood-smoked bacon, chopped

1 tablespoon minced garlic

1 tablespoon minced shallot

3 tablespoons butter

Splash of white wine

1 pound deveined peeled jumbo shrimp

1 portobello mushroom cap, sliced

2 cups chopped fresh spinach

¼ cup chopped scallions

2 cups heavy cream

Salt and pepper to taste

Hot red pepper sauce to taste

For the shrimp, heat a large saucepan over medium gas heat and add the bacon. Cook for about 3 minutes. Stir in the garlic and shallot and sauté. Add the butter and wine. Cook until the butter partially melts and then add the shrimp.

Cook until the sides of the shrimp turn white; turn the shrimp. Stir in the mushroom, spinach and scallions. Sauté for 2 minutes. Remove the shrimp to a bowl using a slotted spoon, reserving the pan juices. Add the cream to the reserved pan juices and mix well.

Simmer until the mixture is reduced by one-third, stirring constantly. Season with salt, pepper and hot sauce. Return the shrimp to the sauce and simmer just until heated through. Spoon the shrimp mixture over equal portions of the grits on serving plates.

Fiesta Seafood Cookbook: A Taste of Pensacola
Energy Services of Pensacola, Florida

LIME GARLIC SHRIMP WITH MANGO MINT SALSA

MANGO MINT SALSA

2 cups chopped mangoes

¾ cup chopped red onion

2 jalapeño chiles, seeded and chopped

1 bunch fresh mint, chopped

Juice of 1 lime

Combine the mangoes with the onion, jalapeño chiles, mint and lime juice in a bowl and mix well. Chill in the refrigerator for 1 hour.

LIME GARLIC SHRIMP

Juice and grated zest of 1 lime

2 garlic cloves, crushed

1 tablespoon olive oil

½ teaspoon coarse salt

½ teaspoon crushed red pepper

¼ teaspoon freshly ground black pepper

24 large shrimp, peeled and deveined

Combine the lime juice, lime zest, garlic, olive oil, coarse salt, red pepper and black pepper in a bowl and mix well. Add the shrimp and stir to coat evenly. Marinate in the refrigerator for 45 minutes. Preheat the grill. Grill the shrimp for 2 minutes on each side or until pink. Serve with the salsa.

Orange County Fare; a culinary journey through the California Riviera
Junior League of Orange County, California

SEAFOOD   201

Cioppino

⅓ cup olive oil

1 medium carrot, peeled, finely chopped

1 red bell pepper, chopped

½ cup chopped onion

3 or 4 garlic cloves, minced

¼ cup chopped celery

2 pounds fresh plum tomatoes, peeled, chopped, or 1 (28-ounce) can Italian plum tomatoes

3 cups fish stock, or 2 cups water and 1 cup clam juice

1 to 2 cups zinfandel

¼ cup tomato paste

2 tablespoons chopped fresh basil, or 2 teaspoons dried basil

1 tablespoon chopped fresh oregano, or 1 teaspoon dried oregano

1 teaspoon freshly ground black pepper

1 teaspoon fennel seeds

1 bay leaf

½ teaspoon red pepper flakes (optional)

⅛ teaspoon sugar

½ teaspoon kosher salt

2 dozen clams in shells, scrubbed

1 cup water or white wine

1 pound raw white fish (halibut, bass, or cod), cut into pieces

1 pound raw shrimp, peeled, deveined, or 1 pound scallops

2 large Dungeness crabs, cooked, cleaned and cracked

¼ cup chopped flat-leaf parsley

Heat the olive oil in an 8-quart stockpot. Sauté the carrot, bell pepper, onion, garlic, and celery for 5 minutes or until the vegetables begin to soften. Add the tomatoes, fish stock, zinfandel, tomato paste, basil, oregano, black pepper, fennel seeds, bay leaf, red pepper flakes, sugar, and salt. Simmer, covered, for 60 to 80 minutes, stirring occasionally. Taste and adjust seasonings, adding more salt if needed. Flavors should be mellow and rich. Discard the bay leaf.

Combine the clams and water or white wine in a saucepan. Steam, covered, over medium heat for 5 minutes or until the shells open. Remove the clams to a bowl with a slotted spoon, reserving the broth. Strain the broth through cheesecloth or a fine strainer into the tomato mixture.

Add the fish and shrimp or scallops to the stockpot and mix well. Simmer for 5 minutes or until the seafood is cooked through and the shrimp turn pink. Stir in the clams and crab and simmer for 1 minute to warm and moisten them. Ladle the cioppino into large soup bowls. Sprinkle with chopped parsley. Have bibs, napkins, shellfish forks, and pliers handy.

This traditional favorite originated in San Francisco in 1900 and is easy to make despite the long list of ingredients.

California Fresh Harvest
Junior League of Oakland-East Bay, California

CRAB CIOPPINO

¼ cup olive oil

4 onions, finely chopped

1 cup chopped celery

1 green bell pepper, chopped

½ cup parsley, chopped

5 green onions, chopped

8 garlic cloves, chopped or pressed

1 tablespoon each red chili pepper flakes, rosemary, oregano, Italian seasoning, sage, thyme, and basil

2 chicken bouillon cubes

2 beef bouillon cubes

½ teaspoon paprika

¼ teaspoon poultry seasoning

¼ teaspoon each ground nutmeg and ground allspice

Pinch ground cinnamon

1 (28-ounce) can diced tomatoes

3 (8-ounce) cans tomato sauce

3 cups water

1 cup white wine

1 cup red wine

2 bay leaves

Meat of 3 Dungeness crabs

3 pounds clams, cleaned (optional)

3 pounds large prawns, peeled and deveined

8 ounces fresh white fish such as sea bass, rock cod or halibut, cut into chunks (optional)

1 lemon, sliced

Salt and pepper to taste

Heat the olive oil in a large stockpot and add the onions, celery, bell pepper, parsley, green onions, garlic, red pepper flakes, rosemary, oregano, Italian seasoning, sage, thyme and basil. Sauté until the vegetables are wilted and brown. Stir in the bouillon cubes, paprika, poultry seasoning, nutmeg, allspice and cinnamon. Add the tomatoes, tomato sauce, water, wine and bay leaves and mix well.

Bring to a boil and reduce the heat. Simmer for 2½ to 3 hours or until thickened, stirring occasionally. Stir in the crab meat, clams and prawns and cook for 1 to 1½ hours; add the fish and lemon slices during the last 30 minutes of the cooking process. Discard the bay leaves. Taste and season with salt and pepper and ladle into soup bowls. You may substitute deveined, peeled and steamed shrimp for the prawns. Add the shrimp a few minutes before the end of the cooking process and cook just until heated through.

California Mosaic
Junior League of Pasadena, California

Celebrate the Ra

EDUCATING THROUGH COOKBOOKS

Stephanie Prade was a perfect choice to co-chair *Herbal Cookery* for the St. Louis Herb Society in Missouri. She loves food, loves growing herbs, and would rather be at the stove than anyplace else.

"It's been a wonderful experience," said Stephanie. "We had so much talent in our group, including dieticians, professional chefs, a food stylist, and a headline writer who worked on recipe titles."

Although the St. Louis Herb Society has a membership of only 60, it's a very active group. It's also fortunate to have its herb garden as part of the Missouri Botanical Garden, which is rated as the number two botanical garden in the world. The Herb Society members devote a two-year provisional period of time and study to become proficient in herb knowledge. The goal then is to take that knowledge to the community...and what better way than through a cookbook that stresses the use of herbs?

"We had a vague idea about what this cookbook should be like, and then we learned that the best ideas are vague ones...the ones that open the doors to creativity," Stephanie said. "The creative process from the group was such a wonderful thing for me to be a part of. It was less of a business process than an artistic one."

HERBAL COOKERY
ST. LOUIS HERB SOCIETY

Encouraging Gardening & Cooking at Home

With the launch of *Herbal Cookery* in 2009, the group is now heavily into the marketing stages. The fact that the 20th annual Tabasco Community Awards, sponsored by McIlhenny Company, awarded the book its second-place winner nationally certainly will help this process. The marketing is so important because the profits made on the cookbook help maintain the herb garden at The Missouri Botanical Garden and fund other projects that follow the group's mission, which is to further the use and knowledge of herbs.

Besides going from shop door to shop door, the society members have been on the radio to promote the book and have done lots of book signings.

"Talking to people one-on-one at book signings—people we would never have an opportunity to encounter—carries our mission even further," Stephanie said. "We've helped to encourage lots of people to grow their own herbs. And then we show them the cookbook and point out the recipes with the herbs as the central part of the food, so it is an easy sell for the book."

ROASTED ASPARAGUS

Serves 6

30 spears asparagus
1/4 teaspoon salt
1/8 teaspoon pepper
2 tablespoons butter

1 tablespoon soy sauce
1 1/2 teaspoons balsamic vinegar
3/4 cup (3 ounces) shaved Parmesan
   cheese curls

Arrange the asparagus spears in a single layer on a baking sheet oiled with olive oil. Sprinkle with the salt and pepper. Roast at 400 degrees for 12 minutes or until tender. Remove to a serving platter and keep warm.

Melt the butter in a small skillet over medium heat. Cook for 3 minutes or until the butter is light brown, shaking the skillet occasionally. Remove from the heat and stir in the soy sauce and balsamic vinegar. Drizzle over the asparagus and top with the cheese.

Serve immediately.

Beach Appétit
Junior League of the Emerald Coast, Fort Walton Beach, Florida

GINGERED GREEN BEANS

SERVES 4 TO 6

1 tablespoon butter
1 1/2 tablespoons peeled and minced
   fresh ginger
2 cloves garlic, minced

1/2 cup pecans, chopped
3 tablespoons light soy sauce
2 tablespoons sherry
1 1/4 pounds green beans, trimmed

Melt the butter in large skillet over medium-high heat. Sauté the ginger, garlic, and pecans for 3 minutes or until the pecans are toasted. Transfer to a small bowl and set aside. Add the soy sauce, sherry, and green beans to the skillet. Cover and simmer for 15 to 20 minutes, stirring occasionally until the beans are cooked. Remove from the heat and toss in the pecan mixture, coating thoroughly before serving.

Dancing on the Table
Junior League of Wilmington, Delaware

Green Beans with Almonds

¼ cup slivered almonds

¼ cup margarine

¼ cup chopped green tomatoes

½ teaspoon salt

4 cups hot cooked green beans

Cook the almonds in the margarine in a saucepan over low heat until golden brown, stirring occasionally. Remove from the heat. Stir in the tomatoes and salt. Mix the almond mixture and the green beans in a serving dish. Serve hot.

Silver Spoons, Blueberry Afternoons
National Association of Junior Auxiliary, Greenville, Mississippi

Wrapped Green Beans

2 cans whole green beans, canned, or
   2 pounds fresh green beans, washed and
   ends snapped off
6 slices of bacon, cut in half, partially cooked

Onion salt

4 tablespoons butter, melted

3 tablespoons packed brown sugar

Wrap 6 to 10 beans at a time with bacon and secure with toothpick. Place bundles in a 9×13-inch baking dish. Sprinkle bundles with onion salt, pour melted butter over bundles and sprinkle with brown sugar. Bake at 350 degrees 15 to 20 minutes or until bacon is done.

Note: To make ahead, complete all steps except the last (pouring the butter and brown sugar over beans.) Put in a glass baking dish and refrigerate overnight until ready to bake. Before putting in oven, pour melted butter over bundles and sprinkle with brown sugar. Also freezes well.

River Road Recipes II,
A Second Helping
Junior League of Baton
Rouge, Louisiana

Community cookbooks eligible for the prestigious Walter S. McIlhenny Hall of Fame award are those which have sold more than 100,000 copies. In the 20-year history of the Tabasco Community Cookbook Awards, 64 classic community cookbooks have been inducted into the Hall of Fame.

LIMAS IN CREAM SAUCE

1 (10-ounce) package frozen lima beans
½ teaspoon Accent
½ teaspoon Lawry's Seasoned Salt

Cracked black pepper
¾ cup half-and-half

Place frozen beans in a buttered 2-quart covered casserole. Sprinkle with Accent, salt and heavily with cracked pepper. Pour cream over the beans. Bake, covered, at 350 degrees, stirring after 20 minutes. Reduce oven to 300 degrees and bake 20 minutes longer or until tender. Do not let cream boil as it will curdle.

Cotton Country Collection
Junior League of Monroe, Louisiana

LOUISIANA RED BEANS AND RICE

1 pound dried red beans
2 onions, chopped
1 bell pepper, chopped
1 pound sausage or ham, sliced
Vegetable oil for sautéing

2 garlic cloves, chopped
1 bay leaf
Salt and pepper to taste
Tabasco sauce to taste
1 (8-ounce) can tomato paste

Rinse the beans thoroughly. Soak the beans in water to cover in a bowl for 8 to 12 hours; drain. Sauté the onions, bell pepper, and sausage in a small amount of oil in a stockpot until the onions are translucent. Add the garlic. Sauté for 1 minute. Add the drained beans, bay leaf, salt, pepper and Tabasco sauce. Cover with water. Bring to a boil over high heat, stirring constantly to prevent the beans from sticking. Stir in the tomato paste. Cover and reduce the heat to low. Cook for 5 to 6 hours or until the beans are tender and the mixture is the desired consistency, adding additional water as needed. Remove the bay leaf. Serve over hot cooked rice.

Roux To Do
Junior League of Greater Covington, Louisiana

Chuckwagon Bean Bake

1 pound bacon, diced
1 pound ground beef
1 medium onion, diced
2 (15-ounce) cans pork and beans
1 (15-ounce) can large butter beans, drained
1 (16-ounce) can kidney beans, drained

¼ cup brown sugar
½ teaspoon liquid smoke
3 tablespoons vinegar
¼ cup ketchup
3 tablespoons molasses

Preheat oven to 350 degrees. Brown bacon, beef, and onion together in large skillet; drain well. Place mixture in oven roasting pan along with remaining ingredients and combine well. Bake 3 hours, stirring occasionally. If mixture becomes dry while cooking, water may be added.

Cafe Oklahoma
Junior Service League of Midwest City, Oklahoma

Savory Beets

3 (16-ounce) cans sliced beets, drained
6 tablespoons vinegar
½ teaspoon ground cloves
1 teaspoon salt

½ cup sugar
1 small onion, sliced
¼ cup butter

Chop enough beets to measure 1 cup. Place remaining sliced beets in saucepan. Process 1 cup chopped beets, vinegar, cloves, salt, sugar, onion and butter in blender until puréed. Pour puréed mixture over sliced beets; mix well. Simmer for 20 minutes, stirring frequently.

The Best of Wheeling
Junior League of Wheeling, West Virginia

Brussels Sprouts and Artichokes au Gratin

1 (10-ounce) package frozen brussels sprouts
1 (14-ounce) can artichoke hearts, drained
1/2 cup mayonnaise
1/4 teaspoon celery salt

1/4 cup Parmesan cheese
1/2 cup butter
2 teaspoons lemon juice

Cook brussels sprouts in 1/2 cup water until just tender; drain. Arrange sprouts and artichokes in greased casserole. Combine remaining ingredients and spoon over sprouts. Bake uncovered at 425 degrees for 8 to 10 minutes.

Viva Tradiciones! South Texas Cooks from Brush to Bay
Junior League of Corpus Christi, Texas

Cauliflower Gratin with Herbed Mornay Sauce

Herbed Mornay Sauce

1/4 cup all-purpose flour
1 teaspoon herbes de Provence
1/4 teaspoon dry mustard
1/2 teaspoon white pepper
1/2 teaspoon cayenne pepper
1/4 cup (1/2 stick) unsalted butter

1 1/2 cups milk
1/2 cup (2 ounces) freshly grated
  Parmesan cheese
1/2 cup (2 ounces) shredded Gruyère cheese
1/2 cup heavy cream or half-and-half

To prepare the sauce, mix the flour, herbes de Provence, dry mustard, white pepper and cayenne pepper in a small bowl. Melt the butter in a medium saucepan over medium-low heat. Whisk in the flour mixture until combined. Cook for 2 minutes, stirring constantly; do not allow to brown. Whisk in the milk gradually. Cook until the sauce thickens and comes to a low boil, stirring constantly. Add the Parmesan cheese and Gruyère cheese and cook until melted. Remove from the heat. Whisk in the cream.

Cauliflower Gratin

1 large head cauliflower, trimmed and cut
  into florets
2 tablespoons salt
1/4 cup (4 ounces) shredded Gruyère cheese

1 cup fresh sourdough bread crumbs
2 tablespoons butter
1/2 cup (2 ounces) freshly grated
  Parmesan cheese

To prepare the gratin, place the cauliflower and salt in cold water in a medium stockpot. Bring to a boil. Reduce the heat and cook until tender. Drain the cauliflower and place in a greased 2-quart baking dish. Preheat the oven to 375 degrees. Pour the sauce over the cauliflower to cover. Sprinkle with the Gruyère cheese and bread crumbs. Dot with the butter and top with the Parmesan cheese. Bake for 15 to 20 minutes or until brown and bubbly.

Herbal Cookery
The St. Louis Herb Society, Missouri

GRANDMOTHER'S FRIED CORN SERVES 6

6 ears white corn	2 tablespoons butter
½ cup water	1 teaspoon cornstarch (optional)
1 tablespoon oil	Salt and pepper to taste
½ cup milk	

Cut corn off the cob; scraping cobs to get corn milk. Add ½ cup water. Heat oil in large skillet. Pour corn and scrapings into skillet and cook for 10 minutes over medium heat, stirring often. Add milk, butter, and cornstarch if mixture seems watery. Salt and pepper to taste.

Cordon Bluegrass
Junior League of Louisville, Kentucky

GREEN CHILE CORN CASSEROLE SERVES 8 TO 10

1 clove garlic, minced	2 (15-ounce) cans cream-style corn
½ cup unsalted butter	2 (4-ounce) cans chopped green chiles
4 cups sour cream	4 eggs, lightly beaten
1 (8-ounce) package corn bread mix	2 tablespoons chili powder
1 (8-ounce) package yellow cake mix	

Preheat oven to 350 degrees. Sweat garlic in the butter in a sauté pan. Combine the garlic, sour cream, corn bread mix, cake mix, corn, green chiles, eggs and chili powder in a bowl and mix well. The mixture will be very sweet. Cut the sweetness by adding salt or hot sauce if desired. Spoon the corn mixture into a 9×13 inch baking pan and bake for 60 to 80 minutes or until brown and bubbly.

Pomegranates & Prickly Pears, flavorful entertaining from the Junior League of Phoenix
Junior League of Phoenix, Arizona

Sautéed Collard Greens

1 bunch collard greens (about 1½ pounds)
3 tablespoons olive oil
2 cloves garlic, crushed
1 shallot, minced

½ cup chicken broth
Salt to taste
Pepper to taste

Discard any yellow, limp or bruised leaves from the collards. Remove and discard the tough central stems of the remaining leaves. Rinse the collards several times in a sink full of cold water to remove any grit. Shake the excess water from the collards and dry on paper towels.

Heat the olive oil in a large skillet. Add the garlic and shallot and sauté over medium heat for 1 to 2 minutes or until the shallot just begins to turn translucent. Tear the collards into fairly large pieces and add to the skillet. Reduce the heat to low.

Cook for about 10 minutes, stirring almost constantly until the collards are wilted but still bright green. Add the broth and continue to cook over low heat for about 10 minutes longer or until most of the broth has been absorbed. Season with salt and pepper.

Excellent Courses, A Culinary Legacy of Ravenscroft
Ravenscroft School, Raleigh, North Carolina

Okra and Tomatoes

4 or 5 fresh medium tomatoes, or
   1 (16-ounce) can tomatoes and
   juice, chopped
1 pound okra

1 large onion, chopped
2 tablespoons bacon grease
Salt and pepper

If using fresh tomatoes, peel and chop. Wash and slice okra into rounds, about ½ inch thick. Sauté onion and okra in grease until browned. Add tomatoes, salt and pepper. Cover and cook slowly for 20 minutes. Add water if necessary to prevent sticking. If too juicy, uncover and cook a little longer. Serve hot.

Southern Sideboards
Junior League of Jackson, Mississippi

ONION PIE

2 pounds sweet onions, thinly sliced and
  separated
½ cup unsalted butter
3 large eggs, lightly beaten
¼ teaspoon salt
½ teaspoon pepper

1 or 2 dashes Tabasco sauce
1 cup sour cream
2 tablespoons Dijon mustard
1 large unbaked (10-inch) deep-dish pie shell
½ cup freshly grated Parmesan cheese

Sauté the onions in the butter in a skillet until translucent; drain. Combine the eggs, salt, pepper, Tabasco sauce, sour cream and Dijon mustard in a bowl and mix thoroughly. Add the onions and mix well. Spoon into the pie shell. Sprinkle with the Parmesan cheese. Bake at 425 degrees for 20 minutes. Reduce the oven temperature to 325 degrees. Bake for 20 minutes longer. Serve hot or at room temperature.

Oh, Shenandoah! A Cookbook from the Museum of the Shenandoah
The Museum of the Shenandoah Valley, Virginia

VIDALIA ONION CASSEROLE

4 large Vidalia onions, sliced ½ inch thick
½ cup butter
½ cup beef broth
½ cup sherry

2 tablespoons flour
1½ cups seasoned soft bread crumbs
½ cup shredded sharp Cheddar cheese
¼ cup grated Parmesan cheese

Preheat the oven to 350 degrees. Sauté the onions in butter in a skillet over low heat until the onions become translucent. Add the beef broth, sherry, and flour; mix well. Cook until slightly thickened, stirring constantly. Spoon the mixture into a greased medium casserole. Sprinkle the bread crumbs, Cheddar cheese, and Parmesan cheese over the onion mixture. Bake at 350 degrees for 20 minutes or until light brown and bubbly.

Sweet Home Alabama
Junior League of Huntsville, Alabama

OPPING JOHN

1 cup dried black-eyed peas

12 ounces smoked ham, chopped

¾ cup chopped celery

¾ cup chopped onion

⅓ cup chopped green bell pepper

1 clove of garlic, finely chopped

½ teaspoon thyme

¼ teaspoon sage

1 medium tomato, peeled, seeded,
  finely chopped

3 tablespoons olive oil

2 tablespoons white wine vinegar

¼ cup chopped parsley

1 cup white rice

Tabasco sauce to taste

Chopped scallions

Rinse and sort the peas. Soak in water to cover in a bowl for 8 to 10 hours; drain well. Combine the peas, ham, celery, onion, green pepper, garlic, thyme and sage in a medium saucepan. Add water to cover. Bring to a boil and reduce the heat. Simmer, covered, for 35 to 40 minutes or until the peas are tender. Drain, reserving the cooking liquid. Stir the tomato into the peas. Add a mixture of the olive oil, vinegar and parsley and mix well. Combine the reserved cooking liquid with enough water to measure 2 cups. Pour into a saucepan and add the rice. Bring to a boil and reduce the heat to low. Cook, covered, for 18 to 20 minutes or until all water is absorbed and the rice is tender. Add the peas. Cook until heated through. Season with Tabasco sauce. Spoon into a serving bowl. Sprinkle with chopped scallions.

Seaboard to Sideboard
Junior League of Wilmington, North Carolina

SPICY BLACK-EYED PEAS

3 slices of bacon

1 (17-ounce) can black-eyed peas

1 (16-ounce) can tomatoes, undrained
  and chopped

1 cup chopped onion

1 large green bell pepper, chopped

⅛ teaspoon garlic powder

1 teaspoon ground dry mustard

½ teaspoon curry powder

½ teaspoon chili powder

1 teaspoon salt

½ teaspoon pepper

Parsley, finely chopped

Cook bacon until crisp in large skillet and crumble into small pieces. Stir the crumbled bacon and remaining ingredients into bacon grease. Simmer covered for 20 minutes.

A Southern Collection—Then and Now
Junior League of Columbus, Georgia

Roasted Red Pepper Boats

4 red bell peppers, cut into halves, stemmed and seeded
1 tablespoon olive oil
8 cups water
4 red potatoes
1½ teaspoons salt
1½ teaspoons dried thyme
1 teaspoon dried rosemary
¾ cup olive oil
¼ cup balsamic vinegar
½ teaspoon salt
Freshly ground pepper
6 ounces chèvre, crumbled
2 tablespoons finely chopped fresh parsley or chives
Sprigs of parsley

Preheat the oven to 500 degrees. Line a baking sheet with foil and arrange the bell peppers cut side down on the foil. Brush the bell peppers with 1 tablespoon olive oil. Roast on the center oven rack for 8 to 10 minutes or until tender and slightly blistered. Set aside. Reduce the oven temperature to 375 degrees.

Bring the water to a boil in a saucepan and add the potatoes and 1½ teaspoons salt. Boil for 25 to 30 minutes or until tender, drain. Cool, peel and cut into ½-inch pieces. Gently toss the potatoes with the thyme and rosemary in a bowl.

Whisk ¾ cup olive oil, the vinegar, ½ teaspoon salt and pepper in a bowl until blended. Reserve 2 tablespoons of the vinaigrette. Pour the remaining vinaigrette over the potato mixture and toss to coat. Add the chèvre and mix well. Taste and adjust the seasonings.

Spoon the potato mixture evenly into the bell pepper shells. Arrange the bell pepper shells filling side up on a baking sheet and drizzle with the reserved vinaigrette. Bake on the center oven rack for 10 minutes. Sprinkle with chopped parsley and arrange on a serving platter. Garnish with sprigs of parsley and serve immediately.

Compliments Of
The Woman's Exchange of Memphis, Tennessee

OWYHEES CRAB-STUFFED POTATOES

4 large baking potatoes

1 tablespoon butter or shortening

½ cup melted butter

½ cup heavy cream

1 teaspoon salt

½ teaspoon cayenne pepper

4 teaspoons grated onion

1 cup shredded sharp Cheddar cheese

1½ teaspoons paprika

1 (6-ounce) can crab meat, picked, drained

Preheat the oven to 400 degrees. Rub the potatoes with 1 tablespoon butter or shortening and bake for 1 hour. Increase the oven temperature to 450 degrees. Cut the potatoes into halves lengthwise and let stand until cool enough to handle. Scoop out the pulp, reserving the shells. Whip the potato pulp with ½ cup butter, cream, salt, cayenne pepper, onion, cheese and ½ teaspoon paprika in a bowl. Gently fold in the crab meat. Spoon into the reserved shells. Sprinkle with the remaining 1 teaspoon paprika. Place on a baking sheet. Bake for 15 minutes or until heated through and light brown.

Idaho a la Carte
Beaux Arts Society, Boise, Idaho

PARTY POTATOES AU GRATIN

1 stick butter

¼ cup sliced green onions

½ cup chopped green pepper

¼ cup chopped pimientos, undrained

2 teaspoons salt

¼ teaspoon pepper

1 tablespoon parsley flakes

1 teaspoon paprika

6 tablespoons flour

4 cups milk

6 cups cubed cooked potatoes

½ pound shredded sharp cheese

In melted butter, sauté onions, green pepper and pimientos about 1 minute. Add seasonings and flour. Blend in milk, stirring, until thickened. Add potatoes and 1 cup cheese. Stir until cheese is melted. Pour into a 3-quart, flat casserole. Spread remaining cheese on top. Bake in a 350-degree oven for 30 to 45 minutes or until bubbly. Make ahead and refrigerate before baking. Freezes perfectly.

Cotton Country Collection
Junior League of Monroe, Louisiana

2 packages frozen chopped spinach	½ teaspoon black pepper
4 tablespoons butter	Red pepper to taste
2 tablespoons flour	½ cup evaporated milk
2 tablespoons chopped onion	2 teaspoons finely chopped fresh
¾ teaspoon celery salt	jalapeño peppers
¾ teaspoon garlic salt	1 teaspoon Worcestershire sauce
Salt to taste	6 ounces Kraft Velveeta

Cook spinach according to directions on package. Drain and reserve liquor. Melt butter in saucepan over low heat. Add flour, stirring until blended and smooth, but not brown. Add onion and cook until soft but not brown. Add ½ cup of the reserved liquor slowly, stirring constantly to avoid lumps.

Cook until smooth and thick; continue stirring. Add the celery salt, garlic salt, salt, black pepper, red pepper, evaporated milk, jalapeño peppers, Worcestershire sauce and the cheese which has been cut into small pieces. Stir until melted. Combine with cooked spinach.

Note: This may be served immediately or put into a casserole and topped with buttered bread crumbs. The flavor is improved if the latter is done and kept in refrigerator overnight. This may also be frozen.

River Road Recipes, The Textbook of Louisiana Cuisine
Junior League of Baton Rouge, Louisiana

Spinach Madeleine, the most famous recipe from the River Road Recipes cookbook series, has undergone a makeover! Kraft Foods has discontinued making its jalapeño cheese roll, which is an important ingredient in the original Spinach Madeleine recipe. As a result, *River Road Recipes* has developed a substitute for the jalapeño cheese roll. We believe your family will never know the difference! This dish freezes well. You may also substitute the Velveeta and jalapeños with 6 ounces Velveeta Mexican Hot Cheese.

Squash Lafayette

2 pounds yellow squash, trimmed and cut
into ½-inch slices

¾ cup butter

1 (8-ounce) package herb-seasoned stuffing
mix, divided

1 (10¾-ounce) can cream of chicken soup

1 cup sour cream

1 medium onion, chopped

2 carrots, grated

1 (2-ounce) jar diced pimiento, drained

Preheat oven to 350 degrees. Boil squash in water to cover in a saucepan 15 to 20 minutes or until tender; drain. Melt butter in a large skillet over medium heat; add half of stuffing mix, chicken soup, sour cream, onion, carrot, and pimiento, stirring well. Stir in squash and spoon into a 7×11×2-inch baking dish. Top with remaining stuffing mix and cover with aluminum foil. Bake at 350 degrees for 45 minutes or until browned.

Creating a Stir
Fayette County Medical Auxiliary, Lexington, Kentucky

The Official Miss Forbus' Squash Casserole

8 yellow squash, sliced

1 cup chopped onion

½ teaspoon salt

Dash of pepper

1 tablespoon margarine

1 cup bread crumbs

3 eggs, beaten

¾ cup milk

1 cup (4 ounces) shredded cheese

Combine the squash, onion, salt, pepper, margarine and a small amount of water in a saucepan. Cook until the squash is tender; drain well. Mix the cooked squash, bread crumbs, eggs and milk in a bowl. Spoon into a baking dish. Bake at 350 degrees for 25 minutes. Top with the cheese and bake for 5 to 6 minutes longer or until the cheese melts.

"Squash casseroles are a popular item throughout the South and a great way to use fresh garden squash. These casseroles were also a popular item in The W dining hall, and several alums submitted recipes purporting to be the authentic squash casserole served there. Miss Mary Cecil Forbus, the legendary 'W' Director of Food Services, assures us that this is her official recipe, however."

Southern Grace
Mississippi University for Women Alumnae Association, Mississippi

BAKED SWEET POTATO FRIES

4 small or 2 medium sweet potatoes
1 tablespoon butter, melted
1 tablespoon olive oil

½ teaspoon seasoned salt
Generous dash of nutmeg

Preheat the oven to 450 degrees. Peel the sweet potatoes, cut lengthwise into thin wedges and then into halves. Combine the butter and olive oil in a 9×13-inch baking pan. Add the salt and nutmeg. Toss the sweet potatoes in the oil mixture. Bake for 20 to 30 minutes or until brown and tender, stirring once or twice.

Steamboat Seasons, A Medley of Recipes
Strings in the Mountains Music Festival, Steamboat Springs, Colorado

CRANBERRY, APPLE AND SWEET POTATO GRILL PACKETS

4 sweet potatoes, peeled and cut into
   ¼-inch slices
2 Golden Delicious apples, thinly sliced
½ cup dried cranberries

½ cup dark brown sugar
6 tablespoons butter, melted
1½ teaspoons cinnamon

Arrange equal portions of the sweet potatoes, apples and cranberries in the center of six sheets of foil and sprinkle equally with the brown sugar. Mix the butter and cinnamon in a bowl and drizzle equally over each portion. Seal the foil, allowing room for the heat to circulate. Grill for 20 to 25 minutes or until the sweet potatoes are tender.
   Note: You may bake this in the oven at 450 degrees for 25 to 30 minutes instead of on a grill.

Five Forks
Kerr-Vance Academy, Henderson, North Carolina

Roasted Sweet Potatoes with Rosemary Honey Vinaigrette

5 cups cubed peeled sweet potatoes

1 tablespoon extra-virgin olive oil

¼ cup honey

3 tablespoons white wine vinegar

1 tablespoon extra-virgin olive oil

3 tablespoons chopped fresh rosemary
  (do not use dried)

2 garlic cloves, minced

½ teaspoon salt

½ teaspoon freshly ground pepper

Combine the potatoes and 1 tablespoon olive oil in a bowl and toss well to coat. Spread in a single layer over a foil-lined 10×15-inch baking pan coated with nonstick cooking spray. Bake at 450 degrees for 35 minutes or until light brown; do not stir. Whisk the honey, vinegar, 1 tablespoon olive oil, the rosemary, garlic, salt and pepper in a bowl. Add the potatoes and toss well to coat. Serve hot or at room temperature.

Recipes of Note
Greensboro Symphony Guild, North Carolina

Sweet Potato Casserole

CASSEROLE

3 cups mashed sweet potatoes

1 cup sugar

1 stick margarine

1 cup coconut

¼ cup milk

2 large eggs

1 teaspoon vanilla

Mix together until creamy; pour into casserole dish.

TOPPING

1 stick margarine

1 cup brown sugar

½ cup plain flour

1 cup chopped pecans

Mix margarine, sugar and flour. Add pecans to mixture; spread over top. Bake at 325 degrees for about 30 minutes.

Dining with Pioneers, Volume 1
AT&T Pioneers, Tennessee Chapter 21

Sweet Potato Crunch

2 (30-ounce) cans mashed sweet
   potatoes, drained
1¼ cups sugar
1 cup milk
½ cup butter, melted
4 large eggs, lightly beaten
1 teaspoon salt

1 teaspoon cinnamon
1 teaspoon vanilla extract
2 cups chopped pecans
2 cups brown sugar
⅔ cup flour
5 tablespoons butter, melted

Combine the sweet potatoes, sugar, milk, ½ cup butter, eggs, salt, cinnamon and vanilla in a bowl and mix well. Spoon into a greased baking dish. Mix the pecans, brown sugar and flour in a bowl. Stir in the 5 tablespoons of butter. Sprinkle over the prepared layer. Bake at 350 degrees for 35 minutes.

Southern On Occasion
Junior League of Cobb-Marietta, Georgia

Sweet Potato-Tangerine Soufflé

3 pounds peeled sweet potatoes
5 tablespoons melted butter
¼ cup dark rum
8 tablespoons brown sugar

¼ teaspoon nutmeg
½ teaspoon salt
5 tangerines
3 tablespoons chopped pecans

Preheat oven to 350 degrees. Boil and mash sweet potatoes. Add 3 tablespoons butter, rum, 6 tablespoons sugar, nutmeg, and salt. Blend together until smooth. Peel tangerines and remove white membranes. Cut the sections from 3 of the tangerines in half. Remove the seeds. Fold seeded tangerines into the sweet potato mixture. Purée in blender. Pour mixture into a greased 2-quart casserole dish. Puncture the centers of the remaining tangerines to remove the seeds. Arrange them on top of the pudding. Combine the remaining sugar and butter with the pecans. Sprinkle over top of the soufflé and bake for 30 minutes.

    Note: Can be made ahead. A pleasant and light accompaniment for roasted poultry.

Of Tide and Thyme
Junior League of Annapolis, Maryland

FRIED GREEN TOMATOES

SERVES 6

1 egg, beaten
1/2 cup milk
1/2 cup cornmeal
1/4 cup all-purpose flour
1 teaspoon salt

1/2 teaspoon pepper
3 medium green tomatoes, cut in
    1/3-inch slices
3 to 4 tablespoons vegetable oil

Combine egg and milk; set aside. Combine cornmeal, flour, salt and pepper. Dip tomatoes in egg mixture; dredge in cornmeal mixture. Heat 3 tablespoons oil in large skillet over medium heat. Arrange a single layer of tomato slices in skillet and cook until golden brown on each side; set aside. Repeat with remaining slices, adding more oil if needed.

    Editor's Note: To add a special touch, serve with Comeback Sauce (page 151).

Let Us Keep the Feast
St. Paul's Episcopal Women, Beaufort, North Carolina

DEEP-DISH TOMATO PIE

SERVES 4 TO 6

3 large tomatoes, thickly sliced, drained
1 baked (9-inch) deep-dish pie shell, cooled
4 medium green onions, chopped
1 handful chopped fresh basil

1 handful chopped fresh chives
Salt and pepper to taste
1 cup mayonnaise
1 cup shredded sharp Cheddar cheese

Layer the tomatoes in the pie shell, sprinkling each layer with green onions, basil, chives, salt and pepper. Combine the mayonnaise and cheese in a bowl and mix well. Spread over the tomatoes. Bake at 350 degrees for 30 minutes.

Oh My Stars!
Junior League of the Roanoke Valley, Virginia

Tomato Pie

3 large tomatoes

1 (9-inch) pie crust

2 green onions, thinly sliced

6 leaves chopped fresh basil

Garlic salt to taste

Ground black pepper to taste

1/4 cup finely grated Swiss cheese

1/4 cup Parmesan cheese

3/4 cup mayonnaise

1 cup grated sharp Cheddar cheese

Preheat oven to 350 degrees. Peel tomatoes. Slice 1/2 inch thick. Arrange one layer in pie shell. Sprinkle tomatoes with onions, basil, garlic salt, pepper, Swiss cheese and Parmesan cheese. Repeat with second layer of tomatoes. Mix mayonnaise and Cheddar cheese together and spread over pie. Bake for 30 minutes or until lightly browned.

Windows Across Missouri
Missouri State Medical Association Alliance, Jefferson City, Missouri

Grate-est Zucchini

4 zucchini

3 shallots

1 teaspoon olive oil or garlic-flavored olive oil

1/3 cup water (optional)

1 teaspoon (or more) freshly grated nutmeg

Salt to taste

Pepper to taste

1/2 cup (2 ounces) grated Parmesan cheese

Use a kitchen knife to cut off and discard the ends of the zucchini. Cut the shallots into thin slices and separate the slices into rings. Use a box grater to grate the zucchini carefully onto a plate.

Heat a large skillet over medium-high heat and add the olive oil. Add the shallots and cook until light brown, stirring frequently. Add the zucchini and mix well. Add the water if the zucchini seems to be dry. Season with the nutmeg, salt and pepper. Cover the skillet and reduce the heat to medium. Cook just until the zucchini is tender; use a pot holder to remove the cover and stir the mixture occasionally to keep it from sticking. Sprinkle the cheese over the top and replace the cover. Cook for 1 to 2 minutes longer or until the cheese melts.

Junior Leagues in the Kitchen with Kids
Association of Junior Leagues International, FRP.INC

Italian Zucchini Crescent Pie

4 cups thinly sliced unpeeled zucchini

1 cup coarsely chopped onion

½ cup butter

2 tablespoons parsley flakes

½ teaspoon salt

½ teaspoon black pepper

¼ teaspoon garlic powder

¼ teaspoon chopped basil

¼ teaspoon oregano

2 eggs

1 cup (4 ounces) shredded mozzarella cheese

1 (8-ounce) package refrigerated
  crescent roll dough

2 teaspoons Dijon mustard

In large skillet, sauté zucchini and onion in butter for about 10 minutes or until tender. Stir in parsley, salt, black pepper, garlic powder, basil and oregano.

Blend eggs with cheese. Add to vegetable mixture.

Separate dough into 8 triangles and place in ungreased 10-inch pie plate, 11-inch quiche dish or 12×8×1½-inch baking pan, pressing dough in bottom and along sides to form crust.

Lightly spread mustard on dough. Spoon vegetable mixture into crust.

Bake at 375 degrees for 20 minutes or until knife tip inserted near center comes out clean. Cover edges with aluminum foil if necessary to prevent over browning. Let stand for 10 minutes before serving.

I'll Cook When Pigs Fly
Junior League of Cincinnati, Ohio

It is believed that the first community cookbook was *A Poetical Cookbook*, published in 1864 and dedicated to the Sanitary Fair held for the Civil War soldiers and their families.

GRILLED SUMMER VEGETABLES WITH MARINADE OR SHALLOT HERB BUTTER

SERVES 6

GRILLED SUMMER VEGETABLES

¼ cup olive oil

2 onions (Georgia Vidalias of course!)

1 medium zucchini, cut lengthwise

1 red or orange pepper, cut in 1-inch lengths

1 yellow squash, cut lengthwise

1 sweet potato or yam, prebaked, sliced
  ½ inch thick

1 small eggplant, sliced ½ inch thick

Clean and prepare vegetables individually. Set vegetables on grill and watch closely remembering that the denser vegetables will take longer to cook so put them on first. The precooked potato or yam will only take about 5 minutes. When vegetables have reached desired doneness, remove from grill directly into marinade or serve hot with shallot butter.

MARINADE FOR CHILLED GRILLED VEGETABLES

5 fresh garlic cloves

2 sprigs fresh rosemary

2 sprigs fresh lemon thyme

1 tablespoon extra-virgin olive oil

2 tablespoons tarragon vinegar

Cracked black pepper and salt

Peel garlic and chop coarsely. Whip into remaining ingredients with food processor. Let mixture sit at room temperature for at least an hour for flavors to develop.

SHALLOT-HERB BUTTER

1 small shallot, minced

1 sprig fresh oregano, chopped

¼ sprig fresh thyme, chopped

4 ounces (1 stick) butter

Salt and pepper to taste

Sauté shallot and herbs in a small amount of butter. Remove from heat and add remaining butter and stir until it has all blended with the herbs and shallots. Replace on heat and wait until butter is frothing. Remove from heat before the butter browns. Spoon off froth until butter is clear. Serve over grilled vegetables.

Note: A delightful and easy way to prepare vegetables for your summer dining pleasure. Serve chilled with the marinade or hot with the shallot-herb butter.

A Taste of Georgia, Another Serving
Newnan Junior Service League, Georgia

LEASANTS

1 to 2 cups flour

1 teaspoon salt

2 teaspoons baking powder

Milk or water

Chicken, beef, venison or rabbit broth

Mix the flour, salt and baking powder in a bowl. Stir in just enough milk to make a soft dough; do not knead. Roll into a thin rectangle on a lightly floured surface. Cut into squares. Drop into hot boiling chicken broth in a large saucepan. Cook, covered, for 20 minutes. Remove from broth. Serve hot as a side or with your favorite cream sauce.

Note: This old French dumpling dish is especially good served with stews.

The Flavors of Mackinac
Mackinac Island Medical Center, Michigan

CLASSIC SCOTCH AND SODA FONDUE

SERVES 6

1 clove garlic

16 ounces Cheddar cheese, shredded

1 tablespoon flour

5½ tablespoons scotch whisky

½ to ¾ cup club soda

1 teaspoon Worcestershire sauce

½ tablespoons butter, melted

1 egg, lightly beaten

French bread, cubed

Rub inside of fondue pot with garlic clove. Place Cheddar cheese in a plastic bag; sprinkle flour over Cheddar cheese; shake bag to coat Cheddar cheese with flour. Place coated Cheddar cheese in a double boiler over simmering water, stirring constantly until all of Cheddar cheese is melted. Stir in scotch whisky, club soda (add only as much club soda as needed; you want the cheese to slowly drip from a spoon), Worcestershire sauce, and butter into cheese mixture; mix until smooth. Take a small amount of melted cheese in a separate dish and add to the beaten egg; mix well. Stir cheese and egg back into double boiler and blend. Pour cheese mixture into fondue pot. Serve with cubed loaves of thick-crusted bread.

Toast to Tidewater
Junior League of Norfolk-Virginia Beach, Virginia

ANCHO CHILE CHEESE ENCHILADAS

SERVES 4 TO 6

ANCHO CHILE SAUCE

4 cups chicken stock

4 large ancho chiles, stemmed and seeded

2 tablespoons corn oil

2/3 large yellow onion, chopped

3 cloves garlic, chopped

2 tablespoons corn oil

2 tablespoons flour

4 teaspoons cumin

1 tablespoon sugar

1 1/2 teaspoons oregano

Salt and pepper to taste

For the sauce, bring the stock and ancho chiles to a boil in a medium saucepan over medium-high heat; reduce the heat to medium-low. Simmer for 10 minutes or until the chiles are tender. Remove from heat, reserving the chiles and cooking liquid.

Heat 2 tablespoons corn oil in a medium skillet over medium-high heat. Add the onion and cook for 3 to 5 minutes or just until it begins to soften, stirring constantly. Combine the sautéed onion, reserved chiles, 1 cup of the reserved cooking liquid, and garlic in a blender and process until the consistency of a smooth paste.

Heat 2 tablespoons corn oil in a large skillet over medium heat. Whisk in the flour until blended. Cook for 2 minutes, stirring constantly with a wooden spoon. Add the reserved chile paste, cumin, sugar, oregano, remaining reserved cooking liquid, salt and pepper and mix well. Reduce the heat to medium-low and simmer for 30 minutes or until thickened, stirring frequently. Cover the sauce and keep warm over low heat.

ENCHILADAS

1 1/2 cups corn oil

12 corn tortillas

5 cups shredded Monterey Jack cheese

1/3 large yellow onion, chopped

For the enchiladas, preheat the oven to 400 degrees. Heat 1 1/2 cups corn oil in a deep skillet over medium heat until hot but not smoking. Fry the tortillas 1 at a time in the hot oil for 2 seconds per side, turning once. Immediately dip the tortillas into the chile sauce to coat. Place the tortillas on a large plate and sprinkle 1/4 cup of cheese over the bottom third of each tortilla. Roll to enclose the cheese and arrange seam side down in a single layer in a baking dish. Spoon the remaining chile sauce over the enchiladas and sprinkle with the remaining 2 cups of cheese and onion. Bake for 10 minutes or until the cheese melts.

Pomegranates & Prickly Pears—flavorful entertaining from the Junior League of Phoenix
Junior League of Phoenix, Arizona

Sesame Noodles with Asparagus

7 tablespoons soy sauce

¼ cup sesame oil

3½ tablespoons dark brown sugar

3 tablespoons dark sesame oil

3 tablespoons balsamic vinegar

2 teaspoons chili oil

¼ cup chopped cilantro

1 tablespoon minced fresh ginger

1 garlic clove, minced

2 teaspoons salt

2 pounds asparagus, trimmed and thinly
   sliced on the diagonal

Salt to taste

16 ounces angel hair pasta

10 scallions, thinly sliced

¼ cup sesame seeds, lightly toasted

Whisk the soy sauce, sesame oil, brown sugar, dark sesame oil, vinegar and chili oil in a bowl until the sugar dissolves. Whisk in the cilantro, ginger, garlic and 2 teaspoons salt. Cook the asparagus in boiling salted water in a large saucepan until tender-crisp; drain and dry on a kitchen towel. Cook the pasta in boiling salted water in the saucepan until cooked through; drain and place in a serving bowl. Reserve some of the asparagus pieces, some of the scallions and some of the sesame seeds. Add the remaining asparagus, scallions and sesame seeds to the pasta. Add the sauce and toss until well coated. Sprinkle the reserved asparagus, scallions and sesame seeds over the top. Serve warm or at room temperature.

A Thyme to Entertain, Menus & Traditions of Annapolis
Junior League of Annapolis, Maryland

Farfalle with Shiitakes, Peas and Sweet Potatoes

2½ cups bouillon

2 cups julienne-cut peeled sweet potatoes

2 cups sugar snap peas (about 8 ounces),
   washed and trimmed

1 cup shiitake mushroom caps without stems
   (about 1 ounce), washed, dried and sliced

1 tablespoon margarine

1 cup thinly sliced onions

4 garlic cloves, minced

¼ teaspoon salt

8 ounces farfalle

Salt for water

¼ cup fresh flat-leaf parsley, chopped

¼ cup fresh chives, chopped

Bring bouillon to a boil in a saucepan and cook sweet potatoes for 1 minute. Add peas and cook, covered, for 2 minutes. Add mushrooms and cook, covered, for 1 additional minute. Drain through a colander, reserving liquid. Return liquid to saucepan and bring to a boil; cook for about 10 minutes or until liquid is reduce to ¼ cup. Set aside.

Heat margarine in the same pot and cook onions and garlic until tender but not brown. Add vegetables, reserved liquid and salt. Bring to a boil and cook 1 minute longer, stirring constantly. cook pasta in boiling salted water until al dente according to package directions. Drain. Add vegetable mixture to hot pasta along with parsley and chives, mixing well. Serve hot.

Note: Can be made dairy or parve. This dish tastes great either way! Add ¼ cup Parmesan cheese to pasta for dairy version. Do not make the pasta ahead of time, as it will be too cool when you add the remaining ingredients.

The Kosher Palette II
Joseph Kushner Hebrew Academy, Livingstone, New Jersey

SPINACH FETTUCCINI

1½ tablespoons butter
1½ teaspoons minced garlic
1½ cups chicken stock, divided
2 ounces cream cheese, softened
3 tablespoons all-purpose flour
3 ounces grated Parmesan cheese
¾ cup half-and-half

1 teaspoon salt
1 teaspoon pepper
1 (10-ounce) package frozen spinach, thawed
1 (16-ounce) package fettuccini, prepared
   according to package directions
10 slices bacon, cooked and crumbled

In large skillet over medium heat, melt butter. Add garlic and sauté 30 seconds. Add ½ cup chicken stock and cream cheese, whisking until cheese melts and mixture is smooth. Add remaining chicken stock and flour. Bring to a boil, stirring constantly. Cook 2 minutes. Remove from heat and add Parmesan cheese, stirring until smooth. Add half-and-half, salt, pepper, and spinach, stirring until thoroughly combined. Place pasta in large bowl. Pour spinach mixture over pasta, tossing well to coat. Serve in individual pasta bowls and garnish with bacon.

Beyond the Hedges
Junior League of Athens, Georgia

8 ounces elbow pasta
2 tablespoons butter
2 tablespoons all-purpose flour
1 cup milk
½ teaspoon salt

¼ teaspoon white pepper
1½ cups shredded Cheddar cheese
1 large egg
1 cup sour cream
½ cup shredded Cheddar cheese

Preheat oven to 350 degrees. Cook the pasta using the package directions and drain. Melt the butter in a saucepan over medium heat. Stir in the flour and cook until bubbly, stirring constantly. Add the milk and cook until thickened. Stir in the salt, white pepper and 1½ cups cheese and cook until blended and of a sauce consistency, stirring constantly.

Whisk the egg in a large bowl and stir in the sour cream. Add the cheese sauce and pasta to the egg mixture and mix well. Spoon the pasta mixture into a greased 2-quart baking dish and sprinkle with ½ cup cheese. Bake for 35 minutes.

Tables of Content
Junior League of Birmingham, Alabama

"I love this recipe so much that each time I make it, I double the recipe. (Use a 9×12-inch baking dish to accommodate the larger quantity.)"

Jennifer Kennedy
FRP Communications Coordinator

"Kitchen Sink" Orzo

10 ounces orzo (about 1½ cups)

2 teaspoons olive oil

1 head radicchio, finely chopped
(about 1 cup)

⅓ cup oil-pack sun-dried tomatoes, drained
and chopped

6 tablespoons olive oil

¼ cup kalamata olives, sliced

¼ cup balsamic vinegar

1 clove garlic, chopped

½ cup fresh basil, chiffonade

½ cup grated Parmesan cheese

½ cup pine nuts, toasted

1 teaspoon kosher salt

1 teaspoon freshly ground pepper

Cook the pasta using the package directions until al dente; drain. Toss the pasta with 2 teaspoons olive oil in a bowl until coated. Let stand until cool.

Toss the radicchio, sun-dried tomatoes, 6 tablespoons olive oil, the olives, vinegar and garlic in a bowl until combined. Add the tomato mixture to the cooled pasta and mix well. Stir in the basil, cheese and pine nuts. Season with the salt and pepper.

Texas Tables
Junior League of North Harris and South Montgomery Counties, Texas

Penne Pasta with Fresh Tomato, Basil and Ricotta Sauce

Makes 3 cups

3 cups chopped ripe tomatoes

1½ cups chopped fresh basil (⅛ to ¼ cup
dried basil)

3 tablespoons minced red onion

1 garlic clove, chopped

1 cup ricotta cheese

⅓ cup olive oil

16 ounces penne pasta, cooked

Salt and freshly ground black pepper, to taste

Combine the tomatoes, basil, onion and garlic. Stir in the remaining ingredients except the pasta and blend well. Toss with hot pasta and serve immediately.

Excellent on rotelle, fusilli, ziti or tubetti pasta.

A Southern Collection—Then and Now
Junior League of Columbus, Georgia

PENNE IN VODKA SAUCE

4 ounces unsalted butter

½ cup olive oil

2 (28-ounce) cans whole peeled tomatoes, drained and chopped

1 teaspoon dill

1 teaspoon crushed red pepper flakes

¼ cup vodka

¼ teaspoon salt

¼ teaspoon sugar

1 cup heavy cream

1 pound uncooked penne

Parmesan cheese to taste

Melt the butter in a heavy saucepan. Add the olive oil, tomatoes, dill, red pepper flakes, and vodka. Cook over medium-high heat for 5 minutes; reduce the heat. Add the salt, sugar, and cream. Simmer until of the desired consistency. Cook the penne in a large pot of boiling water until al dente; drain. Combine the pasta with the sauce in a serving bowl; toss lightly to mix. Serve with the Parmesan cheese.

Note: The vodka sauce may be made ahead and reheated, but do not boil. The red pepper flakes may be steeped in the vodka for 24 hours if desired. Vary the degree of spiciness with the amount of red pepper flakes.

I'll Taste Manhattan
Junior League of New York City, New York

SPAGHETTI WITH ROASTED VEGETABLE SAUCE

8 ounces uncooked spaghetti

2 large ripe tomatoes, cored, halved and seeded

1 small onion, chopped

1 garlic clove, sliced

½ green bell pepper

½ (6-ounce) can tomato paste

¼ cup fresh basil leaves

Salt and freshly ground black pepper, to taste

4 tablespoons freshly grated Parmesan cheese

Preheat oven broiler. Cook pasta according to package directions and drain. Keep warm. Place tomatoes, onion, garlic and bell pepper skin side up on a flat cookie sheet. Roast under the broiler until vegetable skins turn brown and look blistered, approximately 10 minutes. Place vegetables, along with any juices, into a food processor. Add tomato paste and fresh basil; purée until smooth. Pour into a saucepan and heat until warm. Adjust seasoning with salt and black pepper, to taste. Serve over cooked spaghetti and sprinkle with freshly grated Parmesan cheese and cracked black pepper.

Windows Across Missouri
Missouri State Medical Association Alliance, Jefferson City, Missouri

Cashew Pineapple Rice

2 tablespoons butter

1 tablespoon canola oil

1 medium yellow onion

1½ cups long grain rice (don't use instant or quick-cooking)

1 (20-ounce) can pineapple chunks

3 cups reduced-sodium vegetable broth

2 large carrots

½ cup raw cashews

½ teaspoon salt

½ teaspoon red pepper flakes

Heat your oven to 350 degrees. Heat the butter and canola oil in a medium saucepan. Add onion. Cook 4 minutes or until tender. Pour onion and drippings into a 9×11-inch baking dish. Add rice, stirring to coat. Drain pineapple, reserving 1 tablespoon juice. Add pineapple, reserved juice, broth, carrots, cashews, salt, and pepper flakes to rice mixture and stir to combine. Bake, covered, 45 to 55 minutes or until liquid is absorbed. Let stand, covered, 5 minutes.

Boston Uncommon
Junior League of Boston, Massachusetts

Jasmine Rice with Garlic, Ginger and Cilantro

3 cups jasmine rice

3 tablespoons canola oil

⅓ cup finely chopped gingerroot

3 garlic cloves, minced

3½ cups low-sodium chicken broth

1 cup coconut milk

1 pinch salt to taste

¾ teaspoon chopped fresh cilantro

Rinse the rice in a large sieve under cold water until the water runs clear; drain. Heat the canola oil in a large heavy saucepan over medium-high heat. Add the gingerroot and garlic and sauté for 30 seconds or until fragrant. Add the rice and sauté for 3 minutes.

Stir in the broth, coconut milk and salt. Add the cilantro and mix well. Bring to a boil; reduce the heat to medium-low. Cook, covered, for 15 minutes or until the rice is tender. Remove from the heat and let stand, covered, for 10 minutes. Fluff the rice with a fork and serve immediately.

Orange County Fare; a culinary journey through the California Riviera
Junior League of Orange County, California

Fresh Tomato and Basil Risotto with Mozzarella

1½ cups diced plum tomato

2 tablespoons chopped fresh basil

1 tablespoon olive oil

½ teaspoon salt

1 garlic clove, crushed

42 ounces chicken broth

½ cup finely chopped onion

2 teaspoons olive oil

1½ cups uncooked arborio rice

⅓ cup dry white wine

½ cup (2 ounces) diced mozzarella cheese

½ teaspoon ground pepper

3 tablespoons freshly grated Parmesan cheese

Combine tomato, basil, 1 tablespoon oil, salt, and garlic in a small bowl; set aside. Bring broth to a simmer in a medium saucepan; keep warm over low heat. Sauté onion in 2 teaspoons hot oil in a large saucepan over high heat 3 minutes. Add rice and cook, stirring constantly, 1 minute. Add wine to rice mixture and cook, stirring constantly, until liquid is nearly absorbed. Add warm broth, ½ cup at a time, cooking until each portion is absorbed before adding more. Add tomato mixture to rice mixture, stirring well. Remove from heat and stir in mozzarella and pepper. Sprinkle with Parmesan cheese and serve.

Creating A Stir
Fayette County Medical Auxiliary, Lexington, Kentucky

Lone Star Rice

1 cup chopped low-sodium ham

1 cup chopped green onions

¼ cup butter, melted

3 cups cooked rice

1½ cups low-fat sour cream

1 cup shredded sharp Cheddar cheese

1 (4-ounce) can chopped green chiles

⅛ teaspoon ground bay leaves

Salt and white pepper to taste

Preheat the oven to 375 degrees. Sauté the ham and green onions in the butter in a large skillet until the green onions are tender, stirring constantly. Remove from the heat and stir in the rice, sour cream, cheese, undrained green chiles, bay leaves, salt and white pepper. Spoon into a lightly greased 7×11-inch baking pan. Bake for 20 minutes.

Treasures from the Bend, Rich in History and Flavor
Fort Bend Junior Service League, Sugar Land, Texas

BAKED APPLES

6 apples, peeled and thinly sliced
1 cup sugar
½ teaspoon nutmeg
¼ teaspoon cinnamon
3 cups soft bread crumbs
½ cup butter, melted

Mix apples, sugar, nutmeg and cinnamon. Blend bread crumbs with butter. Layer apples and crumbs alternately in buttered 1-quart baking dish. Cover and bake at 350 degrees for 40 minutes.

Treasures of the Smokies
Junior League of Johnson City, Tennessee

SCALLOPED PINEAPPLE

1 (20-ounce) can juice-pack pineapple tidbits
3 tablespoons flour
1 cup shredded sharp Cheddar cheese
⅓ cup sugar
18 butter crackers, crushed
3 tablespoons butter, melted

Drain the pineapple, reserving 3 tablespoons of the juice. Combine the reserved juice and flour in a bowl and mix well. Stir in the pineapple, cheese and sugar. Spoon into an 8×8-inch baking pan.
Combine the cracker crumbs and butter in a bowl and toss to mix. Sprinkle over the prepared layer. Bake at 350 degrees for 25 to 30 minutes or until bubbly. Serve for breakfast or brunch or as a side dish with pork or Kentucky country ham.

Splendor in the Bluegrass
Junior League of Louisville, Kentucky

MEXICAN DRESSING

8 slices bacon, chopped
6 ounces venison sausage or medium-hot bulk pork sausage
½ cup chopped poblano chile
2 serrano chiles, seeded and chopped
1 garlic clove, minced
1 red bell pepper chopped
1 yellow bell pepper, chopped
1 orange bell pepper, chopped
2 celery ribs, chopped
¼ cup chopped Spanish onion
Handful fresh cilantro, chopped
2 small baguettes, or 4 slices white sandwich bread, cubed
1 cup crumbled corn bread
2 cups chicken stock
1 egg, beaten

Cook the bacon and sausage in a large saucepan until the sausage is crumbly and cooked through and the bacon is crisp. Do not drain. Add the poblano chile, serrano chiles, garlic, red bell pepper, yellow bell pepper, orange bell pepper, celery and onion. Sauté for 8 to 10 minutes or until the vegetables are tender. Add the cilantro, bread cubes, crumbled corn bread and chicken stock. Stir to mix well. Remove to a large bowl. Add the egg and stir to mix well. Pour into a 10×10-inch baking dish. Bake at 375 degrees for 20 minutes. Serve warm.

A League of Our Own
Rockwall Women's League, Texas

Baked Oysters

1 cup chopped celery

1 quart oysters, drained and juice reserved

½ cup melted butter

3 cups saltine cracker crumbs

1 cup chopped fresh parsley

3 tablespoons Cajun hot sauce

1½ tablespoons Worcestershire sauce

Salt and pepper to taste

1 pint half-and-half

Sauté celery in oyster juice and butter for 2 minutes. Layer crackers, oysters, and then celery mix in a greased baking dish. Season with parsley, Cajun hot sauce, Worcestershire sauce and black pepper. Pour in part of the carton of half-and-half. Layer everything again in the same order, finishing with the half-and-half. Sprinkle the rest of the cracker crumbs over the dish. Bake at 325 degrees for 45 minutes.

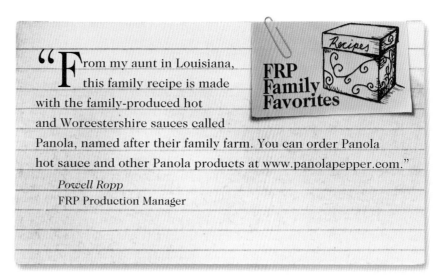

"From my aunt in Louisiana, this family recipe is made with the family-produced hot and Worcestershire sauces called Panola, named after their family farm. You can order Panola hot sauce and other Panola products at www.panolapepper.com."

Powell Ropp
FRP Production Manager

Old Kentucky Bourbon Marinade

MAKES ABOUT 2½ CUPS

½ cup Old Forester bourbon

¾ cup soy sauce

¼ cup canola oil or corn oil

¼ cup water

¼ cup Worcestershire sauce

2 tablespoons brown sugar

4 cloves garlic, minced

1 tablespoon brown mustard

½ teaspoon ground ginger

1 teaspoon white pepper

3 tablespoons coarsely ground black pepper

Combine the bourbon, soy sauce, oil, water, Worcestershire sauce, brown sugar, garlic, mustard, ginger, white pepper and black pepper in a jar with a tight-fitting lid. Cover and shake to mix well. Use to marinate 2 pounds of beef, pork or chicken.

Splendor in the Bluegrass
Junior League of Louisville, Kentucky

Mild Homemade Taco Sauce

1 (16-ounce) can plum tomatoes, undrained
1 large onion, minced
2 large garlic cloves, crushed
1½ tablespoons cooking oil
1 teaspoon oregano
¾ teaspoon ground cumin
¾ teaspoon ground coriander
2 tablespoons (or more to taste) chopped
   green chile

1 tablespoon tomato paste
1½ teaspoons sugar
1 teaspoon chopped fresh cilantro
1 teaspoon white vinegar
Salt to taste
Pepper to taste

In a food processor fitted with the steel blade or in a blender coarsely purée the tomatoes with juice. In a large skillet cook onion and garlic in oil over moderate heat, stirring, until onion is softened. Add oregano, cumin and ground coriander and cook the mixture, stirring, for 2 minutes. Add the tomato purée, chopped green chile, tomato paste, sugar, cilantro, vinegar, salt and pepper. Simmer the mixture, stirring often, for 15 minutes or until sauce is thickened.

Simply Simpatico
Junior League of Albuquerque, New Mexico

First You Make a Roux

2 tablespoons butter, shortening or bacon drippings
2 tablespoons flour

Melt the butter, shortening or bacon drippings in thick pot or skillet. Add the flour and stir constantly until dark brown, being careful not to burn. If there is the slightest indication of over-browning, dispose of the roux and start over. Even a slightly burned sauce will ruin a savory dish. To this basic roux, add seasoning and stock to make various sauces and gravies.

River Road Recipes, The Textbook of Louisiana Cooking
Junior League of Baton Rouge, Louisiana

Tomato Gravy

1 tablespoon vegetable shortening

2 tablespoons flour

1½ cups water

1 (10-ounce) can stewed tomatoes or 9 ripe tomatoes, chopped

Salt and pepper to taste

12 biscuits

Melt the shortening in a 10-inch cast-iron skillet. Add the flour and stir until thickened and browned. Mix ¾ cup of the water with the tomatoes and add the mixture to the flour, stirring constantly. Add enough of the remaining water to make the mixture medium-thick. Add salt and pepper to taste. Serve over biscuits.

Family Secrets
Lee Academy, Clarksdale, Mississippi

Kansas City Rib Rub

1 cup cane sugar

⅓ cup paprika

¼ cup seasoned salt

¼ cup garlic salt

¼ cup celery salt

2 tablespoons onion salt

2 tablespoons barbeque seasoning

2 tablespoons chili seasoning

2 tablespoons black pepper

1 tablespoon lemon pepper

2 teaspoons ground ginger

½ teaspoon thyme

½ teaspoon allspice

½ teaspoon cayenne

Sift cane sugar, paprika, seasoned salt, garlic salt, celery salt, onion salt, barbeque seasoning, chili seasoning, black pepper, lemon pepper, ginger, thyme, allspice and cayenne into bowl; mix well. Rub liberally over ribs. Let stand at room temperature for up to 15 minutes or marinate in refrigerator for up to 24 hours. Store rub in airtight container in cool place.

The Kansas City Barbeque Society Cookbook
Kansas City Barbeque Society, Missouri

CAKES, COOKIES & CONFECTIONS

LESSONS LEARNED

The Junior League of Birmingham, Alabama's first book, *Magic,* helps teach its readers how to cook. The second, *Food for Thought,* emphasizes the importance of cooking, and the latest cookbook, *Tables of Content,* stresses the importance of gathering at the table. In the past 15 years, the league has sold more than $750,000 worth of cookbooks, and the benefits for the community have been overwhelming, including helping the YWCA, the Birmingham Botanical Gardens, and the children's hospital.

Kathryn Tortorici, chairperson for *Tables of Content*, and Nancy Bynon, co-chair, incorporated the importance of gathering at the table through the book's messages, recipes, and photos of tables set up around the city. "…whether modest or lavish, Old South or contemporary, using elaborate recipes or just a few ingredients, it will be the memories of the table—the food, the setting, and the conversation—that stay with us all."

TABLES OF CONTENT
JUNIOR LEAGUE OF BIRMINGHAM

The Best Memories Are Made Gathered Around the Table

One of the most beneficial working tools discovered during the cookbook creation process was attending Favorite Recipes® Press's Cookbook University. Among the many helpful sessions was the guest speaker, a judge for the prestigious Tabasco Community Cookbook Awards, who spoke on 'What Makes an Award-Winning Cookbook'.

"It was not our goal to win an award," Kathryn said. "But we wanted to make a book that was award worthy, making sure we covered all of our bases and incorporated every little thing that makes a cookbook great. If you are going to do something, make it great."

Both women also grew in many ways during the process.

"My communication skills improved," said Kathryn. She also treasures working with her mother, who did all the drawings for the cookbook. "She has since passed away, but I have special memories of this being one of the last projects we worked on together."

Nancy feels her organization skills have improved and that, "I also have become more skilled as a mediator/peacemaker. This is something that's important in the business of working on a cookbook."

APPLE CAKE

3 cups flour	1 cup sugar
2 teaspoons cinnamon	1 cup packed brown sugar
1 teaspoon baking soda	1½ cups vegetable oil
1 teaspoon salt	3 large eggs
1 pound apples, peeled and cut into	3 teaspoons vanilla extract
⅓-inch pieces	¾ cup chopped pecans

Preheat the oven to 350 degrees. Sift the flour, cinnamon, baking soda and salt into a medium bowl. Spray a 12-cup bundt pan with nonstick cooking spray. Spoon 3 tablespoons of the flour mixture into the pan, tilting to coat the pan evenly. Combine the apples and 2 tablespoons of the flour mixture in a bowl and toss to coat. Combine the sugar, brown sugar, oil, eggs and vanilla in a mixing bowl and beat until thickened. Beat in the remaining flour mixture gradually. Fold in the apples and pecans. Spoon into the prepared bundt pan. Bake for 60 minutes or until a cake tester inserted in the center comes out clean. Remove the pan to a wire rack.

CARAMEL SAUCE

½ cup butter	¼ cup milk
1 cup packed brown sugar	1 teaspoon vanilla extract

Melt the butter in a heavy skillet over medium heat. Whisk in the brown sugar and milk. Bring to a boil, whisking constantly until the mixture is smooth. Whisk in the vanilla. Spoon ¼ cup of the hot sauce over the warm cake. Let stand for 15 minutes or until the sauce is absorbed. Invert the cake onto a serving plate. Spoon the remaining sauce over the cake. Let stand for 1 hour before serving.

"I first made this yummy cake as an alternative to the traditional pumpkin pie for Thanksgiving, and my family loved it. Now there is a standing request that I make it every time we get together."

Tanis Westbrook
FRP Project Editor

Grand Temptations
The Junior League of
Grand Rapids, Michigan

Fresh Apple Cake

2 cups sugar

2 large eggs

½ cup water

1 cup salad oil (corn oil)

3 diced apples (2½ cups)

1 cup chopped nuts (optional)

2½ cups flour

2 teaspoons baking powder

1 teaspoon soda

1 teaspoon salt

1 teaspoon cinnamon

1 package butterscotch chips

Combine sugar, eggs, water and oil. Add dry ingredients, mixing well while adding apples and nuts. Pour into greased and floured pan (13×9×2). Sprinkle butterscotch morsels over top of batter. Bake at 350 degrees for 1 hour. Better when served after first day. Use spatula to remove in small squares so the moist part won't be left in the pan.

Dining with Pioneers, Volume 1
AT&T Pioneers, Tennessee Chapter 21

Banana Nut Cake

Cake

1 cup butter or margarine

2 cups sugar

2 eggs

3 cups all-purpose flour

2 teaspoons baking soda

¾ cup milk

1½ cups mashed very ripe bananas

Cream butter and sugar. Add eggs. Alternately add flour, soda and milk. Fold in bananas. Pour into two 9-inch round pans or one 13×9×2-inch baking pan, greased and floured. Bake in a preheated 350-degree oven for 25 minutes.

Icing

1 (8-ounce) package cream cheese

1 (1-pound) box powdered sugar

6 tablespoons butter or margarine

Milk

2 teaspoons vanilla

1 cup chopped pecans

Mix cream cheese, powdered sugar and butter until blended well. Add very small amounts of milk until icing is smooth. Add vanilla, then pecans. Ice cooled cake.

A Southern Collection—Then and Now
Junior League of Columbus, Georgia

ST. LOUIS GOOEY BUTTER CAKE

CRUST

1 cup all-purpose flour

3 tablespoons sugar

1/3 cup butter or margarine

In a mixing bowl, combine flour and sugar. Cut in butter until mixture resembles fine crumbs and starts to cling. Press over the bottom of a baking pan.

FILLING

1 1/4 cups sugar

3/4 cup butter or margarine

1 egg

1 cup all-purpose flour

2/3 cup evaporated milk

1/4 cup light corn syrup

1 teaspoon vanilla

Powdered sugar

In mixing bowl beat sugar and butter together until light and fluffy. Mix in egg until combined. Alternately add flour and evaporated milk, mixing after each addition. Add corn syrup and vanilla. Mix at medium speed until well blended. Pour batter into crust-lined baking pan. Sprinkle with powdered sugar. Bake at 350 degrees for 25 to 35 minutes or until cake is nearly set. Do not overcook. Cool in pan.

Saint Louis Days/Saint Louis Nights
Junior League of Saint Louis, Missouri

Gooey Butter Cake originated in St. Louis in the 1930s. According to legend, a thrifty German baker added the wrong proportions of ingredients into his cake batter. It turned into a gooey, delicious mess that is now a St. Louis tradition. Recipe courtesy of Fred and Audry Heimburger of Heimburger Bakery.

244   MORE RECIPES WORTH SHARING

CHOCOLATE CHOCOLATE CAKE

1½ sticks unsalted butter, softened

2¼ cups packed light brown sugar

3 large eggs, room temperature

3 ounces unsweetened chocolate,
    melted and cooled

2 teaspoons vanilla

2 cups all-purpose flour

2 teaspoons baking soda

¾ teaspoon salt

½ cup buttermilk

1 cup boiling water

Preheat oven to 350 degrees. Grease and flour two 8-inch round cake pans. Set aside.

Using an electric mixer on medium speed, cream butter and add brown sugar. Add eggs, one at a time, beating after each addition. Beat for 5 minutes until mixture is light and fluffy. Add melted chocolate and vanilla. Scrape down side of bowl to make sure ingredients are well blended. In a small bowl, combine flour, baking soda and salt. Add dry ingredients to creamed mixture alternately with buttermilk, beginning and ending with dry ingredients. Blend in boiling water on low speed. Scrape down side of bowl again and mix well.

Divide batter into prepared cake pans. Tap pans on counter several times to make sure batter is evenly distributed and air bubbles are eliminated. Bake on center rake for 35 to 40 minutes or until a cake tester comes out clean. Cool on a wire rack for about 20 minutes before removing from pans. Cool completely before frosting cake. (Cake layers can be frozen at this point.)

CHOCOLATE CHOCOLATE FROSTING

1 stick unsalted butter, softened

1 tablespoon vegetable shortening

2 cups powdered sugar

¼ cup chocolate syrup

½ teaspoon salt

3 ounces unsweetened chocolate,
    melted and cooled

2 teaspoons vanilla

1 large egg yolk, room temperature

2 teaspoons hot coffee

Cream butter and shortening using an electric mixer on medium speed. Blend in 1 cup powdered sugar, scraping side of bowl. Mix in chocolate syrup. Add remaining powdered sugar, salt and melted chocolate. Scrape bowl and mix on medium speed for 1 minute. In a separate bowl, whisk together vanilla and egg yolk. Add hot coffee. Add egg mixture to chocolate mixture and beat on high speed for about 2 minutes or until frosting is light and fluffy. Refrigerate icing for 30 minutes to ensure proper spreading consistency. Place bottom cake layer upside down on a serving plate. Spread frosting between the layers and over the top and side of the cake. Store cake at room temperature.

Note: Don't eliminate the hot coffee. It's the secret ingredient! If you are concerned about using raw egg yolks, use yolks from eggs pasteurized in their shells or use an equivalent amount of egg substitute.

American Pi, The Cookbook
The Paideia School, Atlanta, Georgia

CHOCOLATE ITALIAN CREAM CAKE

SERVES 10 TO 12

CAKE

5 egg whites
½ cup butter, softened
½ cup shortening
2 cups sugar
5 egg yolks
2¼ cups all-purpose flour

¼ cup unsweetened baking cocoa
1 teaspoon baking soda
1 cup buttermilk
1 cup sweetened flaked coconut
⅔ cup finely chopped pecans
2 teaspoons vanilla extract

To prepare the cake, beat the egg whites in a mixing bowl until still peaks form; set aside. Beat the butter and shortening in a mixing bowl until smooth and creamy. Add the sugar gradually, beating constantly until combined. Cream until light and fluffy. Add the egg yolks one at a time, mixing well after each addition. Combine the flour, baking cocoa and baking soda. Add the dry ingredients and the buttermilk alternately to the creamed mixture, beginning and ending with the dry ingredients and mixing well at low speed after each addition. Stir in the coconut, pecans, and vanilla. Fold in the egg whites. Spoon into three greased and floured 8-inch cake pans.

Bake at 325 for 25 to 30 minutes or until a wooden pick inserted in the center comes out clean. Cool in the pans for about 10 minutes. Remove to a wire rack to cool completely.

CHOCOLATE CREAM CHEESE FROSTING

12 ounces cream cheese, softened
¾ cup butter, softened
2½ teaspoons vanilla extract
½ teaspoon cinnamon

1½ packages confectioners' sugar
¾ cup baking cocoa
½ cup buttermilk

To prepare the frosting, beat the cream cheese, butter, vanilla, and cinnamon at medium speed in a mixing bowl until smooth and creamy. Mix the confectioners' sugar and baking cocoa in a bowl. Add to the cream cheese mixture alternately with the buttermilk, beginning and ending with the confectioners' sugar mixture and mixing well at low speed after each addition. Spread between the layers and over the top and side of cooled cake.

Silver Spoons, Blueberry Afternoons
National Association of Junior Auxiliaries, Greenville, Mississippi

THE ROLLING STONE'S CHOCOLATE CAKE SERVES 8 TO 12

CAKE

2 cups flour

2 cups sugar

Pinch salt

1 stick margarine

4 tablespoons cocoa (level)

½ cup cooking oil

1 cup water

2 eggs

½ cup buttermilk

1 teaspoon baking soda

1 teaspoon cinnamon

Sift flour, sugar and salt together in a mixing bowl and set aside. Combine margarine, cocoa, oil and water and bring to a boil in a saucepan. Pour over dry ingredients and mix well. Add eggs, buttermilk, baking soda and cinnamon. Beat together and pour into a 9×13-inch greased baking dish. Bake at 350 degrees for 30 minutes.

ICING

1 stick margarine

4 tablespoons cocoa (level)

4 tablespoons buttermilk

1 box confectioners' sugar (2 cups)

1 teaspoon vanilla

1 cup pecans

Bring to a boil the margarine, cocoa, and buttermilk. Add in the confectioners' sugar, vanilla and nuts. Ice in the pan.

"This was my Grandmother Stone's recipe, which was handed down to my parents and then to me. It is my all-time favorite chocolate cake! We always had it for family gatherings and especially during the holidays. You can never go wrong with chocolate cake!"

Julee Stone Hicks
FRP Communications Editor

FRP Family Favorites

1 cup vegetable shortening	¼ tablespoon baking soda
1 cup unsalted butter	1 cup brown sugar
2 cups sugar	½ cup chopped walnuts
10 large eggs	¼ pound chocolate chips
2 cups sour cream	1½ tablespoons cocoa power
6 cups sifted cake flour	½ tablespoon cinnamon
1½ tablespoons baking powder	

In mixing bowl, cream shortening and butter with sugar. With electric mixer on medium speed slowly add eggs, beating well. Blend in sour cream. Add sifted flour, baking powder and baking soda to batter mixing well.

In a separate bowl, prepare filling by combining brown sugar, nuts, chocolate chips, cocoa and cinnamon.

Pour half the batter into 6 greased 10-inch loaf pans. Sprinkle half the filling over the batter. Pour remaining batter into pans and sprinkle remaining filling on top. In a 375-degree oven, bake loaves for 35 to 40 minutes. Loaves freeze well. Recipe may be cut in half for smaller yield.

Catskill Country Cooking
The Auxiliary of Community General Hospital, Connecticut

"Evening tasting parties were so much fun but when we were done, our spouses suggested we keep the parties going by retesting all the recipes before the book goes to reprint."

STEPHANIE PRADE
HERBAL COOKERY, ST LOUIS HERB SOCIETY

DECADENT CHOCOLATE AND TANGERINE MOUSSE CAKE

CHOCOLATE CAKE

Butter for coating
All-purpose flour for dusting
1 cup (2 sticks) unsalted butter
12 ounces semisweet chocolate

¾ cup sugar
5 eggs, lightly beaten
½ cup ground toasted hazelnuts
Vegetable oil for coating

Coat a 9-inch springform pan with butter and line the bottom with baking parchment. Dust the pan with flour. Melt 1 cup butter and chopped chocolate in a saucepan until blended, stirring occasionally. Remove from the heat and whisk in the sugar, eggs, and hazelnuts. Pour into the prepared pan. Bake for 45 minutes or until the cake tests done. Cool in the pan on a wire rack. Remove the side of the pan and invert the cake onto a hard work surface. Removing the baking parchment. Cut off the outer ½-inch edge of the cake, creating an 8-inch cake and reserving the cake trimmings. Rinse the springform pan and reattach the side. Coat the side with oil. Set the cake in the center of the pan and arrange the reserved cake trimmings on the top. Chill, covered.

TANGERINE MOUSSE AND ASSEMBLY

3 cups strained fresh tangerine juice
⅓ cup sugar
2 envelopes unflavored gelatin
3 tablespoons fresh lemon juice
12 ounces white chocolate, chopped
½ cup sour cream

2 cups whipping cream, chilled
3 ounces white chocolate, shaved
Baking cocoa for garnish
Fresh raspberries for garnish
Sprigs of mint for garnish
Tangerine slices for garnish

Bring the tangerine juice and sugar to a boil in a heavy saucepan and boil for 30 minutes or until reduced to 1½ cups. Sprinkle the gelatin over the lemon juice in a small bowl and let stand for 10 minutes or until softened. Add the gelatin mixture to the tangerine juice mixture and stir until dissolved. Stir in 12 ounces white chocolate and cook over low heat just until the chocolate melts, whisking constantly. Whisk in the sour cream. Pour the tangerine juice mixture into a large bowl and chill for 2 to 3 hours or until thickened but not set, whisking occasionally. Beat the cream in a mixing bowl until stiff peaks form. Fold into the tangerine juice mixture just until incorporated. Pour over the chilled cake, covering the top and side completely. Chill, covered, for 8 to 10 hours. Run a sharp knife around the side of the pan to loosen the cake. Remove the side of the pan and place the cake on a cake plate. Sprinkle the shaved white chocolate over the top of the cake and dust very lightly with baking cocoa. You may cover and chill at this point for up to 1 day. Garnish with raspberries, sprigs of mint and/or tangerine slices.

California Mosaic
Junior League of Pasadena, California

MISSISSIPPI MUD CAKE

CAKE

1 cup butter	Pinch salt
½ cup cocoa	1½ cups nuts, chopped
2 cups sugar	1 teaspoon vanilla
4 eggs, slightly beaten	Miniature marshmallows
1½ cups self-rising flour	Chocolate Frosting

Melt butter and cocoa together on low heat. Remove from heat and stir in sugar and beaten eggs. Mix well. Add flour, salt, nuts and vanilla. Mix well. Spoon batter into a greased and floured 13×9×2-inch pan. Bake at 350 degrees for 35 to 45 minutes. Sprinkle marshmallows on top of hot cake. Cover with chocolate frosting.

CHOCOLATE FROSTING

1 (1-pound) box confectioners' sugar
½ cup whole milk
½ cup cocoa
½ stick butter

Combine sugar, milk, cocoa and soft butter. Mix until smooth and spread on hot cake.

Yesterday, Today & Tomorrow
The Baddour Center,
Senatobia, Mississippi

> "One of many food memories I have of my grandmother, Big Mama, is of the melt-in-your-mouth Mississippi Mud Cake that could be found at most family gatherings. I loved the sticky marshmallows, the rich chocolate cake, and the fudgy thin icing—it was and still is a favorite with young and old. This recipe is the closest I have found to the one of my childhood."

Sheila Thomas
Executive Editor, *More Recipes Worth Sharing*

FRP Family Favorites

Mochaccino Cake

1 package devil's food cake mix

3 eggs

1 cup water

½ cup heavy whipping cream

¼ cup vegetable oil

2 tablespoons baking cocoa

2 tablespoons instant coffee powder

1 cup miniature chocolate chips

2 tablespoons heavy whipping cream

2 tablespoons instant coffee powder

2 (16-ounce) containers vanilla frosting

Preheat oven to 350 degrees. Combine cake mix, eggs, water, ½ cup heavy cream, oil, baking cocoa and 2 tablespoons coffee powder in a bowl. Beat with an electric mixer at low speed until blended. Beat at medium speed for 2 minutes. Stir in the chocolate chips. Pour into 2 greased and floured 9-inch cake pans.

Bake for 25 to 30 minutes or until a wooden pick inserted in the center comes out clean. Cool in the pans for 20 minutes. Remove to a wire rack to cool completely.

Mix 2 tablespoons heavy cream and 2 tablespoons coffee powder in a bowl. Add the vanilla frosting and stir to mix well. Spread between the layers and over the top and side of the cake.

Par 3 Tea Time at the Masters®
Junior League of Augusta, Georgia

Southern Peach Cake

½ cup butter, melted

1 cup sugar

2 eggs, beaten

2 tablespoon milk

1½ cups flour

1½ teaspoons baking powder

¾ cup sugar

2 teaspoons flour

¾ teaspoon cinnamon

3 cups sliced peaches

Preheat the oven to 350 degrees. Beat the butter, sugar, and eggs in a medium bowl until well blended. Add the milk; blend well. Add 1½ cups flour mixed with baking powder; mix well. Pour into a greased 9×13-inch cake pan. Combine ¾ cup sugar, 2 teaspoons flour and cinnamon in a small bowl. Sprinkle half the mixture over the batter. Sprinkle peaches with the remaining cinnamon mixture. Arrange peach slices on top. Bake at 350 degrees for 45 to 50 minutes or until the cake tests done. Serve warm with whipped topping or ice cream.

Sweet Home Alabama
Junior League of Huntsville, Alabama

CINDERELLA PUMPKIN CAKE

CAKE

2 cups sugar

4 large eggs

1 cup vegetable oil

2 cups flour

2 teaspoons baking soda

Cinnamon to taste

2 teaspoons salt

2 cups canned pumpkin

To prepare the cake, combine the sugar and eggs in a mixing bowl and beat until pale yellow and thick. Beat in the vegetable oil. Add the flour, baking soda, cinnamon and salt and mix well. Stir in the pumpkin. Spoon the batter into a greased bundt pan. Bake at 350 degrees for 45 to 55 minutes or until the cake tests done. Cool in the pan for 5 minutes; then remove to a wire rack to cool completely.

CREAMY FROSTING

3 ounces cream cheese, softened

½ cup butter, softened (1 stick)

1 package confectioners' sugar (1 pound)

1 teaspoon vanilla extract

To prepare the frosting, combine the cream cheese and butter in a mixing bowl and beat until creamy. Add the confectioners' sugar and vanilla and mix until smooth. Spread over the cooled cake.

Lone Star to Five Star
Junior League of Plano, Texas

STRAWBERRY CAKE

1 box white cake mix

3 tablespoons flour (heaping)

1 package strawberry gelatin

1 cup frozen sliced strawberries

1 cup salad oil

4 eggs

½ cup water

Mix cake mix, flour, and gelatin. Add oil. Beat in eggs. Add water and strawberries. Mix well. Bake in greased tube pan 35 to 40 minutes in 350 degree oven. Cool on a rack, then carefully remove cake from pan. When completely cool, spread with Strawberry Icing (at right).

STRAWBERRY ICING

½ stick butter

½ cup frozen sliced strawberries

2 cups powdered sugar

Melt butter with ½ cup strawberries. Mash in. Mix in the powdered sugar until spreading consistency. Spread on cooled cake.

River Road Recipes, The Textbook of Louisiana Cuisine
Junior League of Baton Rouge, Louisiana

RED VELVET CAKE WITH CREAM CHEESE FROSTING

SERVES 12

CAKE

4 ounces German's sweet chocolate

½ cup red food coloring (2 small bottles)

2½ cups flour

1 teaspoon baking soda

½ teaspoon salt

1 cup (2 sticks) butter, softened

2 cups sugar

4 egg yolks

1 teaspoon vanilla extract

1 cup buttermilk

4 egg whites, stiffly beaten

Cream Cheese Frosting

Melt the chocolate with the food coloring in a small saucepan. Sift the flour, baking soda and salt together. Cream the butter and sugar in a mixing bowl until light and fluffy. Add the egg yolks, vanilla and chocolate mixture and mix well. Add the flour mixture alternately with the buttermilk, beating well after each addition. Fold in the egg whites. Pour into 3 greased and floured 9-inch round cake pans. Bake at 350 degrees for 35 minutes or until the layers test done. Cool in the pans for 10 minutes. Invert onto wire racks to cool completely. Spread Cream Cheese Frosting between the layers and over the top and side of the cake.

CREAM CHEESE FROSTING

8 ounces cream cheese, softened

½ cup (1 stick) butter, softened

1 (1-pound) package confectioners' sugar

1 teaspoon vanilla extract

Milk

Beat the cream cheese, butter, confectioners' sugar and vanilla in a mixing bowl until smooth. Add enough milk 1 tablespoon at a time to make of the desired spreading consistency.

At Your Service
Junior League of Gwinnett and North Fulton Counties, Georgia

Mrs. Lincoln's White Cake

MAKES 1 (8- OR 9-INCH) LAYER CAKE

Cake

1 cup butter

2 cups sugar

3 cups cake flour

2 teaspoons baking powder

1 cup milk

1 teaspoon vanilla

1 teaspoon almond extract

1 cup chopped blanched almonds

6 egg whites

¼ teaspoon salt

Cream butter and sugar until light and fluffy. Sift together flour and baking powder; remove 2 tablespoons and set aside. Add sifted ingredients, alternating with milk, to creamed mixture. Stir in vanilla and almond extract. Combine almonds with reserved flour and add to batter.

Beat egg whites until stiff; add in salt. Fold into batter. Pour into 3 greased and floured 8- or 9-inch cake pans. Bake at 350 degrees until cake tester comes out clean, 20 to 25 minutes. Cool for 5 to 10 minutes; remove from pans and cool on racks. Frost.

Frosting

2 cups sugar

1 cup water

2 egg whites

⅓ cup chopped candied cherries

½ cup chopped candied pineapple

Five drops vanilla or almond extract

Combine sugar and water in a saucepan, stirring until sugar is dissolved. Bring to a boil; cover and cook about 3 minutes until the steam has washed down any sugar crystals that may have formed on side of pan. Uncover and cook until syrup reaches 238 to 240 degrees.

Whip egg whites until frothy, pour in syrup in thin stream, whipping egg whites constantly until frosting is spreading consistency. Add cherries, pineapple and flavoring.

Honest to Goodness
Junior League of Springfield, Illinois

Vanilla-Mocha Café Cake

2 eggs, lightly beaten
½ cup canola oil
1 cup plain yogurt
1 cup cooled brewed black coffee
2 teaspoons Nielsen-Massey Madagascar
   Bourbon Pure Vanilla Extract
2 teaspoons Nielsen-Massey Pure
   Coffee Extract

1 teaspoon Nielsen-Massey Pure
   Chocolate Extract
2 cups sugar
1-¾ cups all-purpose flour
¾ cup unsweetened cocoa
2 teaspoons baking soda
½ teaspoon salt

Preheat the oven to 350 degrees. Coat a 12-cup bundt pan with nonstick cooking spray. Beat the eggs, canola oil, yogurt, coffee, vanilla extract, coffee extract and chocolate extract in a mixing bowl using an electric mixer on low speed. Add the sugar, flour, cocoa, baking soda and salt. Beat on medium speed for 2 minutes; the batter will be thin. Pour the batter into the prepared cake pan. Bake for 35 to 40 minutes or until the cake tests done. Cool in the pan on a wire rack for 15 minutes. Invert onto a serving platter. Serve with Nielsen-Massey's Cherries Jubilee Sauce.

NIELSEN-MASSEY'S CHERRIES JUBILEE SAUCE   MAKES ABOUT 5 CUPS

2 (21-ounce) cans sweet cherries in
   heavy syrup
¼ cup brandy
¼ cup firmly packed dark brown sugar

1 teaspoon Nielsen-Massey Pure
   Chocolate Extract
2 teaspoons Nielsen-Massey Tahitian Pure
   Vanilla Extract

Combine the cherries, brandy, brown sugar, chocolate extract, and vanilla extract in a large sauté pan. Cook over medium heat for 8 to 10 minutes or until the sauce thickens. Serve over Vanilla-Mocha Café Cake.

A Century of Flavor
Nielsen-Massey Vanillas,
Waukegan, Illinois

Each January as part of FRP's National Meeting, the award-winning cookbooks from the previous year are announced and lunch will often consist of recipes from the winning cookbooks. This cake from *A Century of Flavors*, which celebrates the 100th anniversary of Nielsen-Massey Vanillas, was the perfect choice for a recent luncheon, which was also a surprise 50th birthday party for Mary Margaret Andrews, Director of Marketing and Distribution. This beautiful, scrumptious cake was the highlight of the day.

CREAM CHEESE POUND CAKE

VARIABLE SERVINGS

3 sticks margarine

1 (8-ounce) package cream cheese

3 cups sugar

1½ dashes salt

1½ teaspoons vanilla extract

½ teaspoon butter flavoring

6 large eggs, unbeaten

3 cups sifted plain or cake flour

Cream margarine, cream cheese and sugar until light and fluffy. Add salt, vanilla and butter flavoring; beat well. Add eggs, one at a time, beating well after each addition. Stir in flour. Spoon mixture into well greased and floured 10 inch tube pan or bundt pan. Bake 1½ hours at 325 degrees. This makes a large, very moist cake.

Dining with Pioneers, Volume 1
AT&T Pioneers, Tennessee Chapter 21

SOUR CREAM POUND CAKE

SERVES 12

1 cup butter

3 cups sugar

6 eggs, separated

¼ teaspoon baking soda

3 cups sifted flour

½ pint sour cream

Cream butter and sugar thoroughly. Add egg yolks one at a time. Add baking soda to flour. Alternately add flour and sour cream to creamed mixture. Beat egg whites stiff and fold in. Bake in large tube pan, greased and floured, at 300 for 1½ to 2 hours, or until a toothpick inserted in center of cake comes out clean. Should have nice brown crust on top. Let stand 15 minutes before taking out of pan. No flavoring needed. The longer you keep this cake the more moist it gets!

The Gasparilla Cookbook
Junior League of Tampa, Florida

The Junior League of Tampa works with Connected by 25, a nonprofit organization which serves young adults ages 18 to 25 who have aged out of the foster care system. Our volunteers assist this agency with preparing foster children ages 13 to 17 for adulthood and life after foster care. We also sponsor sibling events to allow the 18- to 25-year-olds to reconnect with their younger siblings who have been living with different families. The youth summit includes speakers and training on life skills not typically available to children in foster care. The Junior League of Tampa also provides 100 move-in kits filled with essential items for making the transition into a first residence.

WHIPPED CREAM POUND CAKE

½ pound butter or margarine

2½ cups sugar

6 eggs

3 cups sifted cake flour

½ pint whipping cream

1 teaspoon vanilla extract

Cream butter and sugar. After adding one egg at a time, beating 1 minute after each, reduce speed of mixer and add flour and cream (not whipped) alternately. Add vanilla extract. Pour into greased, lined tube pan. Put into cold oven and bake at 275 degrees to 300 degrees for 1 hour without opening the door. Then turn the cake around and cook 20 minutes more or until done.

A Taste of Georgia
Newnan Junior Service League, Georgia

LIME-GLAZED POUND CAKE

3¼ cups cake flour

¼ teaspoon baking soda

¼ teaspoon salt

8 ounces cream cheese, softened

1 cup (2 sticks) plus 2 tablespoons unsalted
   butter, softened

3 cups sugar

6 eggs, at room temperature

3 tablespoons fresh lime juice,
   at room temperature

1 teaspoon vanilla extract

2 teaspoons finely grated lime zest

¾ cup sugar

¼ cup fresh lime juice, at room temperature

Position the oven rack in the lower third of the oven. Sift the cake flour, baking soda and salt together. Beat the cream cheese and butter in a mixing bowl at medium speed for 30 to 40 seconds or until creamy and smooth. Add 3 cups sugar and beat for 5 minutes or until light and fluffy, scraping the bowl occasionally. Add the eggs one at a time, beating well after each addition. Beat in 3 tablespoons lime juice and the vanilla until blended. Add the flour mixture one-third at a time, beating constantly at low speed just until smooth after each addition and scraping the bowl occasionally. Fold in the lime zest.

Spread the batter in a greased and floured tube pan, mounding the outside side of the batter higher than the center side. Bake in a preheated 325-degree oven for 1 hour and 30 minutes or until golden brown. Cool in the pan on a wire rack for 10 minutes. Remove to a wire rack. Whisk ¾ cup sugar and ¼ cup lime juice in a bowl until the sugar dissolves. Brush over the top and side of the warm cake.

Excellent Courses, A Culinary Legacy of Ravenscroft
Ravenscroft School, Raleigh, North Carolina

CHOCOLATE CHIP CUPCAKES

CUPCAKES

1½ cups cake flour

1 cup sugar

1 teaspoon baking soda

½ teaspoon salt

½ cup unsweetened baking cocoa

½ cup oil

1 cup water

1 teaspoon vanilla extract

1 tablespoon white distilled vinegar

Topping (below)

Preheat the oven to 350 degrees. Sift together the cake flour, sugar, baking soda, salt and baking cocoa in a medium bowl. Add the oil, water, vanilla and vinegar and mix well.

Place paper baking cups inside muffin tins. Fill each cup ⅓ full with batter. Top with a rounded tablespoonful of Topping. Bake for 18 to 23 minutes.

Note: You may top each cupcake with sliced almonds before baking. These cupcakes freeze well. They are perfect for a picnic.

TOPPING

8 ounces cream cheese

1 egg

½ cup sugar

Dash of salt

6 ounces semisweet chocolate chips

Combine the cream cheese, egg, sugar and salt in a small bowl. Stir in the chocolate chips. Set aside.

California Sizzles
Junior League of Pasadena, California

Chocolate Mint Dessert

4 ounces chocolate

1 cup (2 sticks) butter

2 cups confectioners' sugar

4 eggs

2 teaspoons vanilla extract

3/4 teaspoon peppermint extract

2 cups graham cracker crumbs

1/2 cup finely chopped walnuts

Melt the chocolate with the butter in a saucepan, stirring to blend well. Blend in the confectioners' sugar. Let stand until cool. Beat the mixture until light and fluffy. Beat in the eggs one at a time. Add the vanilla and peppermint extract and mix well. Sprinkle some of the graham cracker crumbs into paper-lined muffin cups. Spoon the chocolate mixture into the cups and sprinkle with the remaining graham cracker crumbs and the walnuts. Freeze until firm or for up to 1 week. Remove to the refrigerator 30 minutes before serving. Peel off the paper liners and place the desserts on a serving tray. Garnish with a dollop of whipped cream.

Note: If you are concerned about using uncooked eggs, use eggs pasteurized in their shells, which are sold at some specialty food stores, or use an equivalent amount of pasteurized egg substitute.

The Bells Are Ringing
Mission San Juan Capistrano Women's Guild, California

Black Bottom Cups

8 ounces cream cheese

1/3 cup sugar

1 egg

1/8 teaspoon salt

1 cup (6 ounces) semisweet chocolate chips

1 1/2 cups flour

1 cup sugar

1/4 cup baking cocoa

1 teaspoon baking soda

1/2 teaspoon salt

1 cup water

1 cup vegetable oil

1 tablespoon vinegar

1 teaspoon vanilla extract

Beat the cream cheese, 1/3 cup sugar, egg and 1/8 teaspoon salt in a mixing bowl until blended. Stir in the chocolate chips. Sift the flour, 1 cup sugar, baking cocoa, baking soda and 1/2 teaspoon salt in a mixing bowl and mix well. Add the water, oil, vinegar and vanilla and beat until blended.

Fill muffin cups 1/3 full with the chocolate batter and top each with 1 heaping teaspoonful of the cream cheese mixture. Bake at 350 degrees for 30 to 35 minutes.

Home Again, Home Again
Junior League of Owensboro, Kentucky

Biscotti alla Rose Marie

1 cup margarine, softened
1³/4 cups sugar
6 eggs

1 ounce anise flavoring
4 cups flour
6 teaspoons baking powder

In a mixer, cream margarine and sugar. Add eggs and anise flavoring; continue to beat for 1 or 2 minutes. Mix flour and baking powder. Add flour to eggs and beat on low speed until well blended.

Dough will be a firm cake batter consistency. Divide the dough into 4 portions and place on a baking sheet. Shape each portion into a loaf using two knives. Bake at 325 degrees for 25 minutes until a light tan in color. Loaves will be cooked but soft.

Remove carefully with a spatula and cut into ³/4-inch-diagonal slices. Return to a 350-degree oven and bake slices to a golden brown. Biscotti will keep for several weeks in a tightly closed metal can lined with paper towel.

Preserving Our Italian Heritage
Sons of Italy Florida Foundation, Tampa, Florida

Care Package Almond Bars

1 package yellow cake mix
½ cup (1 stick) butter, melted
3 large eggs
1 teaspoon vanilla extract

8 ounces cream cheese, softened
1 (1-pound) package confectioners' sugar
4 ounces sliced almonds

Preheat the oven to 350 degrees. Beat the cake mix, butter and 1 of the eggs in a large bowl to form a soft dough. Spread in a greased 9×13-inch baking pan. Combine the remaining 2 eggs, vanilla, cream cheese and confectioners' sugar in a mixing bowl and beat for 3 minutes. Spread over the dough. Bake for 15 minutes. Sprinkle the almonds over the top. Bake for 30 minutes longer or until firm. Cut into bars while warm.

My Mama Made That
Junior League of Hampton Roads, Virginia

"I made these for a party, and I had four people ask for the recipe immediately. These are delicious!"

Jennifer Kennedy,
FRP Marketing Coordinator

FRP Family Favorites

CHOCOLATE MINT BROWNIES

BROWNIES

4 eggs

2 cups sugar

1 cup flour

1 cup baking cocoa

1 cup (2 sticks) margarine, melted

1 teaspoon vanilla extract

1/2 teaspoon peppermint extract

For the brownies, whisk the eggs in a bowl until blended. Stir in the sugar. Add a mixture of the flour and baking cocoa gradually, mixing well after each addition. Stir in the margarine and flavorings. Spoon the batter into a greased and floured 9×13-inch baking pan. Bake at 350 degrees for 20 to 30 minutes. Let stand until cool.

MINT CREAM FROSTING

1/4 cup (1/2 stick) margarine, softened

2-3/4 cups sifted confectioners' sugar

2 to 3 tablespoons milk

1 teaspoon peppermint extract

3 or 4 drops of green food coloring

For the frosting, beat the margarine in a mixing bowl until creamy. Add the confectioners' sugar gradually and beat until light and fluffy. Add the milk. Beat until of a spreading consistency. Stir in the flavoring and food coloring. Spread over the brownies. Freeze for 15 minutes.

CHOCOLATE TOPPING

3 ounces unsweetened chocolate

3 tablespoons margarine

For the topping, heat the chocolate and margarine in a saucepan over low heat until blended, stirring constantly. Spread over the prepared layers. Chill until firm. Cut into squares. Store, covered, in the refrigerator.

Sweet Pickin's
Junior League of Fayetteville, North Carolina

Espresso Chocolate Walnut Brownies

¾ cup chopped walnuts

¾ cup all-purpose flour

¼ cup baking cocoa

¾ teaspoon baking powder

¼ teaspoon kosher salt

2 tablespoons finely ground espresso beans

3 ounces unsweetened chocolate,
    finely chopped

¾ cup unsalted butter, softened (1½ sticks)

1½ cups sugar

3 large eggs, lightly beaten

1 tablespoon vanilla extract

Toast the walnuts in a single layer on baking sheet in a preheated 350-degree oven for 6 to 8 minutes or until lightly browned. Cool completely. Sift the flour, baking cocoa, baking powder and salt together into a small bowl. Stir in the ground espresso beans. Melt the chocolate and butter in a double boiler over simmering water, stirring until smooth. Remove from the heat and stir in the sugar. Beat in the eggs and vanilla. Add the flour mixture and stir just until mixed. Stir in the toasted walnuts. Pour into a 9×13-inch baking pan lined with foil and sprayed with nonstick cooking spray. Bake in a preheated 350-oven for 30 to 35 minutes or until a crust forms and the center is still moist. Cool in the pan on a wire rack. Chill for 2 hours. Cut into small bars.

Peeling the Wild Onion A Collection of Chicago Culinary Culture
Junior League of Chicago, Illinois

Chocolate Chip Bars

2 cups all-purpose flour

1 teaspoon baking powder

½ teaspoon salt

¼ teaspoon baking soda

⅔ cup margarine, softened

2 cups packed brown sugar

2 eggs

2 teaspoons vanilla extract

2 cups (12 ounces) semisweet chocolate chips

2 cups pecans, chopped

Preheat the oven to 350 degrees. Sift the flour, baking powder, salt and baking soda together. Beat the margarine in a mixing bowl until creamy. Add the brown sugar gradually, beating constantly until fluffy. Bet in the eggs and vanilla until blended. Mix in the dry ingredients. Fold in the chocolate chips and pecans. Spread the batter in a greased 9×13-inch baking pan. Bake for 25 minutes. Cool in the pan on a wire rack. Cut into bars. Store in an airtight container.

Texas Tables
Junior League of North Harris and South Montgomery Counties, Texas

ℒUSCIOUS LEMON BARS

SERVES 32

2 cups all-purpose flour

⅛ teaspoon kosher salt

1 cup (2 sticks) unsalted butter, softened

½ cup granulated sugar

6 extra-large eggs, at room temperature

3 cups granulated sugar

2 tablespoons lemon zest
   (zest from 4 to 6 lemons)

1 cup fresh lemon juice

1 cup all-purpose flour

Confectioners' sugar for dusting

Preheat the oven to 350 degrees. Mix 2 cups flour and the kosher salt together in a bowl. Cream the butter and ½ cup granulated sugar in a mixing bowl until light and fluffy. Add the flour mixture and mix with a pastry blender or two round-bladed knives until small crumbs form. Press in a lightly greased 9×13-inch baking pan, being careful to not allow any cracks in the dough. Bake for 15 to 20 minutes or until the crust is light golden brown. Remove to a wire rack to cool. Maintain the oven temperature.

Whisk the eggs, 3 cups granulated sugar, the lemon zest, lemon juice and 1 cup flour in a bowl. Pour evenly over the crust. Bake for 30 to 35 minutes or until the filling is set but not brown. Remove from the oven and cool to room temperature. Cut into bars and dust with confectioners' sugar. Chill until ready to serve.

Note: An alternative method is to cream the butter and sugar with the paddle attachment of an electric mixer in a mixing bowl. Add the flour mixture and mix well. Shape the dough into a ball and flatten the dough with floured hands. Press into the prepared pan.

Sunny Days, Balmy Nights
The Young Patronesses of
the Opera, Coral Gables,
Florida

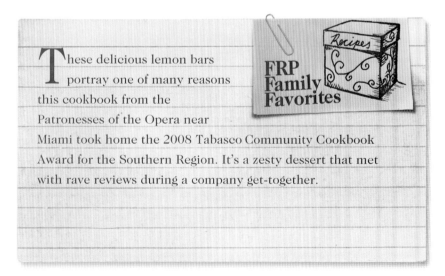

These delicious lemon bars portray one of many reasons this cookbook from the Patronesses of the Opera near Miami took home the 2008 Tabasco Community Cookbook Award for the Southern Region. It's a zesty dessert that met with rave reviews during a company get-together.

# Zebra Bars

BROWNIES

¾ cup (1½ sticks) butter

6 ounces unsweetened chocolate

4 large eggs

4 teaspoons orange-flavored liqueur or orange extract

1 teaspoon vanilla extract

2 cups sugar

1 cup flour

Preheat the oven to 350 degrees. Heat the butter and chocolate in a small, heavy saucepan until melted, stirring constantly. Remove from the heat and allow to cool. Beat the eggs, liqueur and vanilla in a large bowl until thick and lemon-colored. Add the sugar gradually, beating until the mixture is light and fluffy. Stir in the flour until combined. Add the chocolate mixture. Spread in a greased 9×13-inch baking pan. Bake for 25 minutes. Remove from the oven and cool completely.

FROSTING

⅓ cup butter, softened

1⅔ cups confectioners' sugar

2 tablespoons orange-flavored liqueur or orange extract

½ teaspoon vanilla extract

Beat the butter in a small bowl until fluffy. Add the confectioners' sugar, liqueur and vanilla. Beat until smooth and creamy. Spread evenly over the cooled brownies.

GLAZE

1 ounce unsweetened chocolate

1 teaspoon butter

Combine the chocolate and butter in small, heavy saucepan. Melt over low heat, stirring constantly. Drizzle the glaze in a diagonal pattern over the frosted brownies. Cover with plastic wrap and refrigerate for 1 hour or until firm before cutting.

Simply Classic
Junior League of Seattle, Washington

White Chocolate with Raspberry Bars

1 cup (2 sticks) unsalted butter
4 cups white chocolate chips
4 eggs
1 cup sugar
2 cups flour

1 teaspoon salt
2¼ teaspoons almond extract
1 (10-ounce) jar seedless raspberry
 fruit spread, melted
½ cup sliced almonds

Melt the butter in a saucepan over low heat. Remove from the heat. Add 2 cups of the white chocolate chips; do not stir. Beat the eggs in a mixing bowl until foamy. Add the sugar gradually, beating at high speed until pale yellow. Stir in the white chocolate mixture. Add the flour, salt and almond extract. Beat at low speed until just combined. Spread half the batter in a greased and floured 9×13-inch baking pan.

Bake at 325 degrees for 15 to 20 minutes or until light brown. Spread the melted raspberry spread evenly over the baked layer. Stir the remaining 2 cups white chocolate chips into the remaining batter. Spoon gently over the fruit spread. Sprinkle with the almonds. Bake for 30 to 35 minutes or until light brown. Cool completely before cutting into bars.

Settings on the Dock of the Bay
Assistance League of the Bay Area, Houston, Texas

Carmelitas

1 (12-ounce) jar caramel sauce
4½ tablespoons all-purpose flour
1½ cups quick-cooking oats
1½ cups all-purpose flour
1¼ cups packed brown sugar

¾ teaspoon baking soda
⅓ teaspoon salt
1¼ cups (2½ sticks) butter, melted
1½ cups chocolate chips
1½ cups pecans, chopped

Mix the caramel sauce and 4½ tablespoons flour in a bowl and set aside. Combine the oats, 1½ cups flour, the brown sugar, baking soda, salt and butter in a bowl and stir to mix well. Press half the oat mixture in a 9×11-inch baking pan sprayed with nonstick cooking spray. Bake at 350 degrees for 10 minutes. Remove from the oven and sprinkle with the chocolate chips. Pour the caramel mixture over the chocolate chips. Cover with the pecans and sprinkle with the remaining oat mixture. Return to the oven and bake for 20 minutes. Let cool and cut into squares.

Now Serving
Junior League of Wichita Falls, Texas

GOLDEN "ROAD TRIP" BROWNIES

3 cups graham cracker crumbs

12 ounces semisweet chocolate chips

2 cans sweetened condensed milk

Preheat the oven to 350 degrees. Mix all the ingredients in a large bowl with a heavy wooden spoon. The mixture will be very thick. Spoon into a 9×13-inch baking pan generously sprayed with nonstick cooking spray. Cover with a piece of waxed paper, pressing lightly to even out the thick mixture. Bake for 40 to 45 minutes, watching near the end to make sure edges do not get too brown. Remove to a wire rack to cool for 5 to 10 minutes. Invert onto a wire rack until cool to the touch. Place on a cutting board and cut into squares. Store in an airtight container.

Note: If baking in a skillet, reduce the baking time to 30 minutes. These brownies freeze well and are best cooked in a skillet or metal baking pan. Do not use a glass baking dish. Do not bake anything else in the oven along with the brownies or they will not bake evenly.

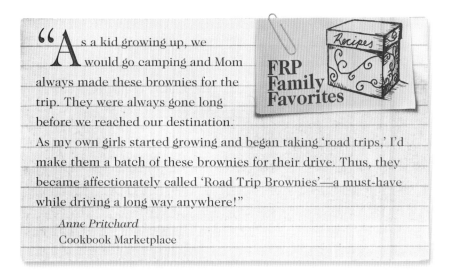

"As a kid growing up, we would go camping and Mom always made these brownies for the trip. They were always gone long before we reached our destination. As my own girls started growing and began taking 'road trips,' I'd make them a batch of these brownies for their drive. Thus, they became affectionately called 'Road Trip Brownies'—a must-have while driving a long way anywhere!"

FRP Family Favorites

Anne Pritchard
Cookbook Marketplace

PECAN DIAMONDS

1 cup (2 sticks) unsalted butter, softened	½ cup honey
⅔ cup confectioners' sugar	¾ cup packed brown sugar
1 medium egg	¼ cup granulated sugar
3 cups flour	3 tablespoons heavy cream
⅔ cup unsalted butter	4 cups pecans, coarsely chopped

Line a 9×13-inch baking dish with aluminum foil and butter the foil. Cream 1 cup butter and the confectioners' sugar in a mixing bowl until light and fluffy. Beat in the egg. Add the flour all at once. Beat at low speed until the dough is smooth and holds together. Press the dough into the prepared pan. Prick all over with a fork. Chill for 15 to 20 minutes. Bake at 375 degrees for 20 minutes or until slightly golden brown.

Melt ⅔ cup butter with the honey in a heavy saucepan. Add the brown sugar and granulated sugar. Bring to a boil. Boil for 1 minutes. Remove from the heat. Add the cream and pecans. Mix until the pecans are coated. Pour over the baked crust. Bake for 20 to 25 minutes. Let stand to cool completely. Lift from the dish using the foil edges and place on a cutting board. Cut into diamond shapes to the desired size. Store in an airtight container.

Fresh from the Pantry and Recipes for Every Day
The Longaberger Company, Newark, Ohio

> "This recipe is one of my favorite desserts to make. Even though it is a little time-consuming, it isn't hard to make and well worth the effort. When I take it to a get-together, there is never any left to take home!"
>
> *Cathy Ropp*
> FRP Project Coordinator

FRP Family Favorites

Best Cookies on Earth

1 cup (2 sticks) butter or margarine
3/4 cup packed light brown sugar
3/4 cup granulated sugar
1 egg
1 teaspoon vanilla extract

1 1/2 cups self-rising flour
1 1/2 cup oats
1 cup semisweet chocolate chips
1 cup chopped dried cranberries
1 (7.5-ounce) package toffee bits

Preheat oven to 350 degrees. Cream butter, brown sugar and granulated sugar in a mixing bowl. Add the egg and vanilla and mix well. Blend in the flour, oats, chocolate chips, cranberries and toffee bits. Drop by teaspoonfuls onto a greased baking sheet. Bake for 10 minutes. Cool slightly before removing to a wire rack. Store in an airtight container.

Under the Magnolias
Athens Academy, Athens, Georgia

Camelback Mountain Cookies

6 cups rolled oats
2 1/2 teaspoons baking soda
1 1/2 cups granulated sugar
1 1/2 cups packed brown sugar
1/2 cup (1 stick) butter or butter-flavor
    shortening, softened

4 medium eggs
1 teaspoon vanilla extract
19 ounces peanut butter
6 ounces chocolate chips

Preheat the oven to 375 degrees. Mix the oats and baking soda in a small bowl. Beat the granulated sugar, brown sugar and butter in a mixing bowl until creamy, scraping the bowl occasionally. Add the eggs and vanilla and beat until blended. Beat in the peanut butter until smooth. Add the oat mixture and beat until combined. Stir in the chocolate chips.

Drop by ice cream scoopfuls onto an ungreased cookie sheet. Bake for 10 to 13 minutes or until light brown and just barely set; do not overbake. Cool on the cookie sheet for 1 minute and then remove to a wire rack to cool completely. Store in an airtight container.

Note: For smaller cookies, bake for 8 to 10 minutes. You may freeze baked cookies for future use.

Pomegranates & Prickly Pears, flavorful entertaining from the Junior League of Phoenix
Junior League of Phoenix, Arizona

Hillary Clinton's Cookies

1 cup shortening
½ cup granulated sugar
1 cup packed light brown sugar
1 teaspoon vanilla extract
2 eggs

1½ cups flour
1 teaspoon baking soda
1 teaspoon salt
2 cups rolled oats
2 cups semisweet chocolate chips

Preheat the oven to 350 degrees. Cream the shortening, granulated sugar, brown sugar and vanilla in a large bowl until light and fluffy. Add the eggs and beat until smooth. Mix the flour, baking soda and salt together. Add to the creamed mixture gradually, mixing well after each addition. Stir in the oats and chocolate chips. Drop by rounded teaspoonfuls onto greased cookie sheets. Bake for 8 to 10 minutes or until golden brown. Cool on the cookie sheets for 2 minutes. Remove to a wire rack to cool completely.

Apron Strings
Junior League of Little Rock, Arkansas

Southwest Spiced Chocolate Chip Cookies

MAKES 4 TO 5 DOZEN COOKIES

½ cup shortening
½ cup (1 stick) butter, softened
½ cup granulated sugar
1 cup packed brown sugar
½ teaspoon baking soda
2 eggs
1 teaspoon vanilla extract
1 teaspoon cinnamon

¼ teaspoon nutmeg
⅛ teaspoon ground cloves
1 pinch of cayenne pepper (optional)
2½ cups all-purpose flour
8 ounces milk chocolate chips
½ cup pine nuts, toasted
½ cup sliced almonds

Cream the shortening and butter in a mixing bowl until light and fluffy. Add the granulated sugar, brown sugar and baking soda and beat well, scraping the side of the bowl occasionally. Beat in the eggs and vanilla. Beat in the cinnamon, nutmeg, cloves, cayenne pepper and flour. Stir in the chocolate chips, pine nuts and almonds. Chill the dough for 1 to 2 hours. Drop the dough by rounded teaspoonfuls 2 inches apart onto an ungreased cookie sheet. Bake in a preheated 375-degree oven for 8 to 10 minutes or until the edges are light brown. Remove to a wire rack to cool.

A Peak at the Springs
Junior League of Colorado Springs, Colorado

URBAN LEGEND COOKIES

2½ cups rolled oats

2 cups flour

1 teaspoon baking powder

1 teaspoon baking soda

½ teaspoon salt

1 cup (2 sticks) butter or margarine, softened

1 cup granulated sugar

1 cup packed brown sugar

2 eggs

1 teaspoon vanilla extract

2 cups (12 ounces) semisweet chocolate chips

4 ounces premium milk chocolate, grated

1½ cups pecans, finely chopped

Process the oats in a food processor or blender to form a fine powder. Mix the processed oats, flour, baking powder, baking soda and salt in a large bowl. Cream the butter, granulated sugar and brown sugar in a large mixing bowl until light and fluffy. Add the eggs one at a time, beating well after each addition. Add the vanilla and mix well. Stir in the flour mixture. Add the chocolate chips, milk chocolate and pecans and stir to mix well. Drop the dough by rounded teaspoonfuls onto ungreased cookie sheets. Bake at 375 degrees for 6 to 8 minutes or until golden brown. Remove to wire racks to cool.

At Your Service
Junior League of Gwinnett and North Fulton Counties, Georgia

FAMOUS "O" COOKIES

1 cup (2 sticks) butter or margarine, softened

1 cup granulated sugar

1 cup packed light brown sugar

2 eggs

1 cup chunky peanut butter

1½ cups flour

1 teaspoon baking soda

1 teaspoon baking powder

1 teaspoon vanilla extract

¼ teaspoon salt

2½ cups rolled oats

1 cup chocolate chips

Cream the butter, granulated sugar and brown sugar in a mixing bowl until light and fluffy. Add the eggs and mix well. Mix in the peanut butter. Add the flour, baking soda, baking powder, vanilla and salt and mix well. Stir in the oats and chocolate chips. Drop by rounded tablespoonfuls 2 inches apart onto an ungreased cookie sheet. Bake at 350 degrees for 10 to 12 minutes. The cookies will not appear to be done. Cool on a wire rack.

Note: For perfect 2½-inch cookies, use a medium cookie scoop that measures about 2 tablespoons.

Once Upon a Time
Junior League of Evansville, Indiana

FLORIDA ORANGE COOKIES

COOKIES

1 cup (2 sticks) butter	2 eggs
2 cups sugar	5 cups flour
4 ounces freshly squeezed orange juice	2 teaspoons baking powder
(about 1½ oranges)	1 teaspoon baking soda
2 tablespoons grated orange zest	1 cup buttermilk

Preheat the oven to 350 degrees. Cream the butter and sugar in a large bowl until light and fluffy. Add the orange juice and orange zest and mix well. Add the eggs and beat until blended. Combine the flour, baking powder and baking soda in a bowl. Add to the creamed mixture alternately with the buttermilk, mixing well after each addition. Drop the dough by ¼ cupfuls 1 inch apart onto a greased or parchment paper-lined cookie sheet. Bake for 14 minutes or until golden brown. Remove to a wire rack to cool completely.

Note: For smaller cookies, drop by teaspoonfuls and bake for 11 to 12 minutes.

ORANGE ICING

2 cups confectioners' sugar	3 tablespoons freshly squeezed orange juice
¼ cup (½ stick) butter, softened	1 teaspoon grated orange zest

Combine the confectioners' sugar, butter, orange juice and orange zest in a bowl and mix well, adding additional orange juice to reach the desired consistency. Spread over the cooled cookies.

EveryDay Feasts, Vol. 2, Culinary Collection
Junior League of Tampa, Florida

Mighty Molasses Cookies

2/3 cup cooking oil

1 cup sugar

1 egg

1/4 cup dark molasses

2 cups plus 2 tablespoons all-purpose flour

1 tablespoon ginger

2 teaspoons baking soda

1 teaspoon cinnamon

1/2 teaspoon salt

1/4 cup sugar

1/2 teaspoon cinnamon

Preheat the oven to 350 degrees. Combine the oil, 1 cup sugar, the egg and molasses in a large mixing bowl with an electric mixer on medium speed. Sift together the flour, ginger, baking soda, 1 teaspoon cinnamon and the salt together into a separate bowl. Add to the molasses mixture, beating well to combine. Refrigerate dough until firm.

Combine 1/4 cup sugar and 1/2 teaspoon cinnamon in a small mixing bowl. Form teaspoon-size balls of dough and roll in sugar-cinnamon mixture. Place on parchment paper-lined baking sheet and bake for 8 to 10 minutes. Cookies will flatten during baking.

Beyond the Hedges
Junior League of Athens, Georgia

Soft Gingersnaps

3/4 cup (1 1/2 sticks) butter, softened

2 cups sugar

2 eggs, beaten

1/2 cup molasses

2 teaspoons vinegar

3 3/4 cups all-purpose flour

1 1/2 teaspoons baking soda

1 tablespoon ginger

1 1/2 teaspoons cinnamon

1/4 teaspoon ground cloves

Cream the butter and sugar in a large mixing bowl. Add the eggs, molasses and vinegar and mix well. Add the flour, baking soda, ginger, cinnamon and cloves and mix well. Shape into 3/4- to 1-inch balls. Place 2 inches apart on a greased cookie sheet. Bake at 325 degrees for 11 to 13 minutes. Do not overbake. Cool on a wire rack. Store in an airtight container. The cookies will rise while baking and then fall when removed from the oven to give the traditional cracked top. A small cookie scoop works well for the desired cookie size.

Note: These cookies disappear so fast you will need to hide them.

Oh Shenandoah!
The Museum of the Shenandoah Valley, Virginia

Hawthorn Hill Coconut Macaroons

½ cup egg whites (about 4 large egg whites),
    at room temperature
1 cup sugar
2½ cups granulated coconut, or
    flaked coconut granulated in food processor or blender
1 teaspoon vanilla

Beat the egg whites until stiff peaks form when beaters are raised. Add the sugar very slowly with beaters at medium speed. Fold in the coconut carefully by hand. Drop by tablespoonfuls onto a nonstick cookie sheet or a cookie sheet lined with parchment paper. Bake in a preheated 325-degree oven for about 18 minutes or until light golden in color. Cool slightly before removing from cookie sheet with a stiff spatula.

Discover Dayton
Junior League of Dayton, Ohio

Mexican Wedding Cookies

MAKES 3 DOZEN COOKIES

1 cup (2 sticks) butter, softened
1 cup confectioners' sugar
2 cups sifted flour

1 cup ground nuts
1 teaspoon vanilla extract
Confectioners' sugar for coating

Beat the butter, 1 cup confectioners' sugar, the flour, nuts and vanilla together in a mixing bowl. Shape into 1½-inch balls. Place on a cookie sheet. Bake at 350 degrees for 10 to 15 minutes or until set. Roll in confectioners' sugar to coat.

A Taste of Enchantment
Junior League of Albuquerque, New Mexico

Potato Chip Cookies

2 cups firmly packed brown sugar, or
    1 cup packed brown sugar and
    1 cup granulated sugar
1 cup (2 sticks) butter, softened
2 eggs
2 cups flour

1 teaspoon baking soda
1 teaspoon vanilla extract
1 cup crushed potato chips
1 cup chopped nuts (optional)
1 cup semisweet chocolate chips or milk
    chocolate chips

Cream the brown sugar, butter and eggs in a mixing bowl until light and fluffy. Stir in the flour, baking soda and vanilla and mix well. Add the potato chips, nuts and chocolate chips and mix well. Drop by teaspoonfuls onto nonstick cookie sheets. Bake at 350 degrees for 10 to 12 minutes or until brown.

Beyond Burlap
Junior League of Boise, Idaho

Snickerdoodles

2 cups all-purpose flour
2 teaspoons cream of tartar
1 teaspoon baking soda
¼ teaspoon salt
1 cup (2 sticks) unsalted butter, softened

1½ cups sugar
2 large eggs
¼ cup sugar
5 teaspoons cinnamon

Preheat the oven to 350 degrees. Grease several cookie sheets. Sift together the flour, cream of tartar, baking soda and salt in a medium bowl. Beat together the butter and 1½ cups sugar in a separate bowl until well blended. Add the eggs, beating until well incorporated. Add the flour mixture to the butter mixture gradually, beating until well mixed and smooth after each addition. Combine ¼ cup sugar with the cinnamon in a small bowl. Pull off pieces of the dough and roll between the palms to form generous 1¼-inch balls. Roll the balls in the cinnamon-sugar mixture. Space about 2¾ inches apart on the cookie sheets. Bake one sheet at a time in the upper third of the oven for 8 to 11 minutes or until the cookies are light golden brown around the edges. Rotate the sheets halfway through baking for even browning. Remove the sheets to wire racks and let stand for 1 to 2 minutes or until the cookies firm up slightly. Remove the cookies to wire racks to cool completely. Be sure to cool the cookie sheets between batches or the cookies may spread too much. Store the cooled cookies in an airtight container for up to 10 days or freeze for up to 1 month.

Dancing on the Table
Junior League of Wilmington, Delaware

RALINE PECAN BITES

1 cup packed brown sugar
½ cup bread flour
⅔ cup butter

2 large beaten eggs
½ cup chopped pecans

Mix together brown sugar and flour. Mix together in a separate bowl pre-softened butter, beaten eggs and pecans. Add pecan mixture to flour mixture until just mixed. Pour into mini-muffin pan and bake at 350 degrees for 15 minutes.

Marshes to Mansions
Junior League of Lake Charles, Louisiana

RIGADEIROS

MAKES 1 DOZEN

1 (14-ounce) can sweetened condensed milk
2 tablespoons baking cocoa
1 tablespoon butter
Sugar, sprinkles or another decorative coating

Combine the condensed milk, baking cocoa and butter in a medium saucepan. Cook for 20 minutes over low heat to 234 to 240 degrees on a candy thermometer, soft-ball stage, stirring frequently and gently. Pour onto a buttered platter and let cool to room temperature. Shape into small 1-inch balls and roll in sugar, sprinkles or another decorative coating.

Note: Kids enjoy helping make this beloved Brazilian treat, traditionally served in little paper cups or miniature baking cups. They are very sweet and have a unique caramel chocolate flavor. Store these chocolates in the refrigerator.

Sunny Days, Balmy Nights
The Young Patronesses of the Opera, Coral Gables, Florida

KENTUCKY BOURBON BALLS

3¼ cups powdered sugar
½ cup butter, softened
8 teaspoons 100-proof Kentucky bourbon
¾ cup chopped pecans
1 to 1½ pounds semi-sweet chocolate chips

Cream sugar, butter, and bourbon until smooth. Add nuts and mix well. Form into ¾-inch balls. Add additional sugar if balls are too soft. Place on metal tray and chill for 1 to 1½ hours. Melt chocolate chips in top of double boiler over hot water. Bring just to boiling, stirring slowly. Remove from heat and cool until warm. Keep warm while dipping candies. Dip balls in chocolate and cool on foil. Refrigerate when cool.

To Market, To Market
Junior League of Owensboro, Kentucky

OLD FORESTER BOURBON BALLS

5 cups vanilla wafer crumbs
2 cups confectioners' sugar
¼ cup baking cocoa
2 cups chopped pecans
6 tablespoons light corn syrup
1 cup Old Forester bourbon
Confectioners' sugar for coating

Combine the cookie crumbs, 2 cups confectioners' sugar, baking cocoa and nuts in a bowl and mix with a large spoon. Add the corn syrup and bourbon and mix well. Shape into small balls and roll in additional confectioners' sugar, coating well. Store in the refrigerator or freezer.

Splendor in the Bluegrass
Junior League of Louisville, Kentucky

Bess's Signature Coconut Balls

2/3 cup sweetened condensed milk

1/8 teaspoon salt

1 teaspoon vanilla extract

1/4 teaspoon almond extract

1 1/2 cups coconut

Combine the condensed milk, salt, vanilla and almond extracts in a bowl and mix well. Stir in the coconut. Shape into 18 balls. Place 2 inches apart on a greased cookie sheet. Bake at 350 degrees for 15 minutes or until lightly browned.

If You Can't Stand the Heat, Get Out of the Kitchen
Junior Service League of Independence, Missouri

No-Bake Irish Coffee Balls

3 tablespoons instant coffee granules

1/3 cup Irish whiskey

3 1/2 cups vanilla wafer crumbs

1 cup pecans, finely chopped

1 1/2 cups confectioners' sugar, sifted

1/3 cup light corn syrup

Dissolve the coffee granules in the whiskey in a small cup. Mix the wafer crumbs, pecans and 1 cup of the confectioners' sugar in a large bowl. Add the whiskey mixture and corn syrup and mix well. Shape into 1-inch balls. Roll in the remaining 1/2 cup confectioners' sugar to coat. Store in an airtight container.

My Mama Made That
Junior League of Hampton Roads, Newport News, Virginia

CRISPY KALEIDOSCOPE EGGS

3 tablespoons butter
2½ cups crisp rice cereal
2 cups fruit-flavored cereal rings

3 cups miniature marshmallows
½ cup jelly beans

Place the butter in a large microwave-safe bowl. Microwave on High for 1 minute or until melted. Add the rice cereal, cereal rings, marshmallows and jelly beans. Microwave for 1 minute. Stir gently to mix without crushing the cereal. Cool for 2 minutes or until easy to handle. Butter your hands well and shape ¼ cup of the mixture at a time into the shape of an egg. Place on a serving plate. The mixture will stay moldable for about 10 minutes.

Pull Up a Chair
Junior League of Columbus, Georgia

ALMOND CRUNCH

MAKES 2 DOZEN

1 cup (2 sticks) butter
1¼ cups sugar
2 tablespoons corn syrup

2 tablespoons water
1 cup slivered almonds, toasted
2 cups (12 ounces) milk chocolate chips

Combine the butter, sugar, corn syrup and water in a heavy saucepan. Cook over medium heat to 300 degrees on a candy thermometer, brittle stage, stirring constantly. If you are not using a candy thermometer, take a spoon and drip one or two drops of the candy mixture into a glass of cold water. Feel the mixture in the water; if it is brittle it is ready. If it is still pliable, the mixture needs to cook longer. Watch for the color of the mixture to go from the original light yellow butter color to a tan caramel color, resembling the color of a baseball glove. Do not allow to become dark brown as this means it has burned.

Remove from the heat and quickly stir in the almonds. Immediately pour into a 9×11-inch heatproof dish or baking sheet lined with buttered foil. Sprinkle with the chocolate chips. Let stand for 5 minutes or until the chocolate is shiny and soft. Spread evenly over the toffee layer. Let stand until room temperature and then chill for 1 hour. Lift the candy out of the dish and remove the foil. Break into 1½-inch pieces. Store in an airtight container.

Excellent Courses, A Culinary Legacy of Ravenscroft
Ravenscroft School, Raleigh, North Carolina

BENNE (SESAME) BRITTLE

VARIABLE SERVINGS

2 cups granulated sugar
1 teaspoon vanilla extract
2 cups parched benne seeds

Melt the sugar in a heavy frying pan or saucepan over a low heat, stirring constantly. When sugar is melted, remove from stove and add vanilla and benne seeds quickly. Pour into a well-buttered pan to about ¼-inch depth (a medium-size biscuit pan is right.) Mark into squares while warm and break along lines when cold.

Charleston Receipts
Junior League of Charleston, South Carolina

CARAMEL CANDY

VARIABLE SERVINGS

1 teaspoon soda
1 cup buttermilk
2 tablespoons white corn syrup
2 cups sugar
1 cup chopped pecans
1 teaspoon vanilla
⅛ teaspoon salt
1 tablespoon butter

Add soda to buttermilk in heavy iron skillet. Add corn syrup and sugar and mix thoroughly. Cook, stirring constantly, until soft ball forms in water. Set aside to cool. Add pecans, vanilla, salt and butter. Drop by teaspoon on waxed paper.

Well Seasoned
Les Passees, Memphis, Tennessee

CRACKER CANDIES

1 sleeve saltine crackers
1 cup sugar
1 cup (2 sticks) butter
2 cups (12 ounces) milk chocolate chips

1 (10-ounce) package peanut butter chips
¾ cup toffee chips
¾ cup chopped pecans
¾ cup shredded coconut (optional)

Line a rimmed baking sheet with baking parchment. Arrange the crackers in a single layer on the prepared baking sheet to completely cover the baking sheet. Combine the sugar and butter in a saucepan and cook until melted and smooth, stirring frequently. Pour evenly over the crackers. Bake at 350 degrees for 12 to 14 minutes or until bubbly. Remove from the oven and sprinkle with chocolate chips, peanut butter chips, toffee chips, pecans and coconut evenly on top. Cover with a sheet of waxed paper and lightly press the toppings into the hot butter mixture. Chill in the refrigerator until firm. Remove the waxed paper and break the candy into pieces.

A Thyme to Entertain—Menus & Traditions of Annapolis
Junior League of Annapolis, Maryland

AUNT MARTHA B'S CHRISTMAS FUDGE

1 (24-ounce) package semisweet
  chocolate morsels
1½ cups butter
4 cups sugar

1 (13-ounce) can evaporated milk
3 tablespoons vanilla
2 cups crushed pecans

Line 17×11-inch jelly roll pan with wax paper. Place morsels and butter in medium glass mixing bowl and set aside. Bring sugar and milk to boil. Continue to boil for 6 minutes, stirring constantly and reducing heat to prevent boiling over. Pour over morsels and butter. Add vanilla and beat to thick consistency 5 to 10 minutes. Add nuts and pour into jelly roll pan. Refrigerate overnight. Cut into small squares. Store in refrigerator.

Full Moon-High Tide
Beaufort Academy, South Carolina

"Night on the Town," sponsored by Mainstreet Beaufort, USA, falls on the first Friday in December and kicks off a month of festive downtown shopping and free parking! On Sunday the Christmas parade delivers Santa and Mrs. Claus atop Beaufort's 1955 American La France Fire Engine to everyone's delight.

STRAWBERRY SHORTCAKE TRUFFLES

3 cups white chocolate candy coating, divided

2/3 cup chopped fresh strawberries or thawed frozen berries

Zest of medium orange

3½ cups prepared yellow cake or pound cake

1 or 2 drops red food coloring

Candy sprinkles or dried strawberries for decoration

Place one cup of white chocolate candy coating into a medium microwave-safe bowl and microwave it until melted, about one minute. Stir until the candy coating is entirely smooth and free of lumps. Set aside to cool slightly.

Blend the berries and orange zest in a food processor or blender until it is a smooth purée. Place the crumbled cake into a large mixing bowl. Gradually add the purée and stir, making a smooth paste. Add the melted candy coating and stir until smooth. Add red food coloring and mix until mixture turns a light pink.

Cover the candy mixture with plastic wrap and refrigerate for 1 hour. Cover baking sheet with foil and set aside.

Once the candy mixture is firm, use a teaspoon to scoop out small balls. Roll gently between your hands and place them on the baking sheet. Place the baking sheet in the freezer for one hour.

Once the candies are chilled enough for dipping, place the remaining 2 cups of white chocolate candy coating in the microwave-safe bowl and microwave until melted, stirring after every 45 seconds to prevent overheating. Stir until the chocolate is melted and smooth.

Using dipping tools or two forks, dip each truffle into the melted white chocolate and return to the baking sheet. Top truffles with sprinkles, dried strawberries, or any other decorative touches while chocolate is still wet so they will adhere.

Place baking sheet with finished truffles in the refrigerator for 15 minutes to finish setting. Store refrigerated in an airtight container for up to one week.

Note: These truffles make a special gift from the kitchen.

You're Invited Back—A Second Helping of Raleigh's Favorite Recipes
Junior League of Raleigh, North Carolina

CHOCOLATE TRUFFLES

1 pound Oreo cookies, finely crushed
8 ounces cream cheese, softened
2 tablespoons Grand Marnier, optional

10 ounces German's Chocolate
2 tablespoons paramount crystals
4 ounces white chocolate, melted

Mix Oreo cookies and cream cheese with an electric mixer on slow speed until completely mixed. Stir Grand Marnier into cookie crumb mixture; mix again. Roll mixture into small balls. Place balls on a cookie sheet lined with waxed paper; freeze for several hours.

Place German's chocolate in a double boiler over low heat; melt. Stir paramount crystals into German's chocolate, as needed, to thin German's chocolate for dipping.

Remove balls from freezer; dip in melted chocolate, covering completely. Place chocolate-covered balls back on a cookie sheet lined with waxed paper; return to freezer.

Drizzle firm chocolate balls with melted white chocolate for garnish. Store in freezer in a freezer-safe container until ready to serve. The chocolate truffles thaw quickly.

Toast to Tidewater
Junior League of Norfolk-Virginia Beach, Virginia

MILLIE'S TRUFFLES

½ cup unsalted butter
4 ounces milk chocolate
4 ounces semisweet chocolate
2 tablespoons confectioners' sugar

3 egg yolks, beaten
2 tablespoons Grand Marnier or other liqueur
Baking cocoa

Combine the butter, milk chocolate and semisweet chocolate in a double boiler. Cook until blended, stirring frequently. Stir in the confectioners' sugar. Stir a small amount of the hot mixture into the egg yolks; stir the egg yolks gradually into the hot mixture. Stir in the liqueur. Spoon into a nonmetal dish.

Chill, covered, for 12 to 24 hours. Shape into 1-inch balls; roll the truffles in baking cocoa.

Great Lake Effects
Junior League of Buffalo, New York

JUNGLE PIECES

3 cups white chocolate chips
1½ cups chunky peanut butter
2 cups chocolate chips

Microwave the white chocolate chips with the peanut butter in a microwave-safe dish until melted using the package directions on the white chocolate chips. Stir until smooth. Pour onto a buttered 10×15-inch baking sheet. Microwave the chocolate chips in a microwave-safe dish until melted using package directions. Pour over the white chocolate layer and swirl with a knife. Chill until set. Slice or break into pieces and serve.

Settings on the Dock of the Bay
Assistance League of the Bay Area, Houston, Texas

PECAN PRALINES I

MAKES APPROXIMATELY 2 DOZEN PRALINES

1 cup white sugar
1 cup brown sugar (½ light and ½ dark)
Dash salt
½ cup milk
2 tablespoons white corn syrup
2 tablespoons butter
1 teaspoon vanilla
1½ cups pecan halves

Mix sugar, salt, milk and corn syrup in heavy 3-quart pan and cook to soft-ball stage. Add butter and vanilla. Beat until cool. Add pecans and drop by tablespoon onto wax paper. When firm, store in closed container.

Talk About Good!
Junior League of Lafayette, Louisiana

1½ packages graham crackers

¾ cup pecans

½ cup (1 stick) butter (do not substitute)

½ cup (1 stick) margarine
(do not substitute)

½ cup sugar

Preheat the oven to 350 degrees. Place the graham crackers side by side (slightly overlapping if needed) on a large, rimmed baking sheet until the entire baking sheet is covered. Break the pecans into small pieces and sprinkle over the graham crackers. Combine the butter, margarine and sugar in a heavy saucepan. Bring the mixture to a boil and boil for 1 minute (no more!), stirring constantly. The mixture will appear slightly thicker. Pour the mixture immediately over the graham crackers and nuts on the cookie sheet. Bake for 10 minutes. Let stand to cool completely. Lift the crackers off the cookie sheet by hand, breaking them apart. Make bite-size pieces, or keep in large cracker sections.

Note: Instead of cutting the pecans, simply place them in a heavy sealable plastic bag. Flatten out the bag and reseal to remove all the air. Then pound the nuts with a large wooden spoon, turning the bag occasionally to make sure all the pecans are beaten into smaller pieces. This is so much easier than trying to cut them and have them fly all over the kitchen! Or, you could use a food processor or nut grinder, but they tend to overprocess the pecans, and the pounding is just more fun.

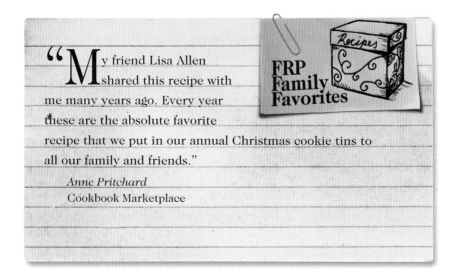

"My friend Lisa Allen shared this recipe with me many years ago. Every year these are the absolute favorite recipe that we put in our annual Christmas cookie tins to all our family and friends."

Anne Pritchard
Cookbook Marketplace

ALMOND TOFFEE

1 cup finely chopped almonds
2 cups sugar
2 cups (4 sticks) butter
¼ cup water

2 tablespoons light corn syrup
2 cups semisweet chocolate chips
3 tablespoons finely chopped almonds

Sprinkle 1 cup chopped almonds in a buttered 9×13-inch baking pan. Combine the sugar, butter, water and corn syrup in a heavy saucepan. Cook over medium heat to 290 degrees on a candy thermometer, soft-crack stage, stirring constantly. Cooking time should be about 20 to 25 minutes.

Pour the candy over the chopped almonds in the pan. Tilt the pan to coat evenly. Sprinkle with the chocolate chips. Let stand for 2 minutes or until the chocolate is melted.

Spread the chocolate evenly over the top of the toffee. Sprinkle with 3 tablespoons chopped almonds. Break into pieces with knife when cool.

Las Vegas: Glitter to Gourmet
Junior League of Las Vegas, Nevada

HONEY DIVINITY

¼ cup honey
2½ cups sugar
⅔ cup water

¼ teaspoon salt
2 egg whites
1 teaspoon vanilla

In a 2-quart saucepan, mix honey, sugar, water, and salt. Stir over low heat until sugar is dissolved. Continue cooking slowly, without stirring, to 265 degrees on candy thermometer (brittle stage.) In a large mixing bowl, beat egg whites at high speed until very stiff. Slowly pour hot syrup on egg whites, beating at high speed until mixture loses its gloss and holds its shape when dropped from a spoon. Add vanilla. Drop by teaspoons onto waxed paper. Store in an airtight container.

Land of Cotton
John T. Morgan Academy, Selma, Alabama

PIES, PUDDINGS & SWEET TREATS

PIONEERING IN VOLUNTEERISM

The Telephone Pioneers of America, now known as the AT&T Pioneers, was founded in 1911 and has become the largest industry-related volunteer organization in the world. Each state is referred to as a chapter and each has its own network of councils and its own fund-raising projects.

The Tennessee Chapter 21 has had tremendous success with cookbook sales. Its 1981 book, *Dining with Pioneers Volume I,* is in its 21st printing and has sold more than 200,000 copies.

"Volume I continues to be our most successful cookbook," said Alene White, past administrator with the Tennessee Telephone Company. "I wasn't involved with that book, but I helped develop *Dining with Pioneers Volume II,* plus *Answering the Call,* a smaller cookbook with healthier recipes, and *Just Kidding Around,* a kid's cookbook."

"We have done so much around Tennessee to help with education and health projects," Alene said. She gets so much pleasure from seeing how much good the cookbook money has done.

Carolyn Paine, who still works for the telephone company and is past president of her chapter, helped develop *Dining with Pioneers Volume III*; in fact, she has sold more of those cookbooks than anyone else.

DINING WITH PIONEERS
AT&T TELEPHONE PIONEERS–
TENNESSEE CHAPTER 21

Celebrating a Century of Service

"I was fortunate to get an article in the local paper, which helped with the sales," said Carolyn. "We did find that people who had Volumes I and II were happy to get Volume III to add to their collection. And Volume III does have a variety of new recipes since we had a younger generation with more varied ethnic backgrounds submitting them."

"Whenever we go to any of the events of the groups we are contributing to, we always take along cookbooks to sell," she said. "And I like pointing out my favorite recipe, Lemon Lust."

Banana Split Pie

3 cups crushed vanilla wafers

1½ sticks butter

2 cups powdered sugar

2 medium eggs

5 medium bananas

1 large can crushed pineapple, drained

1 large tub whipped topping

1 cup chopped pecans

½ jar of maraschino cherries, sliced

Mix the vanilla wafer crumbs and ½ stick of the butter in a 9×13-inch dish, pressing to form a crust. Beat the powdered sugar, remaining butter and eggs together in a bowl for ten minutes; do not underbeat. Pour over the prepared crust. Slice the bananas lengthwise and layer over the filling. Layer with the pineapple. Spread the whipped topping over the pineapple. Sprinkle with the pecans and maraschino cherries. Refrigerate until ready to serve.

Seasoned to Taste
Junior League of Chattanooga, Tennessee

Chocolate Apricot Ice Cream Pie

21 chocolate sandwich cookies, crushed

6 tablespoons butter, melted

1 (15-ounce) can apricot halves

1⅓ cups sugar

¾ teaspoon almond extract

2 quarts French vanilla ice cream, softened

1 cup whipped cream (optional)

Mix the cookies and butter in a bowl. Press over the bottom and up the side of a 10-inch pie plate. Freeze until firm. Cook the apricots and sugar in a saucepan over low heat for 1½ hours or until the apricots fall apart, stirring occasionally. Remove from the heat and stir in the almond extract. Let cool completely. Spread 1 quart of ice cream over the crust. Layer with 1 cup of the apricot sauce and remaining ice cream. Spread ½ cup of the remaining apricot sauce over the top. Freeze until firm. Cut into slices and serve with the remaining apricot sauce and dollops of the whipped cream.

Five Forks
Kerr-Vance Academy, Henderson, North Carolina

 BEST BLUEBERRY PIE

4 cups fresh blueberries

¾ cup sugar

½ cup water

2 tablespoons cornstarch

1 tablespoon butter

¼ cup slivered almonds, toasted

1 tablespoon Cointreau or curaçao

1 baked (9-inch) pie shell

1 cup whipping cream

¼ teaspoon almond extract

Sugar to taste

Bring 1 cup of the blueberries, ¾ cup sugar and water to a boil in a saucepan. Cook for 10 minutes or until soft. Let stand until cool. Combine the cornstarch with a little juice from the blueberry mixture in a bowl and stir until the cornstarch is dissolved. Add to the blueberry mixture. Cook until thickened, stirring constantly. Stir in the butter. Let stand until cool. Add the remaining blueberries, almonds and Cointreau. Pour into the pie shell. Beat the whipping cream, almond extract and sugar to taste in a mixer bowl until soft peaks form. Spread over the pie, sealing to the edge.

More Enchanted Eating
Friends of the West
Shore Symphony,
Muskegon, Michigan

"The best cookbooks are storybooks, their purpose as much to document the communal draw of the meal table as to show the curious cook how to bake a gravity-defying biscuit or stir up a tasty kettle of Brunswick stew. When all the dishes have been cleared from the table, these recipes remain, a tangible link to a time, a place, a people."

JOHN T. EDGE
A GRACIOUS PLENTY

TRIPLE CROWN PIE

4 tablespoons butter, softened
3 ounces cream cheese, softened
1 cup flour
2 eggs
1 stick butter, melted
⅓ cup flour

1 cup semisweet chocolate chips
1 cup nuts, chopped
1 cup sugar
1 tablespoon bourbon or 1 teaspoon vanilla
⅛ teaspoon salt
Whipped cream, for garnish

Cream 4 tablespoons butter and cream cheese. Add 1 cup flour. Mix well. Roll in waxed paper and chill 1 hour. Roll dough out and fit into 9-inch pie pan. Beat eggs until frothy in food processor or blender. Add melted butter, ⅓ cup flour, chocolate, nuts, sugar, bourbon, and salt. Process just until chocolate is coarsely chopped. (Do not overprocess.) Pour into pie shell and bake at 325 degrees for 45 to 60 minutes, or until the center rises and the pastry is tan. Serve topped with whipped cream.

To make miniature tarts, double ingredients for pie crust and, using 1-inch balls of dough, press into tiny muffin tins. Fill the tins ⅔ full and bake at 325 degrees for 25 to 35 minutes, or until done. Yields 48 tarts.

Cordon Bluegrass
Junior League of Louisville, Kentucky

MARY'S COCONUT PIE

1 teaspoon vanilla
½ teaspoon salt
1½ pounds ricotta cheese
4 eggs

½ cup sugar
½ cup milk
½ cup shredded coconut
1 (9-inch) pie shell

Preheat oven to 425 degrees. Combine all of the ingredients. Pour into the pie shell. Bake at 425 degrees for 10 minutes then lower temperature to 350 degrees. Bake for 45 to 50 minutes. Check often. Remove from oven when pie is lightly brown and center is firm. Cool before serving. Garnish with whipped cream.

The Food Court: A Culinary Collective
The Child Advocate Community, Hartford, Connecticut

emon Meringue Pie

5 eggs

3/4 cup sugar

5 tablespoons water

6 to 8 tablespoons fresh lemon juice

Grated rind of 1 lemon

1/4 cup butter or margarine

1 (9-inch) pie crust, baked

1/4 teaspoon cream of tartar

6 tablespoons sugar

Separate 3 eggs, saving 3 whites for meringue. Beat 2 eggs and 3 yolks until light; add sugar gradually, beating constantly. Add water, lemon juice and rind, then put in double boiler over hot water. Add butter and cook until thickened. Pour mixture into baked pie crust. Beat egg whites until frothy. Add cream of tartar and continue beating until stiff enough to hold a point. Gradually beat in sugar and continue beating until mixture is stiff and glossy. Spread on pie filling. Bake in a preheated 300-degree oven for 15 to 20 minutes. Filling can also be used in a lemon cheesecake.

A Southern Collection—Then and Now
Junior League of Columbus, Georgia

Florida Key Lime Pie with Gingersnap Crust

Serves 8 to 10

Gingersnap Crust

1 1/2 cups gingersnap cookies, crumbled (about 18 cookies)

3/4 cup sweetened, flaked coconut

4 tablespoons unsalted butter, melted

In a food processor, pulse gingersnaps until fine crumbs. Add coconut and pulse; add melted butter and pulse. Press into bottom and up sides of 9-inch pie plate. Bake at 350 for 8 to 10 minutes. Cool on wire rack before filling. If food processor is unavailable, crush gingersnaps in plastic bag with mallet until fine crumbs. Place in bowl and add coconut and melted butter and mix. Filling can also be used with traditional graham cracker pie crust. For nuttier flavor, toast coconut before making crust.

Pie Filling

1 (15-ounce) can sweetened condensed milk

1/2 cup Key lime juice

1 teaspoon lime zest

4 egg yolks

Mix all ingredients. Fill cooled pie shell. Bake at 350 for 7 to 10 minutes.

Capture the Coast, Vol. 4, The Culinary Collection
Junior League of Tampa, Florida

CHERRY VANILLA LATTICE PIE

FLAKY PIE CRUST

2½ cups flour

1½ tablespoons sugar

1¼ teaspoons salt

⅔ cup shortening, frozen and cut into
    ½-inch pieces

½ cup (1 stick) cold unsalted butter, cut into
    ½-inch pieces

6 tablespoons ice water

2 teaspoons apple cider vinegar

For the crust, combine the flour, sugar and salt in a food processor. Add the shortening and butter and pulse until the mixture resembles coarse meal. Spoon into a bowl. Combine the water and vinegar in a bowl and mix well. Pour over the flour mixture. Mix with a fork until the mixture forms a ball, adding additional water, 1 teaspoon at a time, if necessary. Shape the dough into 2 balls. Flatten each into a disk. Chill, wrapped in plastic wrap, for 30 minutes to 3 days.

Roll 1 dough disk into an 11-inch circle on a lightly floured surface. Fit into a 9-inch pie plate, leaving ¾-inch overhang. Roll out the remaining dough into an 11-inch circle on a lightly floured surface. Cut into 1-inch-wide strips. Place a piece of waxed paper on a baking sheet. Weave the strips in a lattice pattern on the waxed paper. Chill in the refrigerator or freezer for 20 minutes or until firm.

PIE

1 cup plus 2 tablespoons sugar

¼ cup quick-cooking tapioca

½ teaspoon salt

¼ teaspoon cinnamon

½ teaspoon grated orange zest

6 to 7 cups fresh or frozen tart red cherries,
    pitted

2 to 3 teaspoons vanilla extract

Sugar

Ice cream

For the pie, cover the lower oven rack with foil. Preheat the oven to 400 degrees. Combine the sugar, tapioca, salt, cinnamon and orange zest in a small bowl and mix well. Cook the cherries in a large heavy skillet over medium-high heat for 2 to 5 minutes or until the cherries are slightly soft and the juices begin to run. Remove with a slotted spoon to a bowl. Add the tapioca mixture to the juice in the skillet and bring to a simmer. Simmer for 3 minutes or until thickened, stirring constantly. The tapioca will remain uncooked. Add to the cherries and mix well. Stir in the vanilla. Let stand until cool. Pour into the pastry-lined pie plate. Moisten the edge of the pastry with cold water. Top with the lattice. Let stand for 10 minutes. Trim the edge and crimp together. Brush with cold water and sprinkle lightly with sugar. Bake on the middle oven rack for 40 to 50 minutes or until the edge is golden brown and the filling begins to bubble. Cool on a wire rack. Serve warm or at room temperature with ice cream.

Grand Temptations—Delightful Diversions from the Great Lakes State
Junior League of Grand Rapids, Michigan

Bourbon Pecan Pie

1¼ cups pecan halves

⅓ cup bourbon

1 cup brown sugar, packed

2 tablespoons flour

1 tablespoon margarine, soft

1 cup dark corn syrup

3 eggs, beaten

¼ teaspoon salt

1 (9-inch) pie crust

Toss pecans and bourbon until pecans are coated. Let stand 1 hour or until most of the bourbon is absorbed. Preheat oven to 325 degrees. Mix brown sugar and flour. Beat in margarine until creamy. Beat in corn syrup, eggs, and salt. Stir in pecans and bourbon. Pour into pie shell. Cover edge with ½-inch aluminum foil strip to prevent excessive browning. Remove foil last 15 minutes.

River Road Recipes II, A Second Helping
Junior League of Baton Rouge, Louisiana

Fallen Chocolate Soufflé Cakes

1 cup (2 sticks) butter

8 squares (1-ounce each) bittersweet
chocolate

6 large eggs

10 ounces packed light brown sugar

3 ounces baking cocoa

Melt the butter and chocolate in a double boiler over hot water. Beat the eggs in a large mixing bowl until pale yellow and foamy. Sift in the brown sugar and baking cocoa. Add the chocolate mixture and stir until thickened. Spoon into 6 buttered and sugared 1-cup ramekins.

Bake at 300 degrees for 20 to 25 minutes or until the edges are dry but the centers are still soft. Let cool for 20 to 30 minutes; the centers will fall. Unmold from the ramekins or serve in the ramekins. Serve warm with vanilla ice cream and chocolate or raspberry sauce.

Note: The cakes can be made up to 12 hours ahead and chilled. Reheat in a 300-degree oven for 5 to 8 minutes or microwave for 1 to 2 minutes or until warm.

Savor the Moment, Entertaining Without Reservations
Junior League of Boca Raton, Florida

CHOCOLATE BREAD PUDDING WITH WHISKEY SAUCE

BREAD PUDDING

¼ cup (½ stick) unsalted butter

7 cups French bread cubes
  (crust may be used)

2 cups whipping cream

1 cup milk

8 ounces bittersweet chocolate, chopped

5 egg yolks, lightly beaten

⅔ cup packed light brown sugar

1 teaspoon vanilla extract

Melt the butter in a large heavy skillet over medium heat. Add the bread cubes and cook until golden brown, stirring constantly. Spread in a lightly greased 9×13-inch baking dish.

Bring the whipping cream and milk to a boil in a skillet over medium heat. Remove from the heat. Add the chocolate and whisk until blended. Whisk in the egg yolks, brown sugar and vanilla. Pour over the bread cubes and let stand for 30 minutes. Cover with foil and cut six small holes in the foil and allow the steam to escape. Arrange the baking dish in a large roasting pan. Add enough hot water to the roasting pan to measure 1½ inches. Bake in a preheated 325-degree oven for 1¾ hours or until set. Remove the baking dish from the roasting pan and cool on a wire rack for 30 minutes.

WHISKEY SAUCE

1½ cups milk

1 cup sugar

½ cup (1 stick) butter

3 tablespoons cornstarch

¼ cup water

½ cup bourbon whiskey

Combine the milk, sugar and butter in a heavy saucepan. Cook over low heat until the butter melts and the sugar dissolves, stirring frequently. Mix the cornstarch and water in a bowl until blended and add to the butter mixture. Stir in the bourbon. Bring to a boil over medium heat and boil for 2 minutes, stirring constantly. Serve warm with the warm bread pudding. The sauce makes enough for a double recipe of the bread pudding.

Rendezvous on the Ridge
Junior League of Jonesboro, Arkansas

MOLTON CHOCOLATE CAKE WITH FUDGE SAUCE

SERVES 6

CAKE

5 ounces bittersweet or semisweet
  chocolate, chopped

10 tablespoons unsalted butter

3 eggs

3 egg yolks

1½ cups confectioners' sugar

½ cup all-purpose flour

Preheat oven to 450 degrees. Grease six (½-cup) custard cups or soufflé dishes. Melt chocolate and butter in saucepan over low heat, stirring occasionally. Cook slightly and set aside. Whisk eggs and egg yolks in a large bowl, blending well. Whisk in sugar, then chocolate mixture and flour. Pour equal amount into dishes. (Batter may be prepared one day ahead, covered and chilled.) Bake for 11 minutes or until sides are set but center remains somewhat liquid. Run small knife around cakes to loosen. Invert cakes immediately onto serving plates.

SAUCE

4½ ounces bittersweet or semisweet
  chocolate, chopped

2 ounces unsweetened chocolate, chopped

⅓ cup hot water

¼ cup light corn syrup

¾ teaspoon peppermint extract

½ pint raspberries, for garnish

Mint sprigs, for garnish

Melt chocolates in double boiler on low heat, stirring occasionally. Add water, corn syrup and extract; whisk until smooth. Remove from water and cool slightly. Spoon sauce around cake and garnish with raspberries and mint sprigs.

Note: Sauce may be prepared two days ahead, covered and chilled. Heat in saucepan over low heat, stirring constantly, before serving.

Full Moon—High Tide
Beaufort Academy, South Carolina

HINGHAM PUDDING

2½ cups flour

¼ cup sugar

¼ teaspoon baking powder

1 teaspoon cinnamon

½ teaspoon baking soda

½ teaspoon ground cloves

2 eggs, beaten

¾ cup molasses

¾ cup milk

½ cup melted butter or margarine

½ cup chopped pecans

Poached apples and pears

Mix the flour, sugar, baking powder, cinnamon, baking soda and cloves in a large bowl. Mix the eggs, molasses, milk and butter in a medium bowl. Stir into the flour mixture. Fold in the pecans. Spoon into a greased and floured 8-cup fluted tube pan. Cover the pan with foil, securing with kitchen string if needed. Place the pan on a rack in a deep kettle. Add enough boiling water to the kettle to reach 1 inch up the tube pan. Steam, covered, for 1½ hours or until a wooden pick inserted near the center comes out clean, adding water to the kettle if needed. Let stand for 10 minutes. Unmold carefully. Let stand on a wire rack for 30 to 40 minutes or until slightly cool. To serve, place the pudding on a shallow plate. Arrange poached apples and pears around the pudding. Pour the syrup from the fruit around the pudding. Serve with Sherried Custard Sauce.

SHERRIED CUSTARD SAUCE

MAKES 1 CUP

2 egg yolks, beaten

2 tablespoons sugar

⅛ teaspoon salt

¾ cup milk

1 tablespoon cream sherry

½ teaspoon vanilla extract

Combine the egg yolks, sugar, salt and milk in a small heavy saucepan. Cook over medium heat until the mixture begins to thicken and coats a metal spoon, stirring constantly. Remove from the heat. Pour into a bowl set in a larger bowl of ice water. Stir the sauce constantly for 1 to 2 minutes or until slightly cool. Stir in the sherry and vanilla. Chill, covered, until serving time.

Out of the Ordinary
Hingham Historical Society, Massachusetts

Sopaipilla Cheesecake

2 (8-count) cans crescent rolls
16 ounces cream cheese, softened
1 cup sugar
2 teaspoons vanilla extract

2 sticks butter, softened
¾ cup sugar
1 tablespoon ground cinnamon

Unroll 1 can of the crescent roll dough, pressing the perforations to seal. Place the dough in a greased 9×13-inch baking pan. Beat the cream cheese, 1 cup sugar and the vanilla in a mixing bowl until smooth. Spread over the crescent roll dough layer. Unroll the remaining can of crescent roll dough, pressing the perforations to seal. Place over the cream cheese layer. Cream the butter and ¾ cup sugar in a mixing bowl until light and fluffy. Spread over the top of the crescent roll dough. Sprinkle with the cinnamon. Bake at 350 degrees for 30 minutes.

Now Serving
Junior League of Wichita Falls, Texas

Guava Rum Cheesecake

⅓ cup melted butter
2 tablespoons sugar
1¼ cups graham cracker crumbs
1 cup guava paste
⅓ cup rum
32 ounces cream cheese, softened

2 cups sugar
4 eggs
1 tablespoon lemon zest
2 teaspoons vanilla extract
¼ cup guava jelly
1 tablespoon water

Preheat the oven to 350 degrees. Combine the butter, 2 tablespoons sugar and the graham cracker crumbs in a bowl and mix well. Press the mixture over the bottom and up the side of a buttered 9-inch springform pan. Bake for 8 minutes. Let stand until cool.

Melt the guava paste in a saucepan over low heat. Stir vigorously for 2 to 3 minutes or until smooth. Stir in the rum. Remove from the heat and let stand until cool. Beat the cream cheese in a bowl until light and fluffy. Add 2 cups sugar and beat until blended. Beat in the eggs one at a time. Add the lemon zest and vanilla and mix well. Fold in the guava mixture gently. Pour into the prepared crust. Bake for 1¼ hours, tenting with foil if the top begins to brown. Turn off the oven and let the cheesecake cool in the oven for 20 minutes. Chill for 6 to 8 hours. Heat the guava jelly and water in a small saucepan until the mixture is the consistency of heavy cream, stirring constantly. Let stand until cool. Brush over the cheesecake. Chill, covered, for 30 minutes or longer before serving.

Savor the Seasons, Vol. 3, The Culinary Collection
Junior League of Tampa, Florida

HOKA CHEESECAKE

CRUST

1 cup graham cracker crumbs
½ cup unsalted butter, melted
1 cup sugar
¼ teaspoon cinnamon

Preheat oven to 375. Mix graham cracker crumbs, butter, sugar and cinnamon until combined. Reserve ¼ cup for topping. Press remainder onto the bottom and halfway up the sides of a 9-inch springform pan.

FILLING

24 ounces cream cheese, room temperature
1 cup sugar
½ cup plus 1 tablespoon unsalted butter, melted and cooled
3 eggs
3 tablespoons vanilla

In the bowl of an electric mixer, beat cream cheese and sugar until creamy. Beat in butter, eggs and vanilla. Pour onto crust and bake 60 minutes or until firm. Cool 10 minutes on a wire rack.

TOPPING

½ cup sour cream
1 tablespoon vanilla
2 tablespoons sugar

In a small bowl combine sour cream, vanilla and sugar. Spread over cheesecake and bake an additional 5 minutes. Sprinkle reserved crumbs on top. Refrigerate 12 hours. When ready to serve, remove springform sleeve and transfer cheesecake to serving platter.

Square Table
Yoknapatawpha Arts Council, Oxford, Mississippi

Strawberry Cheesecake with Gingersnap Crust

For the crust

3 cups crushed gingersnaps

¼ cup sugar

¼ cup (½ stick) unsalted butter, melted

Process the gingersnap crumbs, sugar and butter in a food processor until well mixed. Press over the bottom and halfway up the side of a 9-inch springform pan with a 2½ inch side. Bake at 325 degrees on the center oven rack for 10 minutes. Cool on a wire rack.

For the filling

24 ounces cream cheese, softened

¾ cup sugar

1 teaspoon vanilla extract

3 medium eggs

2 cups fresh strawberry halves

Beat the cream cheese and sugar in a mixing bowl until light and fluffy. Add the vanilla and eggs and beat just until blended. Spoon into the prepared crust. Bake at 325 degrees for 1 hour or until the side of the cheesecake is slightly puffed and begins to crack and the center is almost set when gently shaken. Cool on a wire rack and chill, covered, for 8 hours or longer. Place on a serving plate and remove the side of the pan. Arrange the strawberries around the outer edge; cut into wedges to serve.

Oh My Stars!
Junior League of the Roanoke Valley, Virginia

Baked Apple Crisp

1 cup sugar

¾ cup flour

½ teaspoon cinnamon

¼ teaspoon nutmeg

Dash salt

½ cup butter

4 cups Granny Smith apples, peeled and
  cut into chunks

¼ cup orange juice

1 pint vanilla ice cream

Preheat oven to 375 degrees. Combine the sugar, flour, cinnamon, nutmeg and salt in a bowl. Cut in the butter until crumbly; set aside. Place the apples in a 9-inch pie plate. Pour the orange juice over the apples. Top with the crumb mixture. Bake at 375 degrees for 45 minutes or until golden brown. Cool for 5 to 10 minutes. Serve with ice cream.

Boston Uncommon
Junior League of Boston, Massachusetts

Mountain Apple Dumplings

SERVES 8 TO 12

2 Granny Smith apples
2 (8-count) cans refrigerator crescent rolls
1 cup (2 sticks) butter
1½ cups sugar

1 teaspoon vanilla extract
8 ounces Mountain Dew (1 cup)
½ teaspoon cinnamon

Preheat the oven to 350 degrees. Peel the apples. Cut each apple into eight wedges. Unroll the crescent roll dough and separate into triangles. Wrap each apple slice in a triangle of dough to enclose. Place in a buttered 9×13-inch baking pan. Melt the butter, sugar and vanilla in a saucepan. Stir lightly and pour the grainy mixture over the apples. Pour the soda over the top, making sure the edges are well coated. Sprinkle with the cinnamon. Bake for 40 minute or until brown. Serve with ice cream, preferably cinnamon!

My Mama Made That
Junior League of Hampton Roads, Newport News, Virginia

Lemon Blackberry Crisp

SERVES 6 TO 8

4 cups fresh blackberries
¼ cup sugar
2 tablespoons cornstarch
3 tablespoons fresh lemon juice
25 vanilla wafer cookies, crushed
½ cup regular oats

½ cup light brown sugar, firmly packed
¼ cup flour
½ teaspoon cinnamon
½ cup butter or margarine, melted
Ice cream or sweetened whipped cream
 (optional)

Place blackberries in a lightly greased 11×7-inch baking dish. Sprinkle with sugar. Stir together cornstarch and lemon juice; stir into berries. Combine vanilla wafer cookie crumbs, oats, brown sugar, flour and cinnamon, stir in butter until crumbly. Sprinkle over berries. Bake at 400 degrees for 30 minutes or until lightly browned. Serve with ice cream or sweetened whipped cream, if desired.

Substitute blackberries with any fresh fruit of your choice.

Seasoned with Fun
Junior League of El Paso, Texas

Bittersweet Chocolate Fondue with Pomegranate Syrup

Fondue

8 ounces high-quality semisweet chocolate, broken into pieces
½ cup heavy cream

3 tablespoons pomegranate syrup
1 teaspoon vanilla extract

For the fondue, melt the chocolate in a double boiler over low heat. Whisk in the cream and pomegranate syrup. Heat until smooth and warm for serving. Stir in the vanilla. Pour into a fondue pot and keep warm over low heat.

Fondue dipping items

Fortune cookies
Pretzel sticks
Sliced apples
Sliced pears
Sliced kiwifruit
Orange sections

Raspberries
Strawberries
Cubes of angel food cake
Cubes of pound cake

To serve, spear your choice of the dipping items onto small forks or wooden picks and dip into the fondue.

Note: Use Chambord, Grand Marnier or Kahlúa instead of the pomegranate syrup for a variety of flavors.

Main Line Entertains
The Saturday Club of
Wayne, Pennsylvania

My *Mama Made That...Virginia Favorites* from the Junior League of Hampton Roads, Virginia, will go down in cookbook history as the 2009 National Winner of the McIlhenny Company-sponsored Tabasco Community Cookbook Awards. The win by *My Mama Made That* continued the South's domination of the awards. During the 20-year history of the awards program, 23 national awards have been taken by the Southern region.

GINGERBREAD WITH CIDER SABAYON

GINGERBREAD

1½ cups boiling water

1 cup molasses

1 teaspoon baking soda

½ cup unsalted butter, softened

1 cup packed light brown sugar

1 egg

2½ cups flour

1 tablespoon baking powder

2 teaspoons ginger

1¼ teaspoons cinnamon

Pinch of ground cloves

½ teaspoon salt

Cider Sabayon

Bring the water to a boil in a small saucepan and stir in the molasses and baking soda; cool. Cream the butter and brown sugar with the paddle attachment in a mixing bowl for 2 minutes or until light. Mix in the egg. Sift the flour, baking powder, spices and salt together. Add to the creamed mixture alternately with the molasses mixture, mixing constantly at low speed. Spoon into a buttered 9×13-inch baking dish. Bake at 350 degrees for 30 to 35 minutes or until a tester comes out clean. Cool on a wire rack. Cut into 2×3-inch pieces and serve with Cider Sabayon.

CIDER SABAYON

8 large egg yolks

½ cup sugar

½ cup plus 2 tablespoons apple juice

2 tablespoons Calvados

1 cup heavy cream

Combine the egg yolks and sugar in a large stainless steel bowl. Whisk in the apple juice and liqueur. Place over a saucepan of boiling water. Cook for 5 minutes or until the mixture has tripled in volume and is thickened, whisking constantly; the mixture should mound slightly. Place in a bowl with ice water ¼ of the way up the side. Whisk until cold. Whip the cream at high speed in a mixer bowl until soft peaks form. Fold into the custard. Chill until serving time.

Windows, A Tasteful Reflection of Historic Rhode Island
Junior League of Rhode Island, Providence, Rhode Island

Creamy Fruit Delight

SERVES 8 TO 10

Topping

1 cup strawberry yogurt

3 ounces cream cheese, softened

1 tablespoon sugar

2 teaspoon lemon juice

2 cups thawed frozen whipped topping

¼ teaspoon almond extract

Combine the yogurt, cream cheese, sugar and lemon juice in a mixing bowl and beat at medium speed until smooth, scraping the bowl occasionally. Add the whipped topping and flavoring and beat until smooth. Chill, covered, in the refrigerator.

Fruit

2 cups blueberries

3 medium peaches, peeled and sliced

2 cups strawberries, cut in halves

2 cups seedless green grapes

20 ounces mandarin oranges, drained

2 tablespoons sliced almonds

Layer the blueberries, peaches and strawberries in a large glass serving bowl and spread with ½ of the topping. Layer the prepared layers with grapes and oranges and spread with the remaining topping to within 1 inch of the edge of the bowl. Sprinkle with the almonds and chill, covered, until serving time.

Pomegranates & Prickly Pears, flavorful entertaining from the Junior League of Phoenix
Junior League of Phoenix, Arizona

Mackinac Plum Crunch

SERVES 6 TO 8

3 cups pitted blue plums, cut into quarters

3 tablespoons brown sugar

5 tablespoons sugar

¼ teaspoon nutmeg

1 cup flour

1 cup sugar

1 teaspoon baking powder

¼ teaspoon salt

1 egg, beaten

½ cup melted butter

Arrange the plums in a 7×10-inch baking pan. Combine the brown sugar, 5 tablespoons sugar and nutmeg in a bowl and mix well. Sprinkle over the plums. Combine the flour, 1 cup sugar, baking powder, salt and egg in a bowl, mixing with a pastry cutter until crumbly. Sprinkle over the prepared layers; drizzle with the butter. Bake at 375 degrees for 45 minutes. Serve warm.

The Flavors of Mackinac
Mackinac Island Medical Center, Michigan

PEACHES AND CREAM

1½ cups flour
2 (4-ounce) packages vanilla instant
    pudding mix
2 teaspoons baking powder
½ teaspoon salt
6 tablespoons butter, partially melted
1 cup milk

1 egg
2 (15-ounce) cans sliced peaches
16 ounces cream cheese, softened
1 cup sugar
2 teaspoons cinnamon
2 tablespoons sugar

Mix the flour, pudding mix, baking powder and salt in a mixing bowl. Add the butter, milk and egg; beat for 2 minutes. Spoon into a 9×13-inch baking dish. Drain the peaches, reserving the juice. Arrange the peaches over the batter in the baking dish.

Combine 2 tablespoons of the reserved juice with the cream cheese and 1 cup sugar in a mixing bowl; beat for 2 minutes. Spread over the peaches, covering evenly.

Mix the cinnamon and 2 tablespoons sugar in a bowl. Sprinkle over the top. Bake at 350 degrees for 30 to 35 minutes or until golden brown.

Beach Appétit
Junior League of the Emerald Coast, Fort Walton Beach, Florida

LEMON LUST

1½ cups all-purpose flour
¾ cup (1½ sticks) margarine, softened
½ cup broken walnuts
8 ounces cream cheese
1 cup confectioners' sugar
½ cup frozen whipped topping, thawed

3 cups milk
3 (3½-ounce) packages lemon instant
    pudding mix
½ cup frozen whipped topping, thawed
Broken walnuts

Mix the flour, margarine, and ½ cup nuts in a bowl. Press in a 9×13-inch baking pan. Bake at 350 degrees for 20 minutes. Let stand until cool. Beat the cream cheese and confectioners' sugar in a bowl until light and fluffy. Fold in ½ cup whipped topping. Spread over the crust. Combine the milk and pudding mix in a bowl. Beat until thick. Spread over the cream cheese mixture. Top with ½ cup whipped topping and sprinkle with nuts. Cover and chill for 8 to 10 hours.

Dining with Pioneers, Volume 3
AT&T Pioneers, Tennessee Chapter 21

STRAWBERRIES WITH GRAND MARNIER SAUCE

SERVES 4

1 cup milk
1 cup heavy cream
1 teaspoon vanilla extract
4 egg yolks

½ cup sugar
¼ cup Grand Marnier
1 quart strawberries

Heat the milk, cream and vanilla in a double boiler over simmering water until hot but not boiling. Whisk the egg yolks and sugar in a bowl. Stir a small amount of the hot milk mixture into the egg yolks; stir the egg yolks into the hot milk mixture gradually.

Cook for 10 minutes or until the sauce coats the back of a spoon. Do not allow to boil or the sauce will curdle. Remove from the heat and then stir in the liqueur. The sauce will continue to thicken as it cools.

Cut the strawberries into halves or slices. Spoon the strawberries evenly into four wine goblets, martini glasses or dessert bowls. Drizzle the sauce over the strawberries. The sauce may be served warm or chilled.

Excellent Courses, A Culinary Legacy of Ravenscroft
Ravenscroft School, Raleigh, North Carolina

STRAWBERRY RED WINE SORBET

SERVES 4

1 pounds strawberries, cut into halves
    or quarters
1 cup sugar

½ cup dry red wine
1 vanilla bean, split lengthwise into halves
Juice of 1 lemon

This recipe requires 12 hours freezer time. Combine the strawberries, sugar and wine in a bowl and mix well. Scrape the vanilla bean seeds into the strawberry mixture. Add the vanilla bean pod and lemon juice and mix well. Let stand for 45 minutes. Discard the vanilla pod.

Process the strawberry mixture in a blender until puréed. Pour the purée into an ice cream freezer container. Freeze using the manufacturer's directions. Serve immediately. You may store in the freezer for future use. Allow the sorbet to soften slightly before serving.

Texas Tables
Junior League of North Harris and South Montgomery Counties, Texas

PRESERVING TRADITIONS

For almost two decades, Ruth McLeod had been very involved with the Historical League, which is the support arm of the Arizona Historical Society. But when the discussion began about publishing a cookbook, she was one of the naysayers.

"I kept questioning how and where we were going to sell this and was it really going to be a money maker for the league's causes," Ruth said.

Ruth is a naysayer no longer. *Tastes & Treasures* was first published in 2007, and the group sold 10,000 books in 18 months. It's now in its second printing, and even though the economy has taken a downturn, the book continues to sell.

Tastes & Treasures is laid out in three sections. The first section covers history with some recipes from popular hospitality venues around the state. The second section features history makers that have been honored at the museum, with recipes from them or their family members, including Erma Bombeck, noted author and humorist, and Barry M.

TASTES & TREASURES
HISTORICAL LEAGUE

*Preserving Arizona's History
One Cookbook at a Time*

Goldwater, U.S. Senator. The third section is about lunch at the museum. Whenever the league has its monthly meetings, the members bring potluck salads and desserts, which are highlighted in the cookbook.

Tastes & Treasures, a Tabasco Community Cookbook award winner from the Southwest region in 2007, has received five other awards, all of which have contributed valuable publicity for the society. All funds raised from the sale of the cookbook go to the Arizona Historical Society Museum in Tempe, for such projects as education, exhibits, and library archives.

"One example of the cookbook's contribution involves retired Supreme Court Justice Sandra Day O'Connor, a native Arizonan," Ruth said. "The home where she grew up was scheduled to be demolished. With some of the funds, the league was able to have the structure moved to property at the Tempe museum and have it rebuilt brick by brick. It was a structure that needed to be saved and preserved—and the league members were so delighted that we had a hand is seeing that it happened."

KATHERINE'S STRAWBERRY PRESERVES

9 cups small whole strawberries

¼ cup strained fresh lemon juice

8 cups sugar

½ teaspoon unsalted butter

1 (3-ounce) pouch liquid pectin

Gently rinse the strawberries in cool water and drain well. Using a sharp paring knife remove the stems. Discard any hollow berries. In a large bowl, combine the strawberries with the lemon juice, stirring gently to coat the berries. In an 8-quart pan, alternately layer the strawberries and sugar. Cover and let stand 4 to 5 hours. Remove the cover. Over medium-low heat, gradually heat the strawberry mixture, stirring constantly and gently, until the sugar is dissolved. Stir in the butter. Increase the heat to medium-high and bring the mixture to a boil. Reduce the heat and boil gently for 10 minutes, stirring occasionally to prevent sticking.

Increase the heat to medium-high. Bring the mixture to a full rolling boil, stirring constantly and gently. Stir in the entire contents of the pectin pouch. Return the mixture to a full rolling boil stirring constantly. Boil, stirring constantly, for 1 minute. Skim off any foam.

To prevent floating fruit, allow the preserves to cool 5 minutes before filling jars. Gently stir the preserves to distribute the fruit. Ladle the preserves into hot jars, leaving ¼-inch headspace. Wipe the jar rims and thread with a clean, damp cloth. Cover with hot lids and apply screw rings. Process half-pint jars in a 200-degree water bath for 10 minutes, pint jars for 15 minutes.

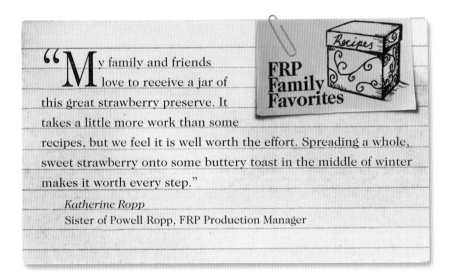

"My family and friends love to receive a jar of this great strawberry preserve. It takes a little more work than some recipes, but we feel it is well worth the effort. Spreading a whole, sweet strawberry onto some buttery toast in the middle of winter makes it worth every step."

Katherine Ropp
Sister of Powell Ropp, FRP Production Manager

FRP Family Favorites

BLACKBERRY JELLY

2 gallons blackberries
Water to cover
Peel from 2 tart apples or crabapples
Sugar

Wash berries. Place with apple skins in large pot and barely cover with water. Bring to boil, cover, and simmer 2 hours. Strain, discard pulp and measure juice. In large pot, put 1 cup juice for every 1 cup sugar, but no more than 4 cups juice at a time. Bring to rolling boil, stirring constantly. When mixture is thick enough for 2 drops to come off spoon together, boil 1 more minute. Mixture should sheet from spoon (drop in sheet, no drops). Pour into hot jars and seal.

Note: Dip a silver fork into boiling jelly, and if it fills in between the tines of the fork, the jelly is done.

The Stuffed Griffen
The Utility Club, Griffin, Georgia

SANGRIA JELLY

1½ cups burgundy
¼ cup orange juice
2 tablespoons lemon juice

2 tablespoons orange-flavored liqueur
3 cups sugar
½ (6-ounce) bottle liquid pectin

Combine wine, juices and liqueur in top of double boiler. Stir in sugar. Place over, but not touching, boiling water and stir until sugar is dissolved, about 3 to 4 minutes. Remove from heat. At once add pectin and mix well. Skim off foam. Pour into clean, hot wine glasses, using metal spoon to prevent breaking. Seal with paraffin.

Simply Simpatico
Junior League of Albuquerque, New Mexico

Miss Ruth Martin's Kumquat Marmalade

3 pounds kumquats

1 lemon

Sugar

1 can crushed pineapple

Thinly slice and seed kumquats and lemon. Weigh and add the same weight of water. Let kumquats soak in water overnight. Boil until tender. Soak for 24 hours and then boil an additional 30 minutes. Weigh mixture again. Add the same weight of sugar and the can of pineapple. Boil for 40 minutes or until syrup begins to jell when placed on a cool saucer. Pour into glass jars and allow to firm before sealing.

Bay Leaves
Junior Service League of Panama City, Florida

Million-Dollar Pickles

4 quarts sliced cucumbers

8 to 10 small onions

2 small green peppers

2 small red peppers

½ cup salt

½ quart cider vinegar

4 cups sugar

½ teaspoon celery seeds

1 teaspoon turmeric powder

2 tablespoons white mustard seeds

1 teaspoon mixed pickling spices

Slice cucumbers, onions and peppers. Put in large crock. Sprinkle salt over them and cover with water. Soak overnight. Drain. Combine vinegar, sugar, celery seeds, turmeric powder, mustard seeds and spices in large kettle; bring to boil. Put drained cucumbers in syrup and cook 20 minutes or until tender. Do not overcook or pickles will become mushy. Pack in hot sterilized jars. Seal.

A fast never-fail recipe—good for the beginner and the experienced!

Cotton Country Cooking
Junior League of Morgan County, Decatur, Alabama

PICKLED OKRA

2 pounds small okra
(enough to fill 5 pint jars)
5 pods hot red or green peppers, or
1¼ teaspoons dried hot pepper flakes
5 cloves garlic, peeled

1 quart white vinegar
½ cup water
6 tablespoons plain salt
1 tablespoon celery seeds

Wash okra. Pack in 5 hot sterilized jars. Place 1 pepper pod (or ¼ teaspoon pepper flakes) and 1 garlic clove in each jar. Bring remaining ingredients to a boil. Pour over okra, spooning some celery seeds into each jar. Seal jars and let stand 8 weeks before using.

Note: For a milder pickle, add ¼ cup sugar to vinegar solution. Dill seeds may be substituted for celery seeds.

Tea-Time at the Masters®
Junior League of Augusta, Georgia

PEACH PICKLES

6 pounds peaches, peeled
3 pounds sugar
1 pint vinegar
1 pint water

1 tablespoon ginger
2 tablespoons crushed whole cloves
4 sticks cinnamon

Blanch and peel peaches. Drop in cold salt and vinegar-water solution (2 tablespoons salt, 2 tablespoons vinegar, 1 gallon water) immediately to prevent discoloration. Put vinegar into preserving kettle with hot water, boil and skim; add spices (tied in cloth bag). Drain peaches well; drop into boiling syrup and cook about 1 minute, until they can be pierced with a straw but are not too soft. Remove from fire and pack in spiced vinegar. Seal and process 20 minutes at simmering in hot water bath.

Pines and Plantations
The Vashti Auxiliary, Thomasville, Georgia

GREEN TOMATO PICKLES

7 pounds green tomatoes

1 pound onions

2 cups lime

2 gallons water

5 pounds sugar

Spices to taste

2 quarts vinegar

Slice tomatoes and onions. Soak in lime and water overnight. Wash to remove lime. Mix in large pot—sugar, spices and vinegar. Bring to boil. Add tomatoes and onions. Boil 15 minutes. Pack in hot jars.

Note: Seven pounds cucumbers can be substituted for green tomatoes.

The Stuffed Griffin
The Utility Club, Griffin, Georgia

CHATTANOOGA CHOW CHOW

16 pounds green tomatoes

12 large onions

15 cucumbers, unpeeled

12 bell peppers

2 large heads cabbage

3 hot peppers

2 cups salt

1 gallon white vinegar

5 pounds sugar

1 cup white mustard seeds

3 tablespoons celery seeds

3 tablespoons turmeric

3 sticks cinnamon

Grind vegetables or chop in food processor. Sprinkle with salt and let stand 6 hours, stirring occasionally. Transfer all to a large mesh strainer and drain overnight.

In large pot, boil vinegar, sugar and spices 15 minutes without stirring. Add chopped vegetables and boil 15 minutes longer, stirring constantly. Remove cinnamon and put in sterile jars; seal.

Dinner on the Diner
Junior League of Chattanooga, Tennessee

GREEN TOMATO CHOW-CHOW

1 head hard cabbage

1 quart onions

1 quart bell peppers

1 gallon green tomatoes

¾ cup salt

2 tablespoons turmeric

4 tablespoons flour

3 tablespoons ground mustard

2 quarts vinegar

2 tablespoons white mustard seeds

1 tablespoon celery seeds

3 cups sugar

Chop vegetables fine. Sprinkle with salt and let stand over night. Drain. Mix turmeric, flour and mustard with enough water to make smooth paste. Let vinegar come to a boil and add mixture. Add all other ingredients, including vegetables. Boil 10 minutes. Seal in jars while hot.

Charleston Receipts
Junior League of Charleston, South Carolina

GINGER PEACH CHUTNEY

1½ cups raisins

½ pound pitted dates, chopped

3 tablespoons lemon juice

3 tablespoons lime juice

½ teaspoon lemon peel

½ teaspoon lime peel

2 cups vinegar cider

3 cups sugar

½ cup chopped candied ginger

10 cups peeled, pitted and thinly sliced
   peaches (about 5 pounds)

In a heavy 4- to 5-quart saucepan, combine raisins, dates, lemon juice, lime juice, lemon and lime peels, vinegar, sugar and ginger. Bring mixture to a boil over high heat; reduce heat to low and simmer, stirring frequently, for 20 minutes. Add peaches to the hot syrup and bring mixture to a boil over high heat. Reduce heat to medium and cook, stirring frequently to prevent sticking, until chutney is thick, about 40 minutes. Ladle hot chutney into 8 clean, hot half-pint canning jars, leaving ⅛-inch headspace. Wipe jar rims with a clean, damp cloth; then put on hot, scalded lids and screw on ring bands. Process jars in a water bath 5 minutes.

Simply Simpatico
Junior League of Albuquerque, New Mexico

# APPLE CHUTNEY

2 quarts apples, cored, peeled and cut into small pieces

2 pounds sugar

2 cups seedless raisins

Rind of 2 oranges, finely chopped

½ cup strong vinegar

⅓ teaspoon cloves

1 cup finely chopped pecans

Boil ingredients until apples and nuts are tender. Place in sterile jars and scald. Good with lamb curry, baked ham, pork or lamb.

Cincinnati Celebrates
Junior League of Cincinnati, Ohio

# MANGO CHUTNEY

16 cups sliced mangoes (11 to 12 medium size)

12 cups sugar (5 pounds) either white or brown or part of each

3 cups vinegar

6 onions, finely chopped

⅔ cup gingerroot, finely chopped

2 to 4 tablespoons garlic to taste, chopped

1 tablespoon salt

1½ cups seeded or seedless white raisins

1 tablespoon cloves

1 tablespoon cinnamon

1 tablespoon nutmeg

1 pound almonds, blanched and cut into slivers (any nuts can be used except peanuts)

¼ pound citron in small slices

1 dozen small hot red peppers, seeded and cut up (1-inch chili peppers)

Peel and slice the mangoes; put in large pot. A porcelain-lined dishpan can be used. Add sugar; pour on vinegar. Let this stand 15 minutes to partly dissolve the sugar and form a liquid in the bottom of the pan. Put on low heat and heat slowly to avoid sticking, stirring often until the sugar is dissolved. Chop the onion, gingerroot and garlic. Add all other ingredients to the mangoes. Cook on medium heat until the mixture is the consistency of thin applesauce, at least 1½ hours. Do not cook too thick as mangoes contain starch and the chutney will thicken as it cools. Remove from heat, immediately place in jars and seal or cover with paraffin.

Note: If green gingerroot is not available, 1 teaspoon of dry ginger powder and, if available, 2 tablespoons of preserved ginger cut very fine may be substituted. Citron is available at Christmas time and can be stored frozen. To speed things along, the mangoes can be sliced the evening before. Measure the sliced mangoes, put in a pot, sprinkle with salt and let stand overnight. Before preparing, pour off liquid but do not wash. The mangoes will shrink overnight but proceed with recipe as above.

Sunsational
Junior League of Orlando-Winter Park, Florida

The Colonel's Green Pear Chutney

MAKES 12 PINTS

½ tablespoon Worcestershire sauce

1½ teaspoons ground pepper

1 tablespoon whole cloves

1½ tablespoons ground cinnamon

Dash red pepper

4½ pounds green pears, sliced

4 lemons, peeled and sliced
   (cut peels into strips)

¾ pound dark raisins

3 pounds dark brown sugar

8 cloves garlic

3 large onions, sliced

⅔ cup crystallized ginger, cut fine

7 cups canned pineapple chunks, drained

1 quart plus 1 cup vinegar

3 tablespoons mustard seeds

½ cup soy sauce

Mix all ingredients and cook slowly until fruit is tender, 45 minutes to 1 hour after boiling. This does not spoil and does not need to be sealed.

Dinner on the Diner
Junior League of Chattanooga, Tennessee

Rhubarb Pear Chutney

MAKES 4 CUPS

1 cup minced red onion

4 cloves garlic, pressed

1 tablespoon minced ginger

¼ cup orange juice

¼ cup apple cider vinegar

⅓ cup sugar, or to taste

2½ cups chopped rhubarb

2½ cups chopped peeled pears or apples

1 stick cinnamon

¼ teaspoon red pepper flakes, or to taste

1 teaspoon salt, or to taste

Combine the onion, garlic, ginger, orange juice, vinegar and ⅓ cup sugar in a heavy 3-quart saucepan. Cook over medium heat until the sugar dissolves and the onion softens. Stir in the rhubarb, pears, cinnamon stick, red pepper flakes and 1 teaspoon salt. Cook for 1 minute. Remove from the heat and keep in a warm place to let the flavors develop and soften. Adjust the salt and sugar to taste.

Tastes & Treasures
Historical League, Tempe, Arizona

CRANBERRY RELISH

1 (16-ounce) package cranberries

2 cups sugar

1 cup water

1 cup orange juice

1 cup celery, chopped

1 medium eating apple, chopped

1 cup golden raisins

1 cup nuts, chopped

1 teaspoon ginger

1 teaspoon orange rind, grated

Bring to a boil the cranberries, sugar and water. Simmer 15 minutes. Remove from heat and add rest of ingredients. Leave this overnight. If cranberries are sold in 12-ounce bag only, reduce sugar to 1½ cups.

America Discovers Columbus
Junior League of Columbus, Ohio

MISS JUDY'S PEPPER RELISH

24 large red pimientos

12 large onions

4 hot peppers

2 tablespoons celery salt

2 tablespoons salt

1 quart vinegar

4 cups sugar

Roast pimientos in slow oven. Cool and peel. Coarsely grind pimientos, onions and hot peppers. Add remaining ingredients and cook slowly. Stir constantly, cooking for about 20 minutes after mixture is thoroughly hot. Pour in jars and seal. This may be doubled easily.

Note: Red and green bell peppers may be substituted for pimientos. Do not roast or peel, just seed and chop.

The Stuffed Griffin
The Utility Club, Griffin, Georgia

HOT TOMATO RELISH

About 20 cups chopped peeled ripe
    tomatoes and juice
6 large yellow onions, chopped
4 bell peppers, chopped
6 hot red or green peppers, chopped,
    with seeds removed

4 jalapeño peppers, chopped
2 tablespoons celery seeds
4 tablespoons or more salt
1 tablespoon coarse ground black pepper
½ cup firmly packed brown sugar
4 cups apple cider vinegar

Combine all ingredients and cook slowly, uncovered, about 3 hours, or until it cooks down and thickens. Pour into sterilized jars and seal.

Cane River Cuisine
Junior Service League of Natchitoches, Louisiana

SPICED FIGS

3 quarts figs
1 cup water
6 cups sugar
1 cup apple cider vinegar

¼ cup pickling spice
3 (3-inch) pieces cinnamon
8 whole cloves

Wash and stem figs. Cover with boiling water; let stand 5 minutes. Make syrup of 1 cup water, sugar, vinegar, and spices tied in a bag. Drain figs and add to syrup. Boil gently for 10 minutes. Remove from heat; cover and let stand for 24 hours. Repeat boiling process for 3 consecutive days. On third day, pack in sterile jars and process in a hot water bath for 15 minutes.

Bay Leaves
Junior League of Panama City, Florida

EZEBEL SAUCE

MAKES 5 CUPS

1 (18-ounce) jar pineapple preserves
1 (18-ounce) jar apple jelly
1 (2½-ounce) jar horseradish
1 (1-ounce) can dry mustard
1 teaspoon white pepper

Thoroughly blend all ingredients. Refrigerate at least 4 hours before using.

Note: As a quick appetizer, serve on cream cheese with crackers. Jezebel Sauce also makes a nice complement for meat. Keeps indefinitely in the refrigerator. (Peach preserves may be substituted for the pineapple preserves.)

Cordon Bluegrass
Junior League of Louisville, Kentucky

ONION TOMATO SAUCE

MAKES 10 TO 12 PINTS

4 quarts coarsely chopped onions
1 quart coarsely chopped celery
6 bell peppers, chopped
2 cups water

2 tablespoons sugar
3 tablespoons salt
4 to 6 quarts peeled, diced tomatoes

Place all ingredients except tomatoes in large kettle. Bring to a boil and simmer 20 minutes. Add tomatoes. Bring to a boil and continue to simmer, partially covered, until thickened, 30 to 45 minutes.

Spoon into sterilized jars allowing ¼-inch space at top of each jar. Adjust lids. Place in boiling water bath for 35 minutes.

Dinner on the Diner
Junior League of Chattanooga, Tennessee

TABASCO COMMUNITY COOKBOOK AWARDS TURN FINAL PAGE AFTER 20 YEARS

Established in 1990 on behalf of the McIlhenny Company, the Tabasco Community Cookbook Awards recognized the achievements of community cookbooks and encouraged the preservation of the vast array of regional food traditions. It was the only program solely created to recognize the best of the thousands of cookbooks issued annually to generate money for charitable causes. As we celebrate the success of *Recipes Worth Sharing* and the release of *More Recipes Worth Sharing*, we also grieve the end of the Tabasco Community Cookbook Awards. Coveted by many and the catalyst of encouraged uniqueness and the honest representation of the people and place, these special awards will be missed. Many of the cookbooks included in *More Recipes Worth Sharing* are winners of this prestigious award, including winners of the first and final awards as well as inductees into the McIlhenny Hall of Fame.

"Over these many years, McIlhenny Company has spotlighted and honored scores of nonprofit organizations and the *Stories, Food, Life* cookbooks they create for fund-raising purposes," said Paul McIlhenny, president and CEO of McIlhenny Company. "While the sun sets on the awards, we leave on a particularly high note, with this year's winners showing exactly why we started this program in the first place, and why community cookbooks will always play an integral role in preserving regional culinary history and traditions."

CONTRIBUTOR LIST

ALABAMA
John T. Morgan Academy
Land of Cotton (1988)

Junior League of Birmingham
* *Tables of Content (2006)*

Junior League of Huntsville
* *Sweet Home Alabama (1995)*

Junior League of Mobile
Bay Tables (1999)

Junior League of Morgan County
* *Cotton Country Cooking (1972)*

ARKANSAS
Junior Auxiliary of Jonesboro
Rendezvous on the Ridge (2008)

Junior League of Little Rock
* *Apron Strings (1997)*
Big Taste of Little Rock (2009)

Junior League of Northwest Arkansas
Add Another Place Setting (2008)

ARIZONA
Arizona Historical League
* *Tastes & Treasures (2007)*

Junior League of Phoenix
* *Pomegranates & Prickly Pears (2005)*

BERMUDA
Bermuda Junior Service League
Island Thyme (2005)

CALIFORNIA
Junior League of Oakland-East Bay
* *California Fresh Harvest (2001)*

Junior League of Orange County
Orange County Fare (2009)

Junior League of Pasadena
* *California Sizzles (1992)*
* *California Mosaic (2007)*

Junior League of Sacramento
Celebrate (2005)

Junior League of San Diego
* *California Sol Food (2004)*

Mission San Juan Capistrano Women's Guild
* *The Bells Are Ringing (2007)*

COLORADO
Guild of Strings in the Mountains Music Festival
* *Steamboat Seasons (2005)*

Junior League of Colorado Springs
A Peak at the Springs, A (2009)

CONNECTICUT
Child Advocate Community, New Haven
The Food Court: A Culinary Collective

DELAWARE
Junior League of Wilmington
Dancing on the Table (2002)

FLORIDA
Junior League of Boca Raton
* *Savor the Moment (2000)*

Junior League of Clearwater-Dunedin
From Grouper to Grits (2005)

Junior League of Ft. Myers
Tropical Settings (1995)

Junior League of Orlando
Sunsational (1982)

Junior League of Pensacola
Some Like it South (1984)

Junior League of Tallahassee
A Thyme to Celebrate (2009)

Junior League of Tampa
* *Gasparilla Cookbook, The (1961)*
Life of the Party, The (2003)
EveryDay Feasts (2005)
Savor the Seasons (2007)
Capture the Coast (2010)

Junior League of the Emerald Coast
Beach Appétit (2004)

Junior League of the Palm Beaches
Worth Tasting (2007)

Junior Service League of Panama City
Bay Leaves (1975)

Micah's Place
A Savory Place (2010)

Sons of Italy Florida Foundation
* *Preserving Our Italian Heritage (1991)*

Young Patronesses of the Opera, Inc., The
Sunny Days, Balmy Nights (2008)

GEORGIA

Athens Academy
Under the Magnolias (1999)

Forward Arts Foundation
The Swan's Palette (2000)

Junior League of Athens
Beyond the Hedges (2007)

Junior League of Augusta
Tea-Time at the Masters® (1977)
Par 3 Tea Time at the Masters® (2005)

Junior League of Cobb-Marietta
Georgia on my Menu (1988)
* *Southern on Occasion (1998)*

Junior League of Columbus
* *A Southern Collection -*
Then and Now (1994)
Pull Up a Chair (2010)

Junior League of Gwinnett and North
Fulton Counties
At Your Service (2001)

Junior League of Savannah
* *Savannah Style (1980)*
Downtown Savannah Style (1996)

Newnan Junior Service League
* *A Taste of Georgia (1977)*
Simply Southern (2008)

St. Andrews School, Savannah
* *First Come, First Served…*
in Savannah (2001)

The Paideida School, Atlanta
American Pi…The Cookbook (2004)

The Utility Club
The Stuffed Griffin (1977)

The Vashti Auxiliary, Thomasville
Pines & Plantations (1976)

Union Mission
* *Starfish Café (2007)*

HAWAII

Child & Family Services Guild
* *Flavors of Hawaii (1998)*

IOWA

Junior League of Waterloo-Cedar Falls
First Impressions (2001)

IDAHO

Beaux Arts Societie
Idaho a la Carte (1995)

Junior League of Boise
Beyond Burlap (1997)

ILLINOIS

Hinsdale Junior Woman's Club
Life is Delicious (2007)

Junior League of Chicago
* *Peeling the Wild Onion (2008)*

Junior League of Springfield
Honest to Goodness (1990)

Nielsen Massey Vanillas
A Century of Flavors (2008)

INDIANA

Junior League of Evansville
* *Once Upon a Time (2003)*

KENTUCKY

Fayette County Medical Auxiliary
Creating a Stir (1999)

Garden Club of Lexington
Entertaining with Blue Grass Winners (2008)

Junior League of Louisville
Cordon Bluegrass (1988)
* *Splendor in the Bluegrass (2000)*

Junior League of Owensboro
To Market, To Market (1984)
Home Again, Home Again (2004)

LOUISIANA

Friends of KEDM Public Radio, Monroe
Variations & Improvisations (2000)

Junior League of Baton Rouge
River Road Recipes:
* *The Textbook of Lousiana*
Cuisine (1959)
River Road Recipes II:
A Second Helping (1976)
* *River Road Recipes III:*
A Healthy Collection (1994)
River Roads Recipes IV:
Warm Welcomes (2004)

Junior League of Greater Covington
* *Roux To Do (2004)*

Junior League of Lafayette
* *Talk About Good! (1967)*

Junior League of Lake Charles
  * *Marshes to Mansions (2007)*

Junior League of Monroe
  * *Cotton Country Collection (1972)*
  Cooking in High Cotton (2008)

Junior League of New Orleans
  Crescent City Moons Dishes and Spoons (2009)

Service League of Natchitoches
  Cane River Cuisine (1974)
  Louisiana Living (1994)

MASSACHUSETTS
Friends of Boston Symphony Orchestra
  * *Cooking with Music (1999)*

Hingham Historical Society
  * *Out of the Ordinary (1998)*

Junior League of Boston
  * *Boston Uncommon (2007)*

MARYLAND
Junior League of Annapolis
  Of Tide & Thyme (1995)
  * *A Thyme to Entertain (2007)*

Maryland Dietetic Association
  Explore the Tastes of Maryland (2002)

MICHIGAN
Friends of the West Shore Symphony
  More Enchanted Eating (1999)

Junior League of Grand Rapids
  Grand Temptations (2004)

Junior League of Saginaw Valley
  * *Between the Lakes (2005)*

Mackinac Island Medical Center, Inc.
  Flavors of Mackinac, The (1997)

MISSOURI
Junior League of Saint Louis
  Saint Louis Days / Saint Louis Nights (1997)

Junior Service League of Independence
  If You Can't Stand the Heat, Get out of the Kitchen (1999)

Kansas City Barbeque Society
  * *Kansas City Barbeque Society Cookbook, The (1996)*

Missouri State Medical Association Alliance
  Windows Across Missouri (2002)

St. Louis Herb Society
  * *Herbal Cookery (2009)*

MISSISSIPPI
Association of Junior Auxiliaries
  Silver Spoons, Blueberry Afternoons (2008)

Baddour Center
  * *Yesterday, Today & Tomorrow (1987)*

Junior Auxiliary of Vicksburg
  Vintage Vicksburg (1986)

Junior League of Jackson
  Southern Sideboards (1975)

Lamar School, Meridian
  Prime Meridian (2001)

Lee Academy, Clarksdale
  Family Secrets (1977)

Mississippi University for Women
Alumnae Association
  Southern Grace (2002)

Yoknapatawpha Arts Council
  * *Square Tables (2005)*

NORTH CAROLINA
Episcopal Church Women of Christ Church
  Back to the Table (1998)

Greensboro Symphony Guild
  Recipes of Note (2006)

Junior League of Fayetteville
  Sweet Pickin's (2001)

Junior League of High Point
  Furniture City Feasts, Restored (2006)

Junior League of Raleigh
  You're Invited Back (2010)

Junior League of Wilmington
  * *Seaboard to Sideboard (1998)*

Kerr-Vance Academy
  Five Forks (2010)

Laurel Garden Club, Highlands
  * *Celebrate the Highlands (2002)*

Ravenscroft School
  Excellent Courses (2008)

St. Paul's Episcopal Church Women
  Let Us Keep the Feast in Historic Beaufort (2001)

NEW JERSEY
Joseph Kushner Hebrew Academy
  The Kosher Palette II (2006)

NEW MEXICO

Junior League of Albuquerque
* *Simply Simpatico (1981)*
A Taste of Enchantment (2001)

NEVADA

Junior League of Las Vegas
Las Vegas: Glitter to Gourmet (2001)

NEW YORK

Auxiliary of Community General Hospital
Catskill Country Cooking (1975)

Junior League of Albany
The Stenciled Strawberry Cookbook (1985)

Junior League of Buffalo
* *Great Lake Effects (1997)*

Junior League of New York City
I'll Taste Manhattan (1994)

OHIO

Junior League of Cincinnati
Cincinnati Celebrates (1974)
* *I'll Cook When Pigs Fly...and they do in Cincinnati! (1998)*

Junior League of Columbus
America Discovers Columbus (1984)

Junior League of Dayton
Discover Dayton (1979)

The Longaberger Company
Fresh from the Pantry (2001)

OKLAHOMA

Cascia Hall Preparatory School
Gourmet Our Way (1995)

Junior League of Tulsa
Oil & Vinegar (2002)

Junior Service League of Midwest City
* *Café Oklahoma (1994)*

Junior Welfare League of Enid
* *Stir-Ups (1982)*

OREGON

Junior League of Eugene
Cooking from the Coast to the Cascades (2002)

PENNSYLVANIA

The Junior Saturday Club of Wayne
* *Main Line Classics II (1996)*
Main Line Entertains (2005)

Sacred Heart Elementary School
* *The Heart of Pittsburgh (1999)*

Devon Horse Show and Country Fair
Appetizers at Devon (2008)

RHODE ISLAND

Junior League of Rhode Island
* *Windows (1995)*

SOUTH CAROLINA

Beaufort Academy
Full Moon - High Tide (2001)

Junior League of Charleston
* *Charleston Receipts (1950)*
* *Charleston Receipts Repeats (1986)*

Junior League of Spartanburg
* *Meet Me at the Garden Gate (2001)*

TENNESSEE

AJLI/Favorite Recipes Press
Junior Leagues In the Kitchen with Kids (2009)

AT&T Pioneers, Tennessee Chapter 21
Dining with Pioneers, Volume 1 (1981)
Dining with Pioneers Volume 3 (2005)

Ducks Unlimited / Favorite Recipes Press
The Hunter's Table (2010)

Germantown United Methodist Women
Be Present At Our Table (2007)

Junior League of Chattanooga
Dinner on the Diner (1983)
Seasoned to Taste (2011)

Junior League of Johnson City
Treasures of the Smokies (1986)

Junior League of Memphis
* *Party Potpourri (1971)*
* *Heart & Soul (1992)*

Junior League of Murfreesboro
Open House (2002)

Junior League of Nashville
Notably Nashville (2003)

Le Bonheur Club, Inc.
Key Ingredients (2002)

Les Passees, Inc.
Well Seasoned (1982)

The Ladies Ministry of Hendersonville
    Church of Christ
    100 Years of Cooking (1993)

The Memphis Symphony League
    Gracious Goodness,
    The Taste of Memphis (1989)

The Woman's Exchange of Memphis
    Compliments Of (2006)

TEXAS

Assistance League® of the Bay Area
    * *Settings on the Dock of the Bay (1999)*
    Settings to Sunsets (2007)

Dallas Junior Forum
    * *Tuxedos to Tailgates (2003)*

Fort Bend Junior Service League
    * *Treasures from the Bend (2009)*

Genesis Women's Shelter
    * *Creating Comfort (2005)*

Junior League of Abilene
    Landmark Entertains (1996)

Junior League of Amarillo
    Beyond the Rim (2003)

Junior League of Beaumont
    Dining Without Reservations (2003)

Junior League of Corpus Christi
    Viva Tradiciones! (1996)

Junior League of Dallas
    Junior League of Dallas Cookbook (1976)
    Dallas Dish (2005)

Junior League of El Paso
    Seasoned with Fun (2000)

Junior League of Lubbock
    A Perfect Setting (2005)

Junior League of North Harris and South
    Montgomery Counties
    * *Texas Ties (1997)*
    Texas Tables (2010)

Junior League of Odessa
    Wild Wild West (1991)

Junior League of Plano
    * *Lone Star to Five Star (2004)*

Junior League of Wichita Falls
    Now Serving (2008)

National Extension Association of Family and
    Consumer Sciences
    Living Well...More Than A Cookbook (2010)

Rockwall Women's League
    A League of our Own (2006)

UTAH
Junior League of Salt Lake City
    Always in Season (1999)

VIRGINIA
Dahlgren United Methodist Church
    Share the Vision Cookbook (2007)

Junior League of Hampton Roads
    * *My Mama Made That (2009)*

Junior League of Lynchburg
    In Good Company (1999)

Junior League of Norfolk-Virginia Beach
    * *Tidewater on the Half Shell (1985)*
    * *Toast to Tidewater (2004)*

Junior League of Roanoke Valley
    Oh My Stars! (2000)

Museum of the Shenandoah Valley
    Oh, Shenandoah! (2009)

WASHINGTON
Junior League of Olympia
    Northwest Inspirations (2009)

Junior League of Seattle
    * *Simply Classic (1993)*
    * *Celebrate the Rain (2004)*

Junior League of Spokane
    Still Gold'n (2007)

Junior League of Yakima
    Fresh from the Valley (2003)

WISCONSIN
Junior League of Madison
    * *Mad About Food (2004)*

WEST VIRGINIA
Junior League of Wheeling
    The Best of Wheeling (1994)

WYOMING
Cheyenne Frontier Days
    * *Cheyenne Frontier Days (1995)*

The University of Wyoming
    Black Tie & Boots (2005)

* *Denotes Tabasco® Community Cookbook Award Winner or McIllhenny Hall of Fame inductee*

INDEX

FRP INC

FRP creates successful connections between organizations and individuals through custom books.

 Favorite Recipes® Press

Favorite Recipes Press, an imprint of FRP, Inc., located in Nashville, Tennessee, is one of the nation's best-known and most respected cookbook companies. Favorite Recipes Press began by publishing cookbooks for its parent company, Southwestern/Great American, in 1961. FRP, Inc., is now a wholly owned subsidiary of the Southwestern/Great American family of companies, and under the Favorite Recipes Press imprint has produced hundreds of custom cookbook titles for nonprofit organizations, companies, and individuals.

Other FRP, Inc., imprints include

BECKON BOOKS   The Booksmith Group
A DIVISION OF **FRP**

CommunityClassics®

Additional titles published by FRP, Inc., are

 Recipes Worth Sharing

The Illustrated Encyclopedia of American Cooking

 Cooking Up a Classic Christmas

 Almost Homemade

 The Vintner's Table

 Junior Leagues In the Kitchen with Kids: Everyday Recipes & Activities for Healthy Living

 *Favorite Recipes of Home Economics Teachers*

To learn more about custom books, visit our Web site, www.frpbooks.com.